Selections from
Early Greek Philosophy

MILTON C. NAHM
Bryn Mawr College

Fourth Edition

New York
APPLETON-CENTURY-CROFTS
Division of Meredith Corporation

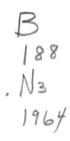

B
188
.N3
1964

PREFACE

THE FRAGMENTS of early Greek philosophy contained in this edition throw light upon the religion and culture of the period and upon the development of Greek science, and offer assistance in the explanation of portions of the later philosophy of antiquity. Interesting and valuable as such uses of early Greek philosophy may be, however, it must still be recognized that the ultimate reason for a return to sources lies in the scope and value of the problems raised and in the technique displayed by the early thinkers in attempting the solution to these problems.

In the period from Thales of Miletus to the Atomists, a speculation new to the world was begun and developed. Moreover, most of the problems of philosophy were raised and to them many solutions were offered, to which later philosophers have given more complete expression. For this speculation, beginning, as Aristotle said, "in wonder," set as its primary problem the reduction of the multiplicity of fact to simplicity of explanatory principle. From this central problem, early Greek thought extended its province to include the explanation of sensation and perception, the construction of cosmologies, hypotheses upon morality, evolution, and "natural law."

Our purpose in *Selections from Early Greek Philosophy* has

been to make available in compact and usable form translations of the source-material of this period from Thales through the Atomists. The inclusion of this speculation in courses in the history of philosophy has presented difficulties which arise not alone because of the importance of the problems treated by the early thinkers but because of the fragmentary state of the source-material itself. The introductions here offered to each collection of sources purport to treat concisely the problems raised and the limitations and value of the solutions offered. Included also are biographical data sufficient to place the man in his time and to give the most important facts known of his life.

No device of editing can overcome the difficulty imposed by the fragmentary state of early Greek philosophy. Nevertheless, the criticism and commentary of the early philosophers offered by Plato, Aristotle, Theophrastus, and the doxographical tradition in general are the indispensable data with which the student must begin. In this edition, the commentary is grouped in categories, that is to say, topically, under the headings of cosmology, perception, biology, etc. It is hoped that such an arrangement will assist the student in following the elaboration and application of the philosophical position held by each man. Further to assist the student, the introductions contain references by letter and number to the passages used for explanation and interpretation.

For the translation of Democritus, portions of which have not hitherto been available in English, I am indebted to Dr. Gordon H. Clark of the Department of Philosophy of the University of Pennsylvania. The translations of the other fragments and doxographical material are those of Dr. Arthur Fairbanks, published in *The First Philosophers of Greece*. Permission to use this material was granted by Routledge and Kegan Paul, Ltd. and I should like to express my thanks for their generosity. The chapter by Theodor Gomperz, used as the introduction to this book, is the Introduction to Gomperz' *Greek Thinkers* and I gratefully acknowledge the permission of Charles Scribners' Sons and John Murray to use it. Footnotes indicate the source of translations supplementary to those prepared by Dr. Clark and those appearing in *The First Philosophers of Greece*.

NOTE TO THE THIRD EDITION

In preparing the third edition of *Selections from Early Greek Philosophy* for publication, I have taken the opportunity to bridge a considerable gap in the philosophical materials accessible to the student of Greek thought prior to the *Dialogues* of Plato. The volume now includes, in the fragments of the writings and conversations of the Sophists, as well as in the valuable commentary upon individual thinkers and the philosophical movement as a whole, a considerable subject matter which follows directly in the tradition of speculation which began in Miletus and which, in turn, has become integral to the tradition of Western thought. Much of this material, although translated, has remained in scattered and somewhat inaccessible sources; some has remained untranslated. For the more advanced student in philosophy, the Sophists have been available for complete study in H. Diels' *Die Fragmente der Vorsokratiker;* but even for him it may be of value to observe the problems raised by the principal Sophistic thinkers in relation to the philosophy in which they originated, as well as in relation to that to which it gave rise. For the less advanced student, the presentation of the philosophies of men of such stature as Protagoras and Gorgias will always have a value, and one the more readily discernible, it may be suggested, once the fragments of their thought are withdrawn, so far as is possible, from the overshadowing context of Plato's writings.

The appearance of the new edition at this time owes much to Professor Alister Cameron's interest in the field of early Greek philosophy. Following my suggestion that he translate the Sophists, Professor Cameron, of the Department of Classics at the University of Cincinnati, generously agreed to defer other research projects in order to make translations of Sophistic material not elsewhere available. I should like to express my gratitude to Professor Cameron and to Miss Elizabeth Caskey, who assisted him in the translations.

The scope of Sophistic writings and the range of interest

evident in the fragments have made it necessary to omit a considerable portion of the collected material. The selections printed here have been chosen primarily for their intrinsic philosophical worth and, secondarily, for their importance in the history of ideas. Fortunately, even in the case of Sophistic rhetoric, the two values are rarely incompatible. Restrictions of space have led, however, to certain omissions—particularly that of the work of Antiphon the Sophist—which I regret. The omission of the Encyclopaedists is of less consequence, inasmuch as the more important extant theories of men like Hippias are readily accessible in Plato's *Dialogues*.

The map of Greater Hellas which appears in this edition is primarily intended to give the location of centers of philosophical speculation, as well as the birthplaces of the philosophers whose work appears in this book.

I should like to acknowledge the kind permission of the Clarendon Press (Oxford) to include translations from Benjamin Jowett's *The Dialogues of Plato* and *The Works of Aristotle Translated into English*, edited by J. A. Smith and W. D. Ross; and of the President and Fellows of Harvard College to include translations from the following volumes of the Loeb Classical Library: Diogenes Laertius' *Lives of the Eminent Philosophers*, translated by R. D. Hicks; Sextus Empiricus' *Outlines of Pyrrhonism* and *Against the Physicists*, translated by R. D. Hicks; and Philostratus' *The Lives of the Sophists*, translated by Wilmer Cave Wright.

NOTE TO THE FOURTH EDITION

The publisher's decision to produce *Selections from Early Greek Philosophy* in a new format has permitted me to make a number of changes in the book and to introduce new material. I have corrected and added to the texts and introductions, provided a new general Introduction, included Richmond Lattimore's translations of the fragments of Heraclitus' and Parmenides' philosophies, and added a second part to the book in which I have treated the life and philosophy of Socrates.

I have been content in this edition to correct and make more intelligible the Introductions to the earlier philosophers. I have added to the biographical details, formalized and made consistent the notations to the fragments, and attempted by various devices of editing both to clarify the material and make it easier to use.

In the general Introduction to the book, I have retained those sections of Theodor Gomperz' Introduction to his "fascinating and imaginative" *Greek Thinkers* which remain among the most illuminating studies of the geographical and cultural background of early Greek philosophy. I have omitted the more archaic portions of Gomperz' writing, especially those relating to primitive religion and early Greek theology. I have used Gomperz' writing not only because of its intrinsic value and interest but because it so well illustrates the *genetic method* of speculation on the origins of philosophy. In my opinion, the genetic method tends to obscure the genuine originality of the early Greek philosophers.

In the second part of the *Selections,* I have tried to show Socrates' knowledge and criticism of natural philosophy and also to argue that his own contribution to philosophy is, despite his debts to his predecessors, as original as that of the Milesians.

I should like to express in this Note my gratitude to Richmond Lattimore for permission to use his translations of the fragments of Heraclitus' and Parmenides' philosophies, as well as to Appleton-Century-Crofts, who first published the translation in Matthew Thompson McClure's *The Early Philosophers of Greece* (New York, 1934). I should like again to thank the publishers who gave permission for the inclusion of material which appeared in the early editions of this book and to express once again my particular gratitude to Gordon H. Clark and A. Cameron for the translations they prepared for those earlier editions.

I should like especially to acknowledge the permission granted by the President and Fellows of Harvard College to reprint excerpts from E. C. Marchant's translation of Xenophon's *Memorabilia of Socrates* and from R. D. Hicks' translation of Diogenes Laertius' *Lives and Opinions of Eminent Philosophers.*

In some instances, I have judged C. D. Yonge's translation of Diogenes Laertius' *Lives* to be superior and have used portions of it. I have availed myself of George Rawlinson's translation of Herodotus' *History* and of North's *Plutarch*. I should like to make a particular mention of my indebtedness to Routledge and Kegan Paul, Ltd. They have generously renewed their permission to use portions of Arthur Fairbanks' *The First Philosophers of Greece*. To them and to Charles Scribners' Sons and John Murray, who also renewed permission to use materials from Theodor Gomperz' *Greek Thinkers*, I should like to express my gratitude. I am no less grateful to the many readers of the previous editions of *Selections from Early Greek Philosophy* who have called my attention to misprints and errors.

M. C. N.

CONTENTS

Preface   v

INTRODUCTION   1

    Introductory: On Philosophy and Philosophers   26

PART I

1. THE MILESIAN SCHOOL   31

    I. Thales   37
    II. Anaximander   39
    III. Anaximenes   43

2. THE PYTHAGOREANS   46

3. HERACLITUS   62

4. THE ELEATIC SCHOOL   78

    I. Xenophanes   79
    II. Parmenides   87
    III. Zeno   98
    IV. Melissus of Samos   103

5. THE PLURALISTS   111

       I. Empedocles   112
      II. Anaxagoras   134

    The Atomists   148

     III. Leucippus   152
      IV. Democritus   154

6. THE SOPHISTS   208

    Introductory   218

    The Sophists of Culture   220

       I. Protagoras   220
      II. Gorgias   229
     III. Anonymus Iamblichi   239

    The Sophists of Eristic   242

      IV. Thrasymachus   243
       V. Callicles   244
      VI. Critias   246

PART II

7. SOCRATES   251

Abbreviations of Authors' Names   295

List of Works Cited   297

Selections from
Early Greek Philosophy

For from wonder, men, both now and
at first, began to philosophize. . . .

Aristotle

INTRODUCTION

I

PHILOSOPHY BEGINS during the first quarter of the sixth century B.C. in the Greek colony of Miletus in Asia Minor. Greek philosophy continues as a single entity until A.D. 529, the year in which the Roman Emperor, Justinian, suppressed the schools of philosophy in Athens.[1]

Justinian's edict brought to a formal close the teaching of the subject, but it did little to diminish the important role played by Greek philosophy in the enormous and enduring influence the civilization of Greece has exerted upon the whole of Western culture. Our debt to Greece has, indeed, been of such scope and depth that it led Sir Henry Maine to maintain that "except the blind forces of nature, nothing moves in this world which is not Greek in origin." Few would subscribe to Sir Henry's judgment and most would dismiss it as hyperbole. Yet, it is not easy for the student of Greek philosophy to avoid similar exaggeration. A proper sense of proportion is difficult to attain and even more difficult to maintain in judging the place in history merited by the speculation from which all subsequent philosophy derives. Nor is the problem only historical. It becomes even more difficult to arrive at a sound evaluation of a philosophy which displays so clearly its authors' extraordinary creative powers

[1] See Edward Gibbon's *The History of the Decline and Fall of the Roman Empire*, Chapter 40.7.

1

and their intention to provide techniques for the intelligible statement of the new ideas.

The fact is that from *ca.* 585 B.C., the year for which Thales of Miletus predicted the solar eclipse of May 28, until 322 B.C., the year of Aristotle's death, there occurs a period of the greatest philosophical productivity ever manifested by a people gifted with extraordinary speculative powers. Indeed, few eras in history are comparable to the two and a half centuries of the earliest philosophy, if the criteria laid down for their evaluation are those of the speculative powers of the thinkers and the influence they exerted.

It is with the earlier portion of this creative period that this book is concerned. More specifically, *Selections from Early Greek Philosophy* contains the principal remaining fragments of the systematic accounts of the universe formulated by the earliest natural philosophers, the similarly fragmented remains of Sophist philosophy of the fifth century B.C., and selections, principally from the writings of Plato, Xenophon, and Aristotle, from which we learn of the life, thought, and death of Socrates. The material for this book is drawn, therefore, from the philosophies constructed between 585 B.C. and 399 B.C., the year of Socrates' death in Athens.

The earlier portion of the book consists primarily of studies of the universe and of its processes. The second part is devoted to Socrates' philosophy of man and of concepts. In spite of the differences in the subject matter which interested the natural philosophers and in that to which Socrates turned his attention, not to speak of the contrasting methods used by the early and the later philosophers, the two parts of the book are integrally related. Socrates searches into himself and into other men and denies any concern with cosmology, geometry, or astronomy. Yet, it is evident that his speculation does continue the interest in central problems of Greek philosophy. It is no less clear, however, that Socrates is not only the heir to early philosophy and an active participant in the speculation which occurred in contemporary Athens, but that his own contribution to the subject is as original as was that of Thales, with whom the subject of philosophy began.

One of the principal problems in *Selections from Early Greek Philosophy* is to indicate the aspects of early Greek theory which make Socratic speculation intelligible and to indicate as well the originality of the successive philosophers and the outstanding creativity of the Socrates with whom philosophy takes a new direction. Philosophy in Greece begins with the attempt to explain the universe in terms of a single principle or cause. Perhaps in its simplest terms, the efforts of philosophers may be described as attempts to discover the simplest and most concise formula for reducing nature's dimensions to intelligible explanation and then elaborating upon the formula by showing in detail precisely how, in philosophical terms, the universe and man are explained in the language and media of speculation. Philosophy proceeds in the persistent effort of natural philosophers to provide sounder and more consistent principles of explanation of the cosmos. With Sophist philosophy, speculation turns to the subject of man, proceeding from the principles examined by such earlier philosophers as Heraclitus, Parmenides, and Zeno. Socrates abandons natural philosophy. He excoriates the Sophists, but proceeds on the path they took in their study of men. But, as we shall see, Socrates sought to know "philosophy" as an art to be distinguished from other arts because its subject matter and technique are unique to it.

The men who produced philosophies between the time of Thales and that of Socrates are of a stature comparable to either that of the first philosopher, who was one of the Seven Sages of ancient times, or of Socrates, who is one of the few authentic original geniuses to appear in history. The systematic philosophies these men produced [2] are examined in detail in the selections pertaining to their lives and thoughts and in the introductions to the individual philosophers and schools of philosophy by which their speculation is interpreted. But we may here turn

[2] The fragments of early Greek philosophy are derived from many sources. A clear account of the contexts in which they appear is given in John Burnet's *Early Greek Philosophy*, 4th ed. (London, A. & C. Black, Ltd., 1930), pp. 31-38. The best account and analysis of the doxographical tradition with which I am acquainted is José M. Ferrater Mora's "Historia de la Filosofía," *Diccionario de Filosofía*, 4th ed. (Buenos Aires, Editorial Sudamericana Sociedad Anónima, 1958).

to the *parerga* or ornaments of their philosophies for some suggestion of their powers and of their influence upon later speculation. Thales is a philosopher because he sought to explain the universe in terms of water. But he also predicted an eclipse and proposed to the Ionians that they adopt Teos as the fittest place for "a single seat of government." Diogenes Laertius tells us, also, that Thales journeyed to Egypt and brought geometry from that land to Greece.

Anaximander, the second Milesian philosopher of whom we have record, offers conjectures which anticipate a theory of evolution and of the survival of the fittest. He is also the "father of maps." Anaximenes, the third of the philosophers of Miletus, tells us that "a rainbow is produced when the sun's rays fall upon thick condensed air." From the evidence of shells and fossils, Xenophanes of Colophon concludes that "these imprints were made when everything long ago was covered with mud, and then the imprint dried in the mud." The philosopher infers that "once the earth was mingled with the sea, but in the course of time it became freed from moisture." Pythagoras invents the geometrical theorem which bears his name and endows posterity with the phrase, "harmony of the spheres." To Zeno of Elea we are indebted for the paradoxes with which logicians and mathematicians still struggle in order to determine whether or not Achilles can pass the tortoise and whether the flying arrow may move either where it is or where it is not. Heraclitus of Ephesus provides us with an image, in illustration of his doctrine that everything changes: "You can not step into the same rivers twice; for other waters pour in upon them." Empedocles of Agrigentum first formulates the conception of the element, but he knows also that hair, leaves, feathers, and reptiles' scales "are the same in origin" and in doing so makes his contribution to comparative morphology. Anaxagoras of Klazomenae constructs a universe in which Mind orders all things, but he also holds that "it is his possession of hands that makes man the most intelligent of the animals." Leucippus and Democritus reduce the universe's dimensions to a minimum in their theories of a cosmos composed of atoms and void, but they also infer that there are innumerable worlds which begin in vortices of atoms. The Sophist Gorgias asks how, if things and words differ, "these things can be indicated to another person"? With Socrates, philosophy moves from speculation upon the universe to reflection upon the nature of man. But the most widely known Socrates is the man whose image and thinking we associate with the words of the Delphic Oracle, "Know thyself," and with Socrates' own injunction: "The unexamined life is not worth living."

These are some among the many contributions these enormously creative men made during one of the seminal periods of speculative philosophy. What accounts most accurately for the *parerga* to their own thinking is "philosophy." If we ask, "What is philosophy?" we do well to note one or two of the interpretations offered by some of these early philosophers and then proceed to Aristotle's view, which has influenced subsequent speculation (see below, *Introductory: On Philosophy and Philosophers*, pp. 26-28). Diogenes Laertius (*ibid.*, 1) offers the most obvious definition, derived from the word, *philosophy*. Heraclitus dissociates philosophy from science and denies that the subject is identical with the "learning of many things" (see below, p. 27). These are mere suggestions compared to the pronouncement of Aristotle, the first book of whose *Metaphysics* is devoted to classifications and examinations of his predecessors who, in his opinion, "lisped" philosophy. What Aristotle does is to approach philosophy in terms of the *causes* by means of which the philosophers explained their world. In the course of Aristotle's discussions, two questions occur. The first is, Why did men begin to philosophize? and the second, What kinds of philosophy have been formulated by philosophers up to the time that the head of the Lyceum offers his own systematic speculation?

Aristotle believes that philosophy begins in "wonder" and that it is "not a science employed in producing." More affirmatively, Aristotle tells us that men philosophized "in order to escape from ignorance" and he adds that "evidently they were pursuing science in order to know, and not from any utilitarian end" (see below, p. 27). The nerve of Aristotle's argument is, however, not that philosophy is the "only free science," the science which "exists for its own sake," but that "men do not think they know a thing till they have grasped the 'why' of it, and this means to grasp its 'primary cause.' " [3]

If we follow Aristotle's argument, however, we discover that our "why" requires for its answer reference to four causes. In their medieval nomenclature, these are: (1) the *material cause*, that out of which a thing comes to be and which persists; (2) the *formal cause*, the statement of the essence; (3) the *efficient cause*, the primary source of the change or coming to rest; and (4) the *final cause* or "that for the sake of which" a thing is done.

As we proceed in *Selections from Early Greek Philosophy*, the meaning and application of Aristotle's classification of causes will become apparent. For him, for example, the Pythagoreans and Socrates formulate philosophies principally in terms of the formal cause; Empedocles and Anaxagoras use efficient causes. But as philosophy begins, Aristotle tells us, "the majority of those who first formed systems of philosophy consider those that subsist in a form of matter to be alone the principles of all things; for wherefrom all entities arise, and wherefrom they are corrupted, . . . this they assert to be . . . a first principle of all things. . . ."

To the details of the philosophies which use the material cause, or that out of which all things come, we shall shortly come. But it is helpful to point out, with reference to early Greek philosophy, that much of the interpretation of this part of the speculative history of the West is best understood if we assume that historians and philosophers approach early Greek philosophy as though they were adapting Aristotle's conception of a *material cause* to the history of the origin and nature of philosophy itself. Most attempts to explain early Greek philosophy indicate that writers have been fascinated by "that out of which it comes and which persists in the change." The reason for this is not far to seek. Early Greek philosophy is the sustained philosophical tradition in which speculation of this kind originates—and at a given time, in a given place, and as the invention of a specific individual. The almost inevitable consequence has been the general adoption of the *genetic* method of explanation, on the

[3] Aristotle, *Physics* II.3. 194 b 16.

assumption that if we are able to make evident the nonphilosophical conditions which prevailed in Greece at the time philosophy emerged we shall also know what emerged. To argue that the genetic hypothesis is faulty as an explanation of philosophy is not to assert that historians, archaeologists, anthropologists, philologists, and other scholars engaged in nonphilosophical disciplines have not made enormously valuable contributions to our knowledge of ancient Greece. It is simply to suggest that it remains open to question whether philosophy must not still be examined as philosophy and not as a subject reducible to that "from which" it emerged on the ground that "that from which" persists throughout the process of change.

Theodor Gomperz' Introduction to his *Greek Thinkers* illustrates the genetic method. The introduction to what John Burnet called this "fascinating and imaginative" study of Greek philosophers may be studied for two reasons. It is, first, a fascinating recreation of the geophysical and cultural background of ancient Greece and its colonies. Secondly, it constitutes a study of the origins of philosophy in which, as Gomperz interprets it, the nature of the subject may be determined and its evolution traced from the instincts which lead first to religion and then to philosophical speculation.

We turn at once to Gomperz' writing on the geographical and cultural background of Greek philosophy, postponing an examination of the validity of the *genetic method.*

II. ON THE GEOGRAPHICAL AND CULTURAL BACKGROUND OF GREEK PHILOSOPHY

Gomperz proceeds on the conviction that we can trace philosophy to its "fount" and that we may then proceed from the "causes" we discover in this process, from "the series of great and tangible factors, plainly manifest or readily to be found, which must have influenced the events to be accounted for, and in which the degree of such influence is the sole subject of doubt."

"All beginnings are obscure," Gomperz writes,[4] "whether owing to their minuteness or their apparent insignificance." In his study of Greek philosophy, he adds, "where we are dealing with the higher intellectual life of a nation," the first place in the influences which must be considered are the "geographical conditions and the peculiar character of its homes."

Gomperz' study proceeds as follows: "Hellas is a sea-girt mountain land. The poverty of her soil corresponds to the narrowness of her river-valleys. And here we find the first clue to some of the essential features of Hellenic evolution proper. It is clear, for instance, that a permanent home and a steady and manifold care and attention were offered to any seeds of civilization which might be deposited in her soil. Her mountain-barriers served her in the office of stone walls, breaking the force of the storm of conquest which sweeps unchecked across the plains. Each hilly canton was a potential seat of culture. Each could develop a separate type of that strongly marked individualism, which was ultimately to prove so favourable to the rich and many-sided civilization of Greece, so fatal to the political concentration of her powers. The country was full of piquant contrasts. Her Arcadia—an inland canton, sunk in torpid provincialism—was matched at the opposite extreme by the extent and curvature of the coast. Her seaboard was larger than Spain's, her mainland smaller than Portugal's. Other conditions, too, fostered this variety of natural gifts. The most diverse trades and professions were practised in the closest proximity. Seamen and shepherds, hunters and husbandmen, flourished side by side, and the fusion of their families produced in later generations a sum of talents and aptitudes complementary to each other. Again, the good fairies who presided at the birth of Greece could have laid no more salutary blessing in her cradle than the 'poverty which was ever her familiar friend.' It . . . lent a forcible impulse to commerce, navigation, emigration, and the foundation of colonies.

"The bays that offer the best harbourage on the Greek

4 From Theodor Gomperz' *Greek Thinkers*, Vol. 1, pp. 3-42. Translated by L. Magnus. Reprinted by permission of John Murray, and Charles Scribner's Sons.

peninsula open towards the east, and the islands and islets, with which that region is thickly sown, afford, as it were, a series of stepping-stones to the ancient seats of Asiatic civilization. Greece may be said to look east and south. Her back is turned to the north and west, with their semi-barbaric conditions. Another circumstance of quite exceptional good fortune may be ranged with these natural advantages. There was Greece in her infancy on the one side, and the immemorial civilizations on the other: who was to ply between them? The link was found—as it were by deliberate selection—in those hardy adventurers of the sea, the merchant-people of Phoenicia, a nation politically of no account, but full of daring and eager for gain. Thus it happened that the Greeks acquired the elements of culture from Babylon and Egypt without paying the forfeit of independence. . . .

"Still, the determining influence in the intellectual life of Greece must be sought in her colonial system. Colonies were founded at all times, and under every form of government. The Monarchy, a period of perpetual conflict, frequently witnessed the spectacle of settled inhabitants giving way to immigrating tribes, and seeking a new home beyond the seas. The Oligarchy, which rested entirely on the permanent alliance between noble birth and territorial possession, was often constrained to expel the 'pauvre gentilhomme,' the type and symbol of disorder, and to furnish him with fresh estates in foreign parts, whither he would speedily be followed by further victims of the incessant party strife. Meantime, the growth of the maritime trade of Greece, the flourishing condition of her industries, and her increasing population, soon made it necessary to establish fixed commercial stations, an uninterrupted supply of raw material, and safe channels for the importation of food. The same outlets were utilized, chiefly under the Democracy, to relieve the indigent poor and to draft off the surplus population. Thus, at an early period, there arose that vast circle of Greek plantations which stretched from the homes of the Cossacks on the Don to the oases of the Sahara, and from the eastern shore of the Black Sea to the coast-line of Spain. Great Greece and Greater Greece, —if the first name belong to the Hellenic portion of Southern Italy, the second might well be given to the sum of these settlements outside. The mere number and diversity of the colonies practically ensured the prospect that any seeds of civilization would happen on suitable soil, and this prospect was widened and brightened to an incalculable degree by the nature of the settlements and the manner of their foundation. Their sites were selected at those points of the coast which offered the best facilities for successful commercial enterprise. The emigrants themselves were chiefly young men of a hardy and courageous disposition, who would bequeath their superior qualities to their numerous issue. . . . Again, though a single city-state took the lead in the foundation of each colony, it would frequently be reinforced by a considerable foreign contingent, and this crossbreeding of Hellenic tribes would be further extended by an admixture of non-Hellenic blood, owing to the preponderance of the men over the women among the original emigrants. Thus, every colony served the purpose of experiment. Greek and non-Greek racial elements were mixed in varying proportions, and the test was applied to their resulting powers of resistance and endurance. Local customs, tribal superstitions, and national prejudices swiftly disappeared before the better sense of the settlers. Contact with foreign civilizations, however imperfectly developed, could not but enlarge their mental horizon in a very appreciable degree. . . . Greece found in her colonies the great playground of her intellect. There she proved her talents in every variety of circumstances, and there she was able to train them to the height of their latent powers. Her colonial life retained for centuries its fresh and buoyant spirit. The daughter cities in most respects outstripped their mother in the race. To them can be traced nearly all the great innovations, and the time was to come when they would steep themselves in intellectual pursuits as well, when the riddles of the world and of human life were to find a permanent home and enduring curiosity in their midst. . . .

"2. The geographical limits of the Greek horizon at this time were likewise wonderfully extended. On the far east and west of the world, as it was then known, the outline emerged from the mist. Precise and definite knowledge replaced the obscurity of legend. Shortly after 800 B.C., the eastern shore of the

Black Sea began to be colonized by Milesians; Sinope was founded in 785, and Trapezunt about thirty years later. Soon after the middle of the same century, Eubœa and Corinth sent out the first Greek settlers to Sicily, where Syracuse was founded in 734 B.C., and before the century's end the ambition and enterprise of Miletus had taken fast foothold at the mouths of the Nile. Three conclusions are involved in the fact of this impulse to expansion. It points to a rapid growth of population on the Greek peninsula and in the older colonies. It presumes a considerable development of Greek industry and commerce; and, finally, it serves to measure the progress in ship-building and in kindred arts. Take navigation, for instance. Where vessels formerly had hugged the shore, and had not ventured in deep waters, now they boldly crossed the sea. The mercantile marine was protected by men-of-war. Seaworthy battleships came into use with raised decks and three rows of oars, the first of them being built for the Samians in 705 B.C. Naval engagements were fought as early as 664 B.C., so that the sea acquired the utmost significance in the civilization of Hellas for the commerce of peace and war. At the same time, the progress of industry was fostered by a notable innovation. A current coinage was created. The 'bullocks' of hoary antiquity and the copper 'kettles' and 'tripods' of a later date successively passed into desuetude, and the precious metals replaced these rougher makeshifts as measures of value and tokens of exchange. Babylonian and Egyptian merchants had long since familiarized the market with silver and gold in the form of bars and rings, and the Babylonians had even introduced the official stamp as a guarantee of standard and weight. A convenient shape was now added to the qualities of worth and durability which make gold and silver the most practical symbols of exchange, and the metals were coined for current use. This invention, borrowed from Lydia about 700 B.C. by the Phocæans of Ionia, conferred remarkable benefits on commerce. It facilitated intercourse and extended its bounds. . . . Similar, if not greater, in effect was the change in the methods of warfare. The old exclusive service of the cavalry, which had flourished in the dearth of pastoral and corn-land as the privilege of wealthy landowners, was now reinforced by the hoplites, or

heavy-armed infantry, who far exceeded the cavalry in numbers. . . . New orders of the population achieved prosperity
and culture, and were filled with a strong sense of self-esteem.
A sturdy middle class asserted itself by the side of the old squire-
archy, and bore with increasing impatience the yoke of the
masterful nobles. But here, as elsewhere, the contradiction between actual conditions of strength and legal dues of preroga-
tive became the cause of civil strife. A battle of classes broke
out. It spread to the peasants, where persistent ill-usage and by
no means infrequent serfdom had sown the seeds of revolt, and
out of the rents and ruins of society there was hatched a brood
of usurpers, who partly destroyed and partly set aside the existing order of things. They constructed in its place a form of government which, though commonly short-lived, was not without
notable results. The Orthagorides, the Cypselides, the Pisistra-
tides, a Polycrates, and many another, may be compared with
the Italian tyrants of the late Middle Ages—the Medici, the
Sforza, or the Visconti—precisely as the party feuds of the one
epoch recall in the other the conflict between the lords and the
guilds. . . .

"Meantime, the stream of intellectual culture found broader
and deeper channels. The ballads of the heroes, which had been
sung for centuries in the halls of Ionian nobles to the accom-
paniment of the lyre, slowly fell into desuetude. New forms of
poetry began to emerge, and with them, in some instances, the
poet's personality emerged from the material of his song. . . .
A new spirit was breathed in the older poetical forms. Myth and
legend were refashioned by the masters of choric song in differing, if not in contradictory, modes. The didactic poets still aimed
at system, order, and harmony in their treatment of the material,
but side by side with those endeavours a manifold diversity was
to be remarked, and a licence in criticism, expressing itself in a
prejudice or preference in respect to this or that hero or heroine
of holy tradition. Thus, the neutral tints of the background were
ever more and more relieved by strong, self-conscious figures
standing out from the uniform mass. Habits of free-will and
feeling were created, and with them there grew the faculty of

independent thought, which was constantly engaged and exercised in wider fields of speculation.

"3. The Greeks were naturally keen-sighted. The faithful representation of sensible objects and occurrences constitutes one of the chief charms of the Homeric poems, and the imitation of figures and gestures by a hand that waxed in cunning now began to succeed to the arts of language and speech. Greece became the apprentice of older civilized countries, turning to Egypt above all for the paramount example of artistic instinct, natural joy, and engaging humour. But even in the limited sphere of the observation of men's ways and manners, fresh material was constantly collected. As travelling grew easier, its occasions would be multiplied. Not merely the merchant, ever intent on new gain, but the fugitive murderer, the exiled loser in the civil strife, the restless emigrant wandering on the face of the earth, the adventurer whose spear was at the service of the highest bidder, who would eat the bread of an Assyrian monarch today and tomorrow would pour down his burning throat the barley-water of Egypt, who was equally at home in the fruit-laden valley of the Euphrates and in the sands of the Nubian desert,—all of these would add to the sum of knowledge about places, peoples, and mankind. The frequent meeting or regular congregation in certain centres of Greeks of all cities and tribes served the purpose of huge reservoirs, in which the observations of individuals and the reports they made to their fellow-townsmen were collected and stored. The shrine of the oracle at Delphi was a chief example of the first, while the second condition was fulfilled by the recurring festivals of the Games, among which those at Olympia held the foremost rank. The sanctuary at Delphi, sacred to Pythian Apollo, was situated in the shadow of steep, beetling crags. Thither would come, and there would meet, an endless line of pilgrims from all parts of Greece and her colonies. . . . The Games which we have mentioned were celebrated in the broad river-valley of the Alpheius, and the attractiveness of that brilliant spectacle increased with each generation. The programme was constantly extended by the inclusion of new kinds of competitions, and the spectators, who at first were drawn merely from the surrounding country, gradually began to arrive—as is shown by the winners' lists, extant since 776 B.C.—from all points in the circumference of the wide Hellenic world. . . .

"The art of writing, the main vehicle for the exchange of thought, helped to distribute the fresh acquisitions of knowledge. Writing, it is true, was no novelty in Greece. . . . All that was wanted was a convenient and easily fashioned material. The want took some time to supply. The remedy was not found till soon after 660 B.C., when Greek trade with Egypt under Psammetich I. received a notable impulse. Then a writing-material of a kind which can hardly be improved was afforded by the pulp of the papyrus shrub, split into slender and flexible strips. From city to city, from land to land, from century to century, the sheets of written symbols now began to fly. The circulation of thought was accelerated, the commerce of intellect enlarged, and the continuity of culture guaranteed, in a degree which can well-nigh be compared with that which marked the invention of the printing-press at the dawn of modern history. . . .

"4. The west coast of Asia Minor is the cradle of the intellectual civilization of Greece. Its line stretches from north to south, but the heart of the movement must be sought in the country enclosing the centre of the line, and in the adjacent islands. There nature poured her gifts with lavish profusion, and those on whom they fell belonged to the Ionian tribe, at all times the most talented among Hellenes. . . . As bold seafarers and energetic traders, they enjoyed every benefit of the keen and fertilizing influence to be derived from intercourse with foreign nations in a more advanced state of civilization. They had the further advantage of intermarrying with other fine races, such as the Carians and Phœnicians, a fact which indisputably increased their original diversity of talent. The Ionians were the furthest removed of all Greeks from that fatal stagnation to which dwellers in isolated countries succumb so readily. It must be added that they lacked the sense of security which friendly mountain-barriers and an infertile soil bestow. The proximity of civilized nations, highly developed and united in a State, was as prejudicial to the political independence of the Ionians as it was beneficial to their intellectual progress. . . . The net result of this cross-series of good influences and bad was the rapid rise and swift decline of a period of prosperity. The ripe fruit fell all too soon, and the seeds it dropped were borne by fugitives from the foreigner's yoke, who would return now and again to the safe protection of Attica's fertile soil."

III. THE "GENETIC METHOD": GOMPERZ ON THE ORIGINS OF GREEK PHILOSOPHY

Theodor Gomperz' study of the conditions under which Greek philosophy arose merits John Burnet's estimate of *Greek Thinkers* as both "fascinating and imaginative." It is true, of course, that since the publication of Gomperz' book scholars have made available much more detailed and accurate information concerning the origins in Greece of the alphabet, the beginnings and developments of trade routes, the various invasions of the land, and the formation of the language. In the more specific area in which the problems of the origins of philosophy in religion arise, the reader is well advised to turn to E. Rohde's *Psyche*, W. Jaeger's *The Theology of the Early Greek Philosophers*, Jane Harrison's *Prolegomena to Greek Religion*, or E. R. Dodds' *The Greeks and the Irrational*. Still, the speculative, rather than the factual portion of Gomperz' study is our primary concern and we may examine the methodology of the study without committing ourselves to the somewhat archaic data from which it derives.

The basic question is this: Is Gomperz' argument such as to justify his explanation of what he calls the "evolution" which occurred in the course of a few centuries and which he believes accounts for "the rise of scientific pursuits and philosophical explanation"?

A brief resume of Gomperz' further argument will show, I believe, that the answer must be in the negative. If we first turn our attention to the method adopted by Gomperz, we discover that he suggests that it is possible to return to the "fount" of the sources of history. This we may do by means of inferences.

Gomperz advises us that inference by deduction, which starts from "causes," provides a more trustworthy method than does the inductive method. If we do start from "causes," Gomperz maintains, as we have observed, that we begin with "the series of great and tangible factors, plainly manifest or readily to be found, which must have influenced the events to be accounted for." We are then told that, having adopted this method, "the degree of such influence," i.e., of "the series of great and tangible factors" is the "sole object of doubt."

We have observed the use Gomperz has made of geophysical factors in Greek culture. We come now to the nerve of the argument concerning the "cause" of philosophical speculation. Gomperz believes that the Greeks offered "new" answers to the "eternal question of mankind—What is the meaning of self, God, and the world?—and these new answers gradually replaced or reshaped the former acceptations of religious belief."

It is, however, the "former acceptations of religious belief" which are the "causes," in Gomperz' sense, of influences which "determine" the intellectual life of Greece and provide the genuine "clue to some of the essential features of Hellenic evolution proper." Gomperz believes that the sources or "founts" of philosophy in religion are accessible. The "ultimate springs" are those, in his view, "from which mankind has derived an infinite variety of figures and forms, partly beautiful and wholesome, partly hurtful and ugly." He holds that Greek religion is grounded on the laws of the association of ideas and, more specifically, upon the law of likeness and the law of contiguity. To the operation of these laws, Gomperz attributes, "directly and inevitably," the conception of natural phenomena "which may be called the personification of nature." By means of the laws of association, on this hypothesis, a savage will "infallibly conclude" that any motion which strikes his mind strongly enough to be of interest is "the outcome of an exercise of will."

The association of movement with willpower, on this theory, is followed by "the observation that a series of frequently recurring effects is to be referred to one and the same natural object." A religion and a cult follow upon the efforts of the savage to mollify the powers so attributed to natural objects and this follows from the fact that natural objects have come to be regarded as "the animate and volitional authors of" the various processes. According to Gomperz, the immediate result is "fetishism," the less immediate, personification. The worship of fetishes and the personification of the gods affect the conception of the gods of Olympus. Despite the fact that the gods are "severed by a yawning gulf" from "the earliest and roughest products of religious imagination," they still retain traces of the "natural fetish" and the "beginning of the anthropomorphic god." An illustration will serve to guide us here. "When Earth is represented by the old theological poet as giving birth to high mountains and to the starry heaven that it may wholly encompass her . . . we are plainly standing with both feet in the realm of the pure worship of nature. Presently, however, we are confronted with a different set of stories. Fair-flowing Xanthus is represented by Homer as subject to a wrathful mood; Achilles fills his bed with dead men; he is sorely pressed by the flames ignited by Hephaestus, smith of the gods. . . ."

There are, in this illustration and others which Gomperz uses, two different kinds of religious imagination at work, and these, he believes, have been hopelessly confused. Spirits and gods have replaced "the volitional and conscious objects of nature." The god is the tenant of the abode and is no longer identical with his place of habitation. The divine being is thus "liberated." This is the "final and decisive step" by means of which polytheism replaced fetishism.

Gomperz regards the Greeks as a people preeminently endowed with the capacities requisite for personifying their Gods. "The process of personification was not confined to mere objects, but was extended to forces, states and qualities. Night, darkness, death, sleep, love, appetite, infatuation, were all looked on by the Greeks as individual beings, more or less successfully personified."

Men began to ask the eternal questions. In pessimistic mood, the Greek asked, "Who and what brought evil in the world?" No clear answer, except the inferences to be drawn from the story of Pandora, was forthcoming and one may accept Gomperz' inference that the lack of clarity evident in the answers and the questions asked is owing to the multiplicity of myths and the crowd of deities. It was Hesiod of Ascra in Bœotia who in the eighth century B.C. took an inventory of Olympus. Not only did he fit the gods into a genealogical system; he also offered in the *Theogony* a cosmogony. His writing on the origin of the gods included an account of the origin of the world.

Gomperz suggests that the sole principle of philosophical interest employed by Hesiod is this, that "the greater is the author of the less." Mountains are born of the Earth. These are "the earliest reflections of a thoughtful and bewildered man." Gomperz argues, however, that this is not all that is involved in Hesiod's work. The ancient writer discusses the origin of the world, but "not a single syllable of explanation is given of the When and How of this process. . . . One thing is as clear as noonday. A wide gulf is fixed between the summary and superficial methods of Hesiod's inquiry into origins and the devotion of those who applied the whole force of their immature philosophy to the solution of the great enigma."

Gomperz clearly means that Hesiod's inventory included not only legend but also "the oldest attempts at speculation" and that the latter are presented in such rough and incomplete fashion that all we know is that such attempts were made. But while Hesiod's attempt is of little value compared to that of the later philosophers, Gomperz does believe that in the Bœotian's writing are present "purely speculative excursions" in which Hesiod "was trusting to his own imagination." Individualism had emerged.

Gomperz has led us in the Introduction to his *Greek Thinkers* from the statement of the bare principles of the theory of the association of ideas, through statements concerning fetishism and personification, to an account of Hesiod's classification of the gods and of this writer's individual interpretation of the relation of the deities to the origin of the world. According to Gomperz, what is significant for and relevant to an understanding of the transition from the "fount" of religion to philosophy are factors such as the following: "the considerable mass of detailed knowledge" which had been collected and the inheritance from the Chaldaeans and Egyptians in astronomy, geometry, and mensuration. It cannot be seriously doubted that, as Greek speculation continued, "the conception of the universe as a playground of innumerable capricious and counteracting manifestations of Will" came to be "more and more undermined" or that "polytheisms inclined more and more to monotheism"; that cosmogony begins to free itself from theogony and "the problem of matter emerged into the foreground of men's thoughts."

For the cultural anthropologist, these factors are significant. The principal issue is, however, a systematic one, and it may be presented in the form of a question: Do these factors "cause" or do they merely serve as "conditions for" the philosophy which began in Miletus?

The answer to this question must take into account the facts that philosophy emerged in Miletus, that philosophers—not as theologians, as mathematicians, as cult-priests, but as philosophers—perfected what emerged, and that what began in Miletus was not religion, theology, astrology, economics, geography, navigational information, nor statecraft. What emerged was philosophy. There is nothing in Gomperz' argument which suggests (a) that a theory of causation taken over from the physical to the social sciences or, for that matter, from physics to logic, is applicable to the new fields or (b) that, granted its applicability to the new fields, the factors arrayed in theory by Gomperz, if they could once more be arrayed in fact, would "cause" philosophy to emerge again.

The issue more relevant to our present problem is clear once we return briefly to a suggestion made earlier in this Introduction. We observed that most explanations of early Greek philosophy are analogous to Aristotle's *material cause*, "that out of which" things come and which "persists" in the change. The point is well illustrated in the account of early Greece given by V. Gordon Childe in *What Happened in History*.[5] Childe argues that early speculation in Greece—he calls it "Iron Age philosophy"—concerned "the One and the Many." This problem, he

[5] (New York, Abelard-Schuman, Ltd., 1953), pp. 208 sq.

maintains, arose primarily from that of "the individual and society" and had its origin in the pursuit of "magical and mystical
ends."

Childe explains this and similar sources of "abstract speculation" in terms of the relation of the individual to society or, more
specifically, to the influence exerted upon the individual by a
serf or slave society. The argument is analogous to that developed by Gomperz. Both Gomperz and Childe suggest that
the "shoots" (philosophical speculation) are wholly accounted
for by the "roots" (nonphilosophical factors). The question remains, however, whether what Aristotle calls "free science,"
philosophy without practical utility, is not essentially different
from the practical activities of colonization or religion or mystical
or ritual observances or state rule which may well have been
its conditions.

The issue is an ancient one. Aristotle raises it concerning
Anaxagoras' assertion that "it is his possession of hands that
makes man the most intelligent of the animals." Aristotle urges,
rather, that "the reasonable point of view is that it is because he
is the most intelligent animal that he has got hands." [6] This is
the systematic problem. In considering it here, we may content
ourselves with the briefest of statements concerning the controversy as it relates to Miletus.

Let us begin with James H. Breasted's estimate [7] of Thales'
contribution to civilization in predicting a solar eclipse for
585 B.C. Breasted argues that in so doing Thales took what was
"probably the most fundamentally important step ever taken"
in human thinking because he interprets the prediction as Thales'
proclamation that the movements of the "heavenly bodies were
in accordance with fixed law. . . ." If we move a step further
with Breasted, we learn that it is precisely the independence of
Thales' prediction from the conditions emphasized by writers
like Gomperz and Childe that is significant in the prediction:
"The gods were thus banished from control of the sky-world
where the eagle of Zeus had once ruled."

[6] Aristotle, *de Partibus Animalium* 687 a 8.
[7] *The Conquest of Civilization* (New York, Harper & Row, Publishers,
Inc., 1926), p. 331.

Breasted's explanation means that something new had emerged in Miletus. It was, moreover, radically different from what had occurred before even though, as Breasted carefully points out, what emerged did not do so *ex nihilo*. Breasted suggests that Thales probably had in his hands the Babylonian lists of observations of the heavenly bodies and had already learned "that eclipses occurred at periodic intervals." One may argue, indeed, that the information Thales drew upon is, for Breasted, the necessary condition for Thales' prediction. Without it, no prediction could have been made; with the Babylonian lists at hand, Thales might still not have made the contribution which Breasted calls "the most fundamentally important step ever taken in human thinking." Babylonian science provides at most the necessary, but certainly not the *sufficient condition* for what occurred. "Hitherto," Breasted writes, "men had believed that eclipses and all other strange things that happened in the skies were caused by the momentary angry whim of some god." Now, men moved into another realm of speculation. These occurrences were explained in terms of the rule of fixed law.

What emerged had emerged from what it was. It had become what it is and the conditions for the "rule of fixed law" did not determine that rule. Thales provided a principle or cause by means of which observed phenomena could be intelligibly classified. By implication, he had laid down a philosophical principle, namely, that the cosmos is to be interpreted, in all its variety and diversity, in terms of an intelligible cause.

The issue is clear enough. It is ordinarily obscured at the outset by several factors which it will be useful to mention. In the first place, Thales did not free his own thinking completely from its reliance upon the gods. The same Thales who predicted the eclipse was the man who maintained that everything is full of gods. Secondly, for the philosopher at any rate, what Breasted holds concerning Thales' contribution to human thinking is more nearly applicable to the explanation of the cosmos in terms of a single principle than to the prediction of an eclipse. Indeed, eclipses are phenomena among other phenomena explained in terms of a single principle or cause by Thales' immediate successor, Anaximander. Thales' principle encompasses the cosmos in its reduction of phenomena to explanation in "accordance with fixed law" and this is of primary significance.

The third point to be noticed is that the implications of Thales' speculation are fully worked out only in the history of Greek natural philosophy. Thales does not wholly rid his speculation of dependence upon the whim of the gods. The traces of the early religious belief manifest themselves as late as the philosophies of Empedocles and Anaxagoras, who employ efficient causes to explain the processes of change in the cosmos. "Love and Hate" and "Mind" evidence the reluctance of philosophers to abandon the interpretation of the cosmos in terms of human feelings and human rationality as these are attributed to the deities.

It is important to notice that early Greek philosophy becomes "philosophy" on the occurrence of two events. Natural philosophy achieves its perfection in classical times in Atomist speculation. It is wholly emancipated when the Atomist philosopher, Leucippus, maintains that "nothing occurs at random, but everything for a reason and by necessity."

Early Greek philosophy is emancipated once again by Socrates. It is perhaps the crowning paradox of this paradoxical man's career that the Athenians, still confused by the resemblances of natural philosophy to religion, put Socrates to death, in part, on a charge of introducing new gods. They seemed to have been unaware that what he had introduced was a new philosophy.

Natural philosophy begun in Miletus and the philosophy of man, the center of Socrates' interest, are both new and original. Neither is wholly unconditioned; neither is wholly determined. Natural philosophy is influenced by the nonphilosophical conditions under which it emerged, Socratic philosophy by nonphilosophical aspects of Greek culture and by the century and a half of speculation upon nature which Socrates inherited.

Socrates dismissed natural philosophy as "sheer folly" and the controversies of its proponents as the talk of madmen. He is, however, thoroughly conversant with the subject and it will be well for us, in the remainder of this introduction, to indicate how what Thales began and what Socrates began again may both be original and yet both be integral parts of "philosophy." This we may do most easily by turning to a classical and important problem with which the early natural philosophers were concerned and by showing how it was transformed in Socrates' speculation.

The Greek natural philosophers, if we except the Eleatics, searched for the cause or principle by means of which they could explain the cosmos and its processes. They searched for the intelligible cause which persists throughout processes of change. They sought, in classical terminology, to "save appearances." This means that they searched for a valid ground for the explanation of what we perceive. The search took place as natural philosophers selected "water," "air," "fire," "the infinite," "atoms," "seeds," as the material cause most suitable to explain continuity and change. With Socrates, what persists becomes the self and concepts; what changes are the actions of men, analogous to the "percepts" of natural philosophy, which must be explained in terms of an abiding self.

Let us turn to the methods employed by the natural philosophers. With but an indistinct notion of the difference between qualities and things qualified, they sought to "save appearances" by accounting for the qualities of things. Anaximander holds that the "world-stuff" is "the infinite," Anaximenes that it is "air." But, in the two Milesian philosophies, the striking difference in explanation, which may well be the guiding thread to the history of natural philosophy in the West, is already made explicit. For Anaximander, the qualities of what we perceive are not derivative but are ultimate. For Anaximenes, the qualities are derivative, not ultimate. Anaximenes implies that qualities are functions of the quantity of the "world-stuff" or "air," the explanatory principle in this system.

The tradition of those who believe that qualities are ultimate is clearly marked out in early Greek philosophy. Anaximander believes that the qualities are not only ultimate but "infinite." For Empedocles, the qualities are ultimate but finite, i.e., the four elements are earth, air, fire, and water, each distinctly qualified. For Anaxagoras, qualities are ultimate and infinite in number, identical with the "seeds" and ordered by Mind or *Nous.* What the Mind orders are "the dense, the moist, the cold, the dark, the rare, the warm, the dry, the bright. . . ."

The tradition of natural philosophy in which quantitative explanation is adopted is no less clear and distinct. It begins with Anaximenes, who implies that all that we perceive is "air" in some state or other of rarefaction and condensation. For the Pythagoreans, the universe is described in quantitative terms, because its structure is mathematical. The material cause is "numbers," the formal cause, "harmony." The greatest achievement of ancient natural philosophy is Atomism. The atoms are infinite in number but, within the system, the explanatory principles are reduced to a minimum. The Atomists anticipate the Newtonian suggestion that "we are to admit no more causes of natural things than such as are both true and sufficient to explain their appearance." As Lucretius makes clear, the Atomists assume that "if . . . you hold that the elements combine without changing their nature, nothing can be created from them, whether animate or inanimate."

Atomism encounters the problem of sensation and perception and fails to cope with it in consistent terms. For Democritus, what is "sensed" is explained both on "realist" grounds, i.e., the structure of the atoms in compounds perceived, and in terms of "subjectivist theory," e.g., that "sweet is by convention." The Sophists, whose interests center wholly upon man, encounter no such difficulty. Having adopted Heraclitean theory, the Sophists examine the problem only as one of "perceiving." The flow of "perceivings" is accepted as the ultimate description of what a man may know, since "Man is," as Protagoras maintained, "the measure" or "the criterion" of all things.

Speculation upon natural philosophy, for Socrates, is of no value and that of the Sophists is both dangerous and unsound. For Socrates, the emancipation of natural philosophy from explanation of percepts in terms of purposes is a denial of the basic explanatory principle in philosophy. Percepts—men's actions—must be understood in terms of ends, which are conceptual. The world of percepts is intelligible only in terms of concepts, precisely as men's specific actions are intelligible in terms of the self. Like the natural philosophers' "fire" and "water" and "air," the self persists throughout change and yet accounts for the differences we perceive. For Socrates, the truth may be beaten out by dialectic. The truth is, for him, that "philosophy" is neither natural philosophy nor Sophism but, rather, a unique art, with its own subject matter and its own technique.

The Atomists abandon the gods for a philosophy without efficient causes. Socrates allocates to gods and men their appropriate tasks. Upon Socrates fell the suspicion that he had meddled with what the people thought "was done by the gods only." Plutarch writes, "Socrates was put to death for the suspicion thereof, . . ." falling victim to the suspicion which had banished Protagoras, and sent Anaxagoras to prison. Plutarch believes that it was Plato who "took away all the ill opinion which the people had of such disputations" concerning whether or not the natural philosophers ascribe "that which was done by gods only, unto certain natural and necessary causes, that worked their effects not by providence nor will, but force, and necessary consequences."

What Plutarch ascribes to Plato is actually Socrates' accomplishment. For Socrates, philosophy is clearly not natural science, which the Athenians confused with religion. What Socrates believed was what we might accurately express as follows: philosophy is a unique universe of discourse.

The philosophers of early Greece emancipate philosophy from its nonphilosophical meanings. For the natural philosophers, it is the cosmos as a whole for which they seek an explanation. Lucretius sums up [8] the goal of the Atomists:

> Name o'er creation with what name thou wilt,
> Thou'lt find but properties of those first twain,
> Or see but accidents those twain produce—
> [As] state of slavery, pauperhood, and wealth,
> Freedom, and war, and concord, and all else
> Which come and go whilst nature stands the same,
> We're wont, and rightly, to call accidents. . . .

[8] Titus Lucretius Carus, *de Rerum Natura*, I. 449 sq., translated by William Ellery Leonard, *Lucretius: Of the Nature of Things* (New York, E. P. Dutton & Co., 1921), p. 18.

To suggest that philosophy is emancipated by both the Atomists and by Socrates is not to suggest that they were in agreement concerning the answer to the question, What is philosophy? For Socrates, the effort to explain his presence in the prison cell solely in terms of muscles, bones, and nerves—in terms of mechanism and materialism—is fruitless. It confuses, Socrates argues, "condition and cause." Socrates believes that he is in prison, condemned to death, because of "the best." He explains his own state neither in terms of the whims of the gods nor in terms used by the natural philosophers. His explanation is one which requires concepts, ends, and knowledge of the self. Men's actions are analogous to the percepts which were the primary interest of the natural philosophers and the Sophists.

While philosophy, whether it be Milesian or Socratic, is a single speculative art, the foci of interest for philosophers shift from 585 B.C. to 399 B.C. and the principal interests in the cosmos and in man diverge. They are reunited in the systematic philosophies of Plato and Aristotle, but our immediate concern in this book of selections is with the natural philosophy which begins in Miletus. It is to this form of speculation that science in the West owes its inception and early development. It is here, also, as I have indicated, that the two traditional explanations of nature emerge. One explains qualities in terms of mathematics, the other in terms of what is believed to be implicit in things and not a function of quantity.

We turn now to speculation in Miletus and to the diverse explanations of the cosmos which followed and from this to the philosophies of the Sophists and of Socrates, in which the basic interest is man.

INTRODUCTORY: ON PHILOSOPHY AND PHILOSOPHERS

1. D. L., *Lives* 1. 12. But[1] Pythagoras was the first person who invented the term Philosophy, and who called himself a philosopher; for he said that no man ought to be called wise,

[1] Translated by C. D. Yonge, *The Lives and Opinions of Eminent Philosophers* (London, Henry G. Bohn, 1863), pp. 9-10.

but only God. For formerly what is now called philosophy was called wisdom and they who professed it were called wise men, as being endowed with great acuteness and accuracy of mind; but now he who embraces wisdom is called a philosopher.

2. HERA., *Fr.* 16. Learning of many things does not teach one to have understanding; else it would have taught Hesiod and Pythagoras, and also Xenophanes and Hecataeus.

3. ARIST., *Met.* 982 b 12.[2] That it is not a science of production is clear even from the history of the earliest philosophers. For it is owing to their wonder that men both now begin and at first began to philosophize; they wondered originally at the obvious difficulties, then advanced little by little and stated difficulties about the greatest matters, e.g., about the phenomena of the moon and those of the sun and of the stars, and about the genesis of the universe. And a man who is puzzled and wonders thinks himself ignorant (whence even the lover of myth is in a sense a lover of Wisdom, for the myth is composed of wonders); therefore since they philosophized in order to escape from ignorance, evidently they were pursuing science in order to know, and not for any utilitarian end. And this is confirmed by the facts; for it was when almost all the necessities of life and the things that make for comfort and recreation had been secured, that such knowledge began to be sought. Evidently then we do not seek it for the sake of any other advantage; but as the man is free, we say, who exists for his own sake and not for another's, so we pursue this as the only free science, for it alone exists for its own sake. . . .

4. ———— 983 b 23. Evidently we have to acquire knowledge of the original causes (for we say we know each thing only when we think we recognize its first cause), and causes are spoken of in four senses. In one of these we mean the substance, i.e., the essence (for the 'why' is reducible finally to the definition, and the ultimate 'why' is a cause and principle); in another the matter or substratum, in a third the source of the change,

[2] Translated by W. D. Ross, *The Works of Aristotle Translated into English,* Vol. VIII, ed. by W. D. Ross (Oxford, The Clarendon Press, 1928).

and in a fourth the cause opposed to this, the purpose and the good (for this is the end of all generation and change. . . .) [3]

5. D. L., *op. cit.* I. 10. But [4] of Philosophy there arose two schools. One derived from Anaximander, the other from Pythagoras. Now, Thales had been the preceptor of Anaximander, and Pherecydes of Pythagoras. And the one school was called Ionian, because Thales, being an Ionian . . . had been the tutor of Anaximander;—but the other was called the Italian from Pythagoras, because he spent the chief part of his life in Italy. . . . I. 13. Now there are three divisions of philosophy, Natural, Ethical, and Dialectic. Natural philosophy occupies itself about the world and the things in it; Ethical philosophy about life and the things which concern us; Dialectics are conversant with the arguments by which both the others are supported. . . .

6. PLATO, *Apology.* 38 A. Socrates: . . . the unexamined life is not worth living.

[3] See Aristotle's *Physics* 194 b 23, quoted above, p. 6.
[4] C. D. Yonge, *op. cit.*

PART I

THE MILESIAN SCHOOL

IN THE FIRST book of the *Metaphysics,* Aristotle provides a critical history of preceding philosophical speculation. As we have observed in the Introduction, Aristotle's procedure leads him to remark upon many aspects of philosophy. He writes that the subject begins in "wonder"; that the knowledge men seek when they philosophize is not practical; that they desire this knowledge in order to avoid ignorance; and that men seek by means of philosophy to answer the question, "Why?" which means that their queries will be answered in terms of "causes" (see above, pp. 5-6 sq. and below, I. B. 2, 3).

Philosophy begins in Miletus. The first men to pursue the subject are Thales, Anaximander, and Anaximenes, citizens of that Greek colony in Asia Minor. In his examination of Milesian philosophy, Aristotle maintains that the men of this school sought to answer the question, "Why?" in terms of the *material cause.* He means by this that they attempted to explain the cosmos by discovering the "matter" or "substratum" out of which things come and which persists throughout the change (see above, p. 6).

Once speculation upon the cosmos begins, however, a second problem confronts the earliest philosophers. They attempt to answer not only the question, "Why?" but also, "How?" Again, as was indicated in the Introduction, (see above, pp. 23-24). Thales' successors, Anaximander and Anaximenes, offer antithetical replies to the questions concerning the "how" of the

transformation of matter into the world we observe. The qualities of things and events are held by Anaximander to be inherent
in the matter, whereas Anaximenes holds that the qualities of
things are to be explained as functions of the quantity of the
"matter" in clouds or stone or earth.

In both instances, however, Milesian speculation is directed
to the reduction of the diversity, variety, and multiplicity of the
phenomenal world to a unity of explanatory or causal principle.
As philosophers first approach the problem, the unifying principle is interpreted to be a fundamental "world-substance" or
"world-stuff" which, in its transformations, produces the observed beginnings and endings, changes and recurrences, processes and stabilities in the world.

It is soon evident, also, that the adequacy of the principle of
explanation is not the sole criterion used by the early Greek
philosophers to justify their choice of "causes." The new speculation implicitly requires that the principle adopted must not be
involved in direct conflict with any other principle unless a
satisfactory explanation of the relation of the two principles is
provided (see Anaximander, below, pp. 39-40 sq. and Heraclitus,
Ch. 3).

Thales [1] is the first philosopher of whom we have record
who set himself the problem of explaining the universe in terms
of one principle or "world-stuff." In philosophizing in terms of
what Aristotle was later to call the "material cause," Thales was
no doubt speculating out of wonder and for no utilitarian
reason. Nevertheless, by tradition Thales was one of the Seven
Wise Men. Writers who have left information concerning his
many-sided genius leave little doubt that much of his life was
devoted to activities of decidedly practical character. He is at
once a lawgiver and politician, who offers a plan for the con-
federation of the Hellenic states; civil engineer, who diverts the
course of the Halys river; mathematician, who brings back to
Greece certain geometrical propositions he had learned in Egypt
and who applies his acquired knowledge to the measurement of
the Pyramids and the calculation of the distances of ships at sea.
As we have already observed, (see above, p. 2) he predicted

[1] The selections relating to Thales' life and thought begin below, p. 37.

a solar eclipse for the year 585 B.C. and we have already re-marked upon Breasted's suggestion that this astronomical feat is probably the most fundamentally important step ever taken in human history. In any case, the occurrence of the eclipse on May 28, 585 B.C. had a practical consequence. It is said to have stopped a war (see below, I. A. 2). It is interesting, also, that Aristotle, who tells us that philosophy begins in "wonder" and is a subject of no practical value, also takes pains to recount an anecdote concerning Thales as a practical man. By securing a monopoly on olive presses in Chios and Miletus, Thales made a quantity of money and so showed the world that philosophers "can easily be rich if they like, but that their ambition is of an-other sort." [2]

Our interest in Thales primarily concerns his philosophy. He selects a natural substance or material, water, as the principle explaining change and transformation while yet remaining the same. Aristotle explains the selection of water on the grounds that moisture is essential to the origin of life and, consequently, to growth and change (see below, I. B. 2). It is possible that Thales, possessed of the Greek predilection for thinking in con-crete, image-making fashion, proceeded from the imagined trans-formations of earth into dews, mists, and springs to the more sophisticated view that water is suitable for selection as the primary substance because it undergoes transformation into gaseous and solid states in the forms of steam and ice. This ex-planation would involve temperature changes as a further ex-planatory factor, and it is perhaps possible that Thales was aware of the general problem involved, since Aristotle (see below, I. B. 4) suggests that Thales regarded the soul as the source of movement and cites as an example Thales' belief in the power of the lodestone to move iron.

Thales' selection of water as the substance that explains change satisfies the requirement that the substance assume various states. Difficulties remain, however, some of which are perceived by the Milesians themselves. Anaximander, son of Praxiades,[3]

[2] Aristotle, *Politics* I. 1259 a 6.
[3] The selections relating to Anaximander's life and thought begin below, p. 39.

"associate of Thales," attempts to meet one of the deficiencies in Thales' theory. Of Anaximander's life, we know little more than that he was sixty-four years of age in 547 B.C., that he constructed a map, probably for use in trade routes in the Black Sea, that he invented the gnomon, and that he conducted a colony to Appollonia, where a statue was erected in his honor.

The problem presented by Thales' theory to Anaximander may be stated simply: Granted that water may be selected to explain change because of the variety of forms or states it assumes in the world we experience, would not this substance, or, indeed, any similar natural substance like air or fire destroy the rest? If, for example, water be selected, ordinary experience demonstrates that its moistness is destructive of the heat of fire. The clarity with which Anaximander saw the difficulty is indicated in the one remaining fragment of his work (see below, II. B. a. 1) involving the germ of the Platonic theory of justice as "minding one's own business" and of not encroaching upon another's task. To avoid this difficulty, Anaximander identifies the fundamental substance with no one of the natural substances, earth, air, fire, or water. He selects, rather, the "infinite," a mixture, which may be thought of as a boundless stock from which all things come and to which all things return. The infinite is timeless and in motion. It surrounds all the worlds (see below, II. B. a. 2) and since it is not identical with any natural substance, the conflict of contraries will not cause its destruction and "becoming" or change may continue eternally. As a consequence of the eternal motion of the "infinite," substances are separated off. The first separated are heat and cold (see below, II. B. b. 2). On Zeller's [4] view, these combine to give the moist, which in turn gives rise to air, fire, and water. This view is supported by Alexander's explanation of the origin of the sea as the remainder of the original moisture (see below, II. B. b. 3), and is consistent with Anaximander's view (see below, II. B. c. 2) that life began in moisture and followed a course of evolution. Burnet suggests that of the opposites, heat and cold, heat makes its empirical ap-

[4] Edward Zeller, *A History of Greek Philosophy*, from the English translation of *The Pre-Socratic Philosophy* by S. F. Alleyne (London, Longmans, Green, and Co., Inc., 1881).

pearance as fire, while cold is differentiated into air and earth.

The abstract "infinite" is abandoned by the third member of the Milesian school, Anaximenes.[5] The son of Eurystratos and an associate of Anaximander, Anaximenes lived until *ca.* 525 B.C. Anaximenes selects air as the fundamental substance persisting through change. The volatility of air and its seeming inexhaustibility apparently lead to this choice. One important consequence of Anaximenes' adoption of air as the primary substance is to be seen in his reinterpretation of Thales' theory that soul is diffused throughout the universe. Anaximenes identifies air and breath, discovering in this substance the basis for life and change in living beings. Drawing upon the microcosm for his analogy, Anaximenes interprets the macrocosm as a living, breathing organism in which, by inference, change and movement occur because of the presence of breath (see below, III. B. a. 1).

Thales suggests that soul is the source of motion. Anaximander offers motion and separation as the cause of the variation of objects in the world. Anaximenes improves upon the views of his fellow Milesians by offering an ordered sequence of change and by submitting for examination a specific process by which the varied states of objects in the world of experience could have been produced from air. Air, we are told, assumes different states through a process of rarefaction and condensation (see below, III. B. b. 1, 2). Rarefied air is fire. As air is condensed more and more, it is, in order, wind, water, earth, and stones. No explanation is given of the means by which the process begins but with the theory of rarefaction and condensation, Milesian philosophy has advanced far. In the first place, Anaximenes' hypothesis is one suitable for experimental verification. Secondly, it offers a possibility for reducing to quantitative differences such intangible qualitative differentiations as hardness, softness, etc. Once this step has been taken, the way is prepared for the experimental assumption of the Atomists that an adequate explanation of phenomena may be obtained by the determination of the ratio between the amount of matter and the extent of the space it occupies.

Milesian cosmology may be regarded as an application of

[5] The selections from Anaximenes' philosophy begin below, p. 43.

the theory of substance to the universe and its general character is dominated by Thales' theory that the earth is a disc floating on water. Anaximenes, for example, adopts the general hypothesis of a flat earth but tells us that it floats on air. From Anaximenes' description of the motion of the stars as similar to the motion of a cap turning upon the head and with the added hypothesis that the stars disappear behind high places, we infer that the Milesian universe was one terminated by the surface of earth and the vault of heaven. Anaximander elaborates the theory with important consequences for later cosmology. The earth is a cylinder, with flat ends, one of which is our habitat. The cylinder swings unattached in the middle of the universe, maintained in this position by its equidistance from the boundaries of the world and by its heaviness, since in the motion of the infinite, heavy objects move towards the center. This obviates any need for an hypothesis of the earth floating on any substance. Out of the original differentiation of hot and moist from the infinite come earth and air as a core, surrounded by a circle of fire. This circle, broken into three hoops or rings, is surrounded by air. Through apertures in the air that surrounds it, fire shines forth as the stars, sun, and moon. In Anaximander's cosmos, the earth is the center of a cosmic eddy and is enclosed within circles or "cartwheels." The hypothesis of circles is adopted and elaborated upon by the Pythagoreans.

Aristotle explains the Milesian philosophy in terms of the material cause.

ARIST., *Met.* I. 983 b 7. Now the majority of those who first formed systems of philosophy consider those that subsist in a form of matter to be alone the principles of all things; for wherefrom all entities arise, and wherefrom they are corrupted,—ultimately the substance, indeed, remaining permanent, but in its passive states undergoing a change—this they assert to be an element, and this a first principle of all things. And for this reason they are of the opinion that nothing is either generated or annihilated, since this primary entity always persists. . . .

I. THALES

A. LIFE

1. D.L., *Lives* 1. 13. Now these were they who accounted wise men: Thales, Solon, Periander, Cleobolus, Chilon, Bias, Pittacus. . . . 1. 37. Apollodorus, in his Chronicles, says that Thales was born in the first year of the 35th Olympiad (640 B.C.); and he died at the age of seventy-eight years, or according to Sosicrates, at the age of ninety, for he died in the 58th Olympiad, having lived at the time of Crœsus, to whom he promised that he would enable him to pass the Halys without a bridge, by turning the course of the river. . . . 1. 22. Herodotus, Duris, and Democritus are agreed that Thales was the son of Euxamius and Cleobule; of the family of the Thelidæ, who are Phoenicians by descent. . . .

2. HEROD., *Hist.* Ch. 74-75. . . . War broke out between the Lydians and the Medes and continued for five years. . . . Another combat took place in the sixth year, in the course of which, just as the battle was growing warm, day was on a sudden changed into night. This event had been foretold by Thales, the Milesian, who forewarned the Ionians of it, fixing for it the very year in which it actually took place (May 28, 585 B.C.). The Medes and the Lydians, when they observed the change, ceased fighting, and were alike anxious to have terms of peace agreed on. . . .

3. ———— Ch. 170. Before their [the Ionians'] misfortunes began, Thales, a man of Miletus, of Phoenician descent . . . counselled them to establish a single seat of government, and pointed out Teos as the fittest place for it, "for that," he said, "was the center of Ionia. Their other cities might still continue to enjoy their own laws, just as if they were independent states." This also was good advice.

4. D.L., *op. cit.* 1. 23. He (Thales) seems by some accounts

to have been the first to study astronomy, the first to predict eclipses of the sun and to fix the solstices. . . .

B. Thought

1. Aet., *Plac.* 1. 3. *Dox* 276. Thales the Milesian declared that the first principle of things is water.

2. Arist., *op. cit.* I. 983 b. 18. As to the quantity and form of this first principle, there is a difference of opinion; but Thales, the founder of this sort of philosophy, says that it is water (accordingly he declares that the earth rests on water), getting the idea, I suppose, because he saw that the nourishment of all things is moist, and that warmth itself is generated from moisture and persists in it (for that from which all things spring is the first principle of them); and getting the idea also from the fact that the germs of all beings are of a moist nature, while water is the first principle of the nature of what is moist. And there are some who think that the ancients, and they who lived long before the present generation, and the first students of the gods, had a similar idea in regard to nature; for in their poems Oceanos and Tethys were the parents of generation, and that by which the gods swore was water,—the poets themselves called it Styx; for that which is most ancient is most highly esteemed, and that which is most highly esteemed, is an object to swear by. Whether there is any such ancient and early opinion concerning nature would be an obscure question; but Thales is said to have expressed this opinion in regard to the first cause.

3. ———, *de Caelo.* II. 13. 294 a 28. Some say that the earth rests on water. We have ascertained that the oldest statement of his character is the one accredited to Thales the Milesian, to the effect that it rests on water, floating like a piece of wood or something else of that sort.

4. ———, *de Anima* I. 2. 405 a 19. And Thales, according to what is related of him, seems to have regarded the soul as something endowed with the power of motion, if indeed he said that the lodestone has a soul because it moves iron. I. 5. 411 a 7.

Some say that soul is diffused throughout the whole universe; and it may have been this which led Thales to think that all things are full of gods.

II. ANAXIMANDER

A. LIFE

1. D.L., *op. cit.* II. 1. Anaximander, the son of Praxiades, was a citizen of Miletus. . . . 3. He also was the first discoverer of the gnomon; and he placed some in Lacadæmon on the sundials there . . . and they showed the solstices and the equinoxes. . . . He was the first person, too, who drew a map of the earth and sea. . . . 4. And Apollodorus, in his Chronicles, states, that in the second year of the 58th Olympiad (547-546 B.C.), he was sixty-four years old. . . . They say that when he sang, the children laughed. . . .

B. THOUGHT

a. The infinite.

1. SIMP., *Phys.* 6 r. 24, 26 (from Theophrastus, *Dox.* 476). Among those who say that the first principle is one and movable and infinite, is Anaximander of Miletus, son of Praxiades, pupil and successor of Thales. He said that the first principle and element of all things is infinite, and he was the first to apply this word to the first principle; and he says that it is neither water nor any other one of the things called elements, but the infinite is something of a different nature, from which came all the heavens and the worlds in them.

2. HIPP., *Phil.* 6. *Dox.* 559. And this (first principle) is eternal and does not grow old, and it surrounds all the worlds.

3. SIMP., *op. cit.* 6 r. And from what source things arise, to that they return of necessity when they are destroyed; for they

suffer punishment and make reparation to one another for their injustice according to the order of time, as he says in somewhat poetical language.

4. HIPP., *loc. cit.* Besides this, motion is eternal, and as a result of it the origin of the worlds was brought about.

5. SIMP., *loc. cit.* Evidently when he sees the four elements changing into one another, he does not deem it right to make any one of these the underlying substance (substratum), but something else besides them. And he does not think that things come into being by change in the nature of the element, but by the separation of the opposites which the eternal motion causes.

6. ——— 32 r. 150, 20. There is another method, according to which they do not attribute change to matter itself, nor do they suppose that generation takes place by a transformation of the underlying substance, but by separation; for the opposites existing in the substance which is infinite matter are separated, according to Anaximander, who was the earliest thinker to call the underlying substance the first principle. And the opposites are heat and cold, dry and moist, and the rest.

7. ARIST., *Phys.* III. 5. 204 b 22. But it is not possible that infinite matter is one and simple; either, as some say, that it is something different from the elements, from which they are generated, or that it is absolutely one. For there are some who make the infinite of this character, but they do not consider it to be air or water, in order that other things may not be destroyed by the infinite; for these are mutually antagonistic to one another, inasmuch as air is cold, water is moist, and fire hot; if one of these were infinite, the rest would be at once destroyed. Accordingly, they say that the infinite is something different from these elements, namely, that from which they come.

b. The application of the infinite to the cosmos.

1. SIMP., *op. cit.* 5. Those who assumed innumerable worlds, e.g., Anaximander, Leucippus, Democritus, and, at a later date, Epicurus, held that they came into being and passed away *ad*

infinitum, some always coming into being and others passing away.

2. PLUT., *Strom.* 2. *Dox.* 579. Anaximander says that at the beginning of this world something productive of heat and cold from the eternal was separated therefrom, and a sort of sphere of this flame surrounded the air about the earth, as bark surrounds a tree; then this sphere was broken into parts and defined into distinct circles, and thus arose the sun and the moon and the stars.

3. ALEX., *Meteor.* 91 r. *Dox.* 494. Some of the physicists say that the sea is what is left of the first moisture; for when the region about the earth was moist, the upper part of the moisture was evaporated by the sun, and from it came the winds and the revolutions of the sun and moon, since these made their revolutions by reason of the vapors and exhalations, and revolved in those regions where they found an abundance of them. What is left of this moisture in the hollow places is the sea; so it diminishes in quantity, being evaporated gradually by the sun, and finally it will be completely dried up. Theophrastus says that Anaximander and Diogenes were of this opinion.

4. PLUT., *loc. cit.* Anaximander says that the earth is a cylinder in form, and that its depth is one-third of its breadth.

5. HIPP., *op. cit.* The earth is a heavenly body, controlled by no other power, and keeping its position because it is the same distance from all things; the form of it is curved, cylindrical like a stone column; it has two faces, one of these is the ground beneath our feet, and the other is opposite to it. ————. The stars are a wheel (circle) of fire, separated from the fire about the world, and surrounded by air. There are certain breathing-holes like the holes of a flute through which we see the stars; so that when the holes are stopped up, there are eclipses. The moon is sometimes full and sometimes in other phases as these holes are stopped up or open. The circle of the sun is twenty-seven times that of the moon, and the sun is higher than the moon, but the circles of the fixed stars are lower.

6. Aet., *op. cit.* 2. 13. *Dox.* 342. The stars are wheel-shaped masses of air, full of fire, breathing out flames from pores in different parts. 15. 345. Anaximander (*et al.*): The sun has the highest position of all, the moon is next in order, and beneath it are the fixed stars and the planets. 16. 345. The stars are carried on by the circles and the spheres in which each one moves. 20. 348. The circle of the sun is twenty-eight times as large as the earth, like a chariot wheel, having a hollow center and this full of fire, shining in every part, and sending out fire through a narrow opening like the air from a flute. 21. 351. The sun is equal in size to the earth, but the circle from which it sends forth its exhalations, and by which it is borne through the heavens, is twenty-seven times as large as the earth. 24. 354. An eclipse takes place when the outlet for the fiery exhalations is closed. 25. 355. The circle of the moon is nineteen times as large as the earth, and like the circle of the sun is full of fire; and eclipses are due to the revolutions of the wheel; for it is like a chariot wheel, hollow inside, and the center of it is full of fire, but there is only one exit for the fire. 28. 358. The moon shines by its own light. 29. 359. The moon is eclipsed when the hole in the wheel is stopped. 3, 3. 367. Anaximander said that lightning is due to wind; for when it is surrounded and pressed together by a thick cloud and so driven out by reason of its lightness and rarefaction, then the breaking makes a noise, while the separation makes a rift of brightness in the darkness of the cloud.

c. The theory of the origin and evolution of man.

1. Hipp., *loc. cit.* Animals came into being through vapors raised by the sun. Man, however, came into being from another animal, namely the fish, for at first he was like a fish.

2. Aet., *op. cit.* V. 19. Anaximander said that the first animals were generated in the moisture, and were covered with a prickly skin; and as they grew older, they became drier, and after the skin broke off from them, they lived for a little while.

3. Plut., *loc. cit.* Anaximander says that at the beginning man was generated from all sorts of animals, since all the rest can quickly get food for themselves, but man alone requires

careful feeding for a long time; such a being at the beginning could not have preserved his existence.

4. ———, *Symp.* VIII. 730 E. Wherefore they (the Syrians) reverence the fish as of the same origin and the same family as man, holding a more reasonable philosophy than that of Anaximander; for he declares, not that fishes and men were generated at the same time, but that at first men were generated in the form of fishes, and that growing up as sharks do till they were able to help themselves, they then came forth on the dry ground.

III. ANAXIMENES

A. LIFE

1. D.L., *op. cit.* II. 3. Anaximenes, the son of Eurystratos, a Milesian, was a pupil of Anaximander; but some say that he was also a pupil of Parmenides. . . . And he lived, according to the statements of Apollodorus, in the 63rd Olympiad (528-525 B.C.), died about the time of the taking of Sardis.

2. HIPP., *op. cit.* 1. 7. *Dox.* 560-561. Anaximenes, himself a Milesian, son of Eurystratos . . . flourished about the first year of the 58th Olympiad. . . .

B. THOUGHT

a. Anaximenes' principle of explanation: air.

1. AET., *loc. cit. Dox.* 278. *Fr.* "As our soul which is air," he says, "holds us together, so wind [πνεῦμα] and air encompass the whole world."

2. SIMP., *op. cit.* 6 r. *Dox.* 476. Theophrastus. Anaximenes of Miletus, son of Eurystratos, a companion of Anaximander, agree with him that the essential nature of things is one and infinite, but he regards it as not indeterminate but rather determinate, and calls it air.

3. Hipp., *op. cit.* 7. *Dox.* 560. Infinite air is the first principle, from which arise the things that have come and are coming into existence, and the things that will be, and gods and divine beings, while other things are produced from these.

b. Anaximenes' explanation of phenomena in terms of air.

1. Simp., *loc. cit.* . . . The air differs in rarity and in density as the nature of things is different. . . .

2. Hipp., *op. cit.* 7. *Dox.* 560. And the form of air is as follows: When it is of a very even consistency, it is imperceptible to vision, but it becomes evident as the result of cold or heat or moisture, or when it is moved. It is always in motion; for things would not change as they do unless it were in motion. It has a different appearance when it is made more dense or thinner; when it is expanded into a thinner state it becomes fire, and again winds are condensed air, and air becomes cloud by compression, and water when it is compressed farther, and earth and finally stones as it is more condensed. . . .

3. Plut., *Strom.* 3. *Dox.* 579. By compression of the air the earth is formed, and it is very broad; accordingly he says that it rests on air. . . .

4. Aet., *op. cit.* 3. 10. *Dox.* 377. The form of the earth is like a table.

5. Hipp., *op. cit.* 7. *Dox.* 560. Similarly, the sun and the moon and all the rest of the stars, being fiery bodies, are supported on the air by their breadth. And stars are made of earth, since exhalations arise from this, and these being attenuated become fire, and of this fire when it is raised to the heaven the stars are constituted. There are also bodies of an earthy nature in the place occupied by the stars, and carried along with them in their motion. He says that the stars do not move under the earth, as others have supposed, but around the earth, just as a cap is moved about the head. And the sun is hidden not by going underneath the earth, but because it is covered by some of the higher parts of the earth, and because of its greater distance from us. The stars do not give forth heat, because they are so far away.

Winds are produced when the air that has been rarefied is set in motion; and when it comes together and is yet further condensed, clouds are produced, and so it changes into water. And hail is formed when the water descending from the clouds is frozen; and snow, when these being yet more filled with moisture become frozen;—And a rainbow is produced when the sun's rays fall upon thick condensed air.

6. AET., *op. cit.* 2. 1. *Dox.* 327. Anaximenes *et al.:* Infinite worlds exist in the infinite in every cycle. 4. 331. The world is perishable. 11. 339. The sky is the revolving vault most distant from the earth. 14. 344. The stars are fixed like nailheads in the crystalline (vault). 19. 347. The stars shine for none of these reasons, but solely by the light of the sun. 22. 352. The sun is broad [like a leaf]. 23. 352. The stars revolve, being pushed by condensed resisting air.

🏛🏛🏛🏛🏛 2

THE PYTHAGOREANS

Two aspects of the complicated Pythagorean philosophy [1] are dominant. They are the religious or moral and the mathematical or formal. These aspects are not mutually exclusive in the speculation of the philosophers of the "Italian School" but, rather, are integrally related in the Pythagorean view that the portion of a man's soul which possesses reason is superior to that which lacks reason (see below, C. d. 6) and that the best life is one in which ritual observances and intellectual discipline are designed to guide the life of the good man (see below, C. e. 4).

In the course of their philosophizing, the Pythagoreans conceived the cosmos as a mathematical structure. Their speculation was enormously influential in establishing the quantitative interpretation of the world and of its processes (see above, p. 24). In the course of their speculation concerning the soul and the problem of immortality, the Pythagoreans most radically influenced the thought of Socrates and Plato (see below, C. d. 1 and Ch. 7).

Of Pythagoras' life little is known, but the presence of Milesian elements in his thought lends weight to the tradition that he was a disciple of Anaximenes. A native of Samos, Pythagoras migrated from Greece to Croton, in southern Italy, *ca.*

---

[1] The selections from Pythagorean philosophy begin below, p. 52.

46

532 B.C. and there established his school (see below, A. 1 sq.). The development of Pythagorean philosophy in the hands of the followers was so varied that the group may be termed a school only in the sense that one man, the founder, stimulated an interest in one or the other of the aspects that dominated his own thought. Pythagoras, himself, was a religious teacher and a mathematician of native gifts. To him are attributed the first cosmology in which the earth is a planet rather than the center of the universe, the discovery of the Pythagorean theorem, and the formulation of the theory of harmony. Continued persecutions of the Pythagoreans in Croton forced Pythagoras to flee to Mesopontum, where his death occurred *ca.* 495 B.C. His most renowned disciples were Alcmæon of Croton, Hippasus of Mesopontum, and Philolaus of Croton (see below, B. 1).

Pythagoreanism, as a religious or ethical school, is influenced by the tenets and ritual of the cult of Orpheus. Perhaps the most important factor in the teaching of the cult of Orpheus was purification, by which man could recover the godlike character he once had. In this, Orphism is reminiscent of the teachings of the cult of Dionysus, in which the preoccupation with man's immortality owed its origin to the myth of Dionysus' capture by the Titans. In the myth, Dionysus was killed and eaten by his captors who, in turn, were destroyed by Zeus' thunderbolts. From the ashes of the Titans, containing as they did part of the divine Dionysus, man was created. Orphism, retaining the conception of the fallen god, added the theory of the transmigration of the soul. Every human soul, preexisting with the gods, must occupy a human body. Upon the conduct of the human being depended the future state of the soul, in that the soul returned to the gods or was punished for its sins by a return to the earth. For the Orphic, good conduct consisted largely in the observance of the stringent rules of life, including prohibitions upon particular kinds of food and participation in the mysteries or sacred pantomimes. Pythagoreanism incorporated much of Orphism in its teachings, including the belief in immortality and in metempsychosis (see below, C. d, e) and an observance of many rules of conduct. The sacrifice of animals was prohibited and the ritual was directed towards the end of demonstrating the superiority of the intellectual life, rather than to the mere performance of fixed ceremonies.[2]

In his mathematical philosophy, Pythagoras adopted number as the principle essential to an explanation of the universe. Perceiving "many qualities of numbers in bodies perceived by sense" (see below, C. a. 2), the founder and his disciples generalized their observations into a philosophy.

It seems probable that the beginnings of their explanations are to be found, as Aristotle suggests (*ibid.*), in Pythagoras' discovery of the relationship of concord in music to number. By experimentation with the lengthening and shortening of a vibrating string, the concordant intervals of the scale could be reduced to the numerical ratios of 1:1, 4:3, 3:2, and 2:1. These ratios, in turn, when reduced to their lowest common denominator, can be represented by the numbers 6, 8, 9, 12. Since these numbers, in turn, form a ratio in which means and extremes are equal, limit or form or unity is said by the Pythagoreans to have been brought into a concord of tones by the union of disparate or contrary elements. The simplicity and precision with which such a concord could be expressed had a wide influence upon Greek formal or mathematical theories of beauty, particularly upon the Platonic aesthetic.[3]

In the Pythagorean application of the theory of concord in music, *harmonia,* which originally signified the octave or a musical scale, comes to mean a system of relations and eventually the plan, scheme, or system which things compose. For later speculation, it is likewise the form or ratio as contrasted to the matter. In these meanings, *harmonia* is applied by the Pythagoreans to sciences as varied as medicine and cosmology. Medicine, on Pythagorean grounds, must have as its end the proper restoration of the complex harmony of the body, a harmony disturbed by illness. The soul is considered to be a harmony or attunement of the body, a theory to which Plato and

[2] For a discussion of the relation between mathematical studies and the purgation of the soul, see John Burnet's *Greek Philosophy: Part I Thales to Plato* (London, Macmillan and Co., Ltd., 1928), pp. 40-42.

[3] See my *Aesthetic Experience and Its Presuppositions* (New York, Harper & Row, Publishers, Inc., 1946), Ch. III.

Aristotle offer objections (see below, C. d. 1, 2; and Ch. 7, pp. 270 sq.).

There is also a *harmonia* of the cosmos (see below, C. b). The Pythagorean construction of the universe is fundamentally influenced by the Milesians and, in particular, by the teaching of Anaximander. Corresponding to the infinite of Anaximander or the boundless air of Anaximenes is the dark, a substance unlimited, cold, and dense. As a Pythagorean addition, there is also light, which is limited and formed. By attraction, portions of the dark are drawn to the limited, as if the universe were breathing, and these portions are given form or limit (see below, C. b. 1). As a consequence of the "breaths" of the universe, the astronomical system is evolved. Ten heavenly bodies revolve from west to east around the central fire. Between the central fire and earth, a planet moving as do other heavenly bodies, is counter-earth. Counter-earth, according to Aristotle (see below, C. b. 2), is included in order to construct a universe with ten heavenly bodies, as ten was considered to be a sacred number. The earth always presents the same side to the central fire and to counter-earth and we see neither of them. Earth is round, a planet, and receives light and heat from the sun, which shines by reflected light from the central fire (see below, C. a. 3, C. b). In the cosmos, after earth and in succession towards the limit of the universe, are the moon, the sun, the five planets, Mercury, Venus, Mars, Jupiter, and Saturn. At the limit of the cosmos is the sphere of the fixed stars.

The Pythagorean cosmology derives from that of Anaximander. Certain suggestions in the Milesian's hypothesis indicate the method by which *harmonia* was introduced into the Pythagorean system. Anaximander believed that the movement of the infinite produced wheels of fire and he adopted as a unit of measurement of the universe the radius of the earth. The wheel of the stars was nine times the size of the earth, that of the moon eighteen times that of the earth, that of the sun twenty-seven times the earth's size, from which it is evident that the cosmology is based upon an arithmetical progression. The Pythagoreans assume that the heavenly bodies move at distances from the central fire corresponding to the intervals of the octave. Since all moving bodies produce sound, the Pythagoreans, thinking perhaps of the speed of revolution of the bodies around the central fire or perhaps of the distance by which the bodies were separated from the central fire, assumed that a *harmonia* existed, with the resultant "music of the spheres" (see below, C. b. 3). The theory suggests at once a difficulty in the Pythagorean employment of hypotheses. The *harmonia* could not relate to the original ten heavenly bodies, as the theory was based either upon seven sounds, if the harmonic system of the heptachord is adopted, or upon eight sounds, if the harmonic system of the octochord is adopted.

The conception of the limited and the unlimited is based upon a similar arbitrary method of definition. All numbers are divided into odd and even. Since odd and even are the components of numbers and numbers are the essence and material of things in the world, things will likewise be odd or even. The next identification is that of odd with limited and of even with the unlimited (see below, C. a. 3). The reason for this identification is apparent if it be remembered that the Pythagorean number system was exhibited spatially. Numbers were represented by dots or alphas as demarcations of figures. The dots or alphas are disposed in straight lines in order to form geometrical figures. The Pythagoreans designated numbers by their shapes. These included "triangular," "square," and "oblong" numbers.

The first number after 1 which can be represented as a triangular number is 3. The sum of the first n natural numbers can be presented as a triangle and is represented in the Pythagorean *tetraktys* (see Fig. 1). The *tetraktys* is, for the Pythagoreans, the sacred symbol and the source of all numbers and shows how the number 10 is represented.

In Pythagorean mathematics, "square" numbers are formed by the addition of odd numbers to 1 (see Fig. 2). To form the figures, the Pythagoreans used the *gnomon,* said to have been invented by Anaximander (see above, Ch. 1, II. A. 1). This is an instrument for drawing right angles. *Gnomons* of odd numbers of dots or *alphas* placed around 1 always give a square, i.e.,

$1 + 3 = 4$ or 2^2; $1 + 3 + 5 = 9$ or 3^2. Similarly, *gnomons* of odd numbers added to a square give other squares, e.g., $1 + 3 = 2^2$; $2^2 + 5 = 3^2$; $3^2 + 7 = 4^2$. On the other hand, beginning with the even number 2, *gnomons* of even numbers give the series 2, 6, 12, 20, called by the Pythagoreans "oblong," owing to their spatial representation in the set figure (see Fig. 3).

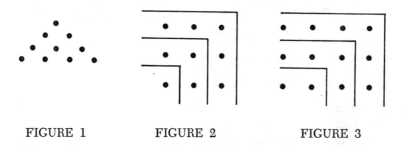

FIGURE 1   FIGURE 2   FIGURE 3

The Pythagoreans identified odd and even with limited and unlimited, the limited resisting division, the second open to endless division. Having identified things with limited and unlimited, the Pythagoreans assumed that the cosmos is constructed of conflicting elements. All things are combinations of the limited and the unlimited, reconciled by *harmonia* (see below, C. a. 3, for the list of ten pairs of opposites).

Proceeding further, the Pythagoreans apply their theory to earth, air, fire, and water. Beginning with the identification of *one* with the point, *two* with the line, *three* with the plane, and *four* with the solid, they formally identify the cube with earth, the tetrahedron with fire, etc. (see below, C. c. 1, 2).

The brilliant discovery that ratios and number are applicable to music results eventually in definition. The conception of form, as contrasted to matter, is applied to physical things as well as to geometrical and musical relations. The strength of Pythagorean philosophy derives from the reduction of multiple phenomena to formal ratios. Its weakness lies in the arbitrary application to phenomena of ratios and numbers which are not strictly applicable or are applicable only by altering the phenomena.[4] Counter-earth, included in order to make the heavenly bodies add to ten, is one example but there are many others. Justice, for example, is identified with four or with nine, since if one multiplies two by two or three by three and then takes the square root of the result "equals are returned to equals," a term synonymous with Pythagorean justice. For all of its weaknesses, however, Pythagoreanism pointed the way to and the necessity for definition and exerted perhaps its most important influence upon the Platonic theory of ideas.

PYTHAGORAS

A. LIFE AND TEACHING

1. HEROD., *Hist.* IV. 95. But I learn from the Greeks who dwell in the Hellespont and in the Pontus, this Salmoxis was a man, and a slave in Samos, the slave of Pythagoras the son of Mnesarchus. . . .

2. D.L., *Lives* VIII. 1. . . . We will now proceed to treat of the Italian School, which was founded by Pythagoras, the son of Mnesarchus, a seal engraver. . . . And as he was a young man and devoted to learning, he quitted his country, and got initiated into all the Grecian and barbarian sacred mysteries. Accordingly, he went to Egypt, on which occasion Polycrates gave him an introduction to Amasis; and he learnt the Egyptian language. . . . Then he returned back again to Samos, and finding his country reduced under the absolute dominion of Polycrates, he set sail, and fled to Croton in Italy. . . . 44. According to Heraclides, the son of Serapion, he was eighty years old when he died. . . .

---

4 See, for example, the identification of things with the "limited" and the "unlimited," above, p. 50; the identification of numbers "as the elements of all things," below, C. a. 3; the use of pebbles to "make," i.e., construct or delineate living things, below, C. a. 6; and the introduction of "counter-earth," to produce the "harmony of the spheres" and the "music of the spheres," below, C. b. 2, 3. See, also, Aristotle's criticism, below, C. a. 3. Cf. the Socratic method of definition, Ch. 7, pp. 252 and 268.

3. HIPP., *Phil.* 2. *Dox.* 555. . . . He perished in a conflagration with his disciples in Croton in Italy. And it was the custom when one became a disciple for him to burn his property and to leave his money under a seal with Pythagoras, and he remained in silence sometimes three years, sometimes five years, and studied. . . . The esoteric class were called Pythagoreans, and the others Pythagoristæ. . . .

4. POL., *Hist.* II. 39.[5] When, in the district of Italy, then known as Greater Hellas, the club-houses of the Pythagoreans were burnt down, there ensued, as was natural, a general revolutionary movement, the leading citizens of each city having thus unexpectedly perished, and in all the Greek towns of the district murder, sedition, and every kind of disturbance were rife. . . .

5. HERA., *Fr.* 17. Pythagoras, son of Mnesarchos, prosecuted scientific investigations beyond all other men, and making a selection of these writings, he made a wisdom of his own. . . .

6. EUC., *Elem.* 1. 47. In right-angled triangles the square on the side subtending the right angle is equal to the squares on the sides containing the right angle.

7. PROC., *On Euclid* 1. (ed. Friedlin 428.6-14). If we listen to those who relate ancient history, we find some of them attributing this theorem to Pythagoras and saying that he sacrificed an ox upon the discovery. . . .

B. LIVES AND TEACHINGS OF PYTHAGOREANS

1. D.L., *op. cit.* VIII. 7. 1. Philolaus was a native of Crotona, and a pupil of Pythagoras. It was from him that Plato wrote to Dion to take care and purchase the books of Pythagoras. 2. And he died under suspicion of having designed to seize on the tyranny. . . . 4. He wrote one book, which Hermippus reports, on the authority of some unknown writer, that Plato the philosopher purchased when he was in Sicily. . . . 15. Down to the

---

[5] Polybius, *The Histories*, translated by W. R. Paton (London, W. Heinemann, 1922-27).

time of Philolaus it was not possible to acquire knowledge of any Pythagorean doctrine, and Philolaus alone brought out those three celebrated books which Plato sent a hundred minas to purchase. Not less than six hundred persons went to his evening lectures. . . .

2. ——— VIII. 79. 1. Archytas was a native of Tarentum, and the son of Innesagoras; or, as Aristoxenus relates, of Histiæs. . . . 3. He was also a Pythagorean; and he it was who saved Plato's life by means of a letter, when he was in danger of being put to death by Dionysius.

C. Pythagorean Theory and Doctrines

a. The theory of numbers and harmony.

1. Arist., *Met.* XII. 6. 1080 b 16. The Pythagoreans say that there is but one number, the mathematical, but things of sense are not separated from this, for they are composed of it; indeed, they construct the whole heaven out of numbers, but not out of unit numbers, for they assume that the unities have quantity; but how the first *one* was constructed so as to have quantity (magnitude), they seem at a loss to say.

2. ——— XIII. 3. 1090 a 20. But the Pythagoreans, because they see many qualities of numbers in bodies perceived by sense, regard objects as numbers, not as separate numbers, but as derived numbers. And why? Because the qualities of numbers exist in a musical scale (*harmonia*), in the heavens and in many other things.

3. ——— I. 5. 985 b-986 b 8. With these and before them (Anaxagoras, Empedocles, Atomists) those called Pythagoreans applying themselves to the sciences, first developed them; and being brought up in them they thought that the first principles of these [i.e., numbers] were the first principles of all things. And since of these (sciences) numbers are by nature the first, in numbers rather than in fire and earth and water they thought they saw many likenesses to things that are and that are coming to be, as, for instance, justice is such a property of numbers, and

soul and mind are such a property, and another is opportunity, and of other things one may say the same of each one.

And further, discerning in numbers the conditions and reasons of harmonies also; since, moreover, other things seemed to be like numbers in their entire nature, and numbers were the first of every nature, they assumed that the elements of numbers were the elements of all things, and that the whole heavens were harmony and number. And whatever characteristics in numbers and harmonies they could show were in agreement with the properties of the heavens and its parts and with its whole arrangement, these they collected and adapted; and if there chanced to be any gap anywhere, they eagerly sought that the whole system might be connected with these (stray phenomena). To give an example of my meaning: inasmuch as ten seemed to be the perfect number and to embrace the whole nature of numbers, they asserted that the number of bodies moving through the heavens were ten, and when only nine were visible, for the reason just stated they postulated the counter-earth as the tenth. We have given a more definite account of these thinkers in other parts of our writings. But we have referred to them here with this purpose in view, that we might ascertain from them what they asserted as the first principles and in what manner they came upon the causes that have been enumerated. They certainly seem to consider number as the first principle and as it were the matter in things and in their conditions and states; and the odd and the even are elements of number, and of these the former is limited, the latter unlimited, and unity is the product of both of them, for it is both odd and even, and number arises from unity, and the whole heaven, as has been said, is numbers.

A different party in this same school say that the first principles are ten, named according to the following table: limited and unlimited, even and odd, one and many, right and left, male and female, rest and motion, straight and crooked, light and darkness, good and bad, square and oblong. After this manner Alcmæon of Croton seems to have conceived them, and either he received this doctrine from them or they from him; for Alcmæon arrived at maturity when Pythagoras was an old man, and his teachings resembled theirs. For he says that most human affairs are twofold, not meaning opposites reached by definition, as did the former party, but opposites by chance—as, for example, white-black, sweet-bitter, good-bad, small-great. This philosopher let fall his opinions indefinitely about the rest, but the Pythagoreans declared the number of the opposites and what they were. From both one may learn this much, that opposites are the first principles of things; but from the latter he may learn the number of these, and what they are. But how it is possible to bring them into relation with the causes of which we have spoken if they have not clearly worked out; but they seem to range their elements under the category of matter, for they say that being is compounded and formed from them, and that they inhere in it.

4. ——— I. 8. 989 b 32-990 a 32. Those, however, who carry on their investigation with reference to all things, and divide things into what are perceived and what are not perceived by sense, evidently examine both classes, so one must delay a little longer over what they say. They speak correctly and incorrectly in reference to the questions now before us. Now those who are called Pythagoreans use principles and elements yet stranger than those of the physicists, in that they do not take them from the sphere of sense, for mathematical objects are without motion, except in the case of astronomy. Still, they discourse about everything in nature and study it; they construct the heaven, they observe what happens in its parts and their states and motions; they apply to these their first principles and causes, as though they agreed entirely with the other physicists that being is only what is perceptible and what that which is called heaven includes. But their causes and first principles, they say, are such as to lead up to the higher parts of reality, and are in harmony with this rather than with the doctrines of nature. In what manner motion will take place when limited and unlimited, odd and even, are the only underlying realities, they do not say; nor how it is possible for genesis and destruction to take place without motion and change, or for the heavenly bodies to revolve. . . .

5. HIPP., *loc. cit.* Number is the first principle, a thing which is undefined, incomprehensible, having in itself all num-

bers which could reach infinity in amount. And the first principle of numbers is in substance the first monad, which is a male monad, begetting as a father all other numbers. Secondly the dyad is a female number, and the same is called by the arithmeticians even. Thirdly the triad is male number; this the arithmeticians have been wont to call odd. Finally the tetrad is a female number, and the same is called even because it is female.

All numbers, then, taken by classes are fours (for number is undefined in reference to class), of which is composed the perfect number, the decad. For the series, one two three and four, becomes ten, if its own name is kept in its essence by each of the numbers. Pythagoras said that this sacred tetraktys is "the spring having the roots of ever-flowing nature" in itself, and from this numbers have their first principle. For the eleven and the twelve and the rest derive from the ten the first principle of their being. The four parts of the decad, this perfect number, are called number, monad, power, and cube. And the interweavings and minglings of these in the origin of growth are what naturally completes nascent number; for when a power is multiplied upon itself, it is the power of a power; and when a power is multiplied on a cube, it is the power of a cube; and when a cube is multiplied on a cube, the cube of a cube; thus all numbers, from which arises the genesis of what arises, are seven:— number, monad, power, cube, power of a power, power of a cube, cube of a cube.

6. Arist., *op. cit.* XIV. 1092 b 10. Once more, it has in no sense been determined in which way numbers are the causes of substances and of being—whether . . . as limits (as points are of spatial magnitudes). This is how Eurytus decided what was the number of what (e.g., of man or of horse), viz., by imitating the figures of living things with pebbles, as some people bring numbers into the forms triangle and square.

b. The cosmos and the harmony of the spheres.

1. Arist., *Phys.* IV. 6. 213 b 22. And the Pythagoreans say that there is a void, and that it enters into the heaven itself from the infinite air, as though it (the heaven) were breathing; and

this void defines the natures of things, inasmuch as it is a certain separation and definition of things that lie together; and this is true first in the case of numbers, for the void defines the nature of these.

2. ————, *de Caelo* II. 13. 293 a 19. These [the Pythagoreans] say that fire is at the center and that the earth is one of the stars, and that moving in a circle about the center it produces night and day. And they assume yet another earth opposite this which they call counter-earth, not seeking reasons and causes for phenomena, but stretching phenomena to meet certain assumptions and opinions of theirs and attempting to arrange them in a system.—And farther the Pythagoreans say that the most authoritative part of the All stands guard, because it is specially fitting that it should, and this part is the center; and this place that the fire occupies, they called the guard of Zeus, as it is called simply the center, that is, the center of space and the center of matter and of nature.

3. ———— II. 9. 290 b 15. Some think it necessary that noise should arise when so great bodies are in motion, since sound does arise from bodies among us which are not so large and do not move so swiftly; and from the sun and moon and from the stars in so great number, and of so great size, moving so swiftly, there must necessarily arise a sound inconceivably great. Assuming these things and that the swiftness has the principle of harmony by reason of the intervals, they say that the sound of the stars moving on in a circle becomes musical. And since it seems unreasonable that we also do not hear this sound, they say that the reason for this is that the noise exists in the very nature of things, so as not to be distinguishable from the opposite silence; for the distinction of sound and silence lies in their contrast with each other, so that as blacksmiths think there is no difference between them because they are accustomed to the sound, so the same things happen to men. II. 9. 291 a 7. What occasions the difficulty and makes the Pythagoreans say that there is a harmony of the bodies as they move, is a proof. For whatever things move themselves make a sound and noise; but whatever things

are fastened in what moves or exist in it as the parts in a ship, cannot make a noise, nor yet does the ship if it moves in a river.

c. The mathematical structure of the cosmos.

1. Aet., *Plac.* II. 6. *Dox.* 334. Pythagoras: The universe is made from five solid figures, which are called also mathematical; of these he says that earth has arisen from the cube, fire from the pyramid, air from the octahedron, and water from the icosahedron, and the sphere of the all from the dodecahedron.

2. Herm. *I.G.P.* 16. *Dox.* 655. The monad is the first principle of all things. From its forms and from numbers the elements arose. And he declared that the number and form and measure of each of these is somehow as follows: Fire is composed of twenty-four right-angled triangles, surrounded by four equilaterals. And each equilateral consists of six right-angled triangles, whence they compare it to a pyramid. Air is composed of forty-eight triangles, surrounded by eight equilaterals. And it is compared to the octahedron, which is surrounded by eight equilateral triangles, each of which is separated into six right-angled triangles so as to become forty-eight in all. And water is composed of one hundred and twenty triangles, surrounded by twenty equilaterals, and it is compared to the icosahedron, which is composed of one hundred and twenty equilateral triangles. And æther is composed of twelve equilateral pentagons and is like a dodecahedron. And earth is composed of forty-eight triangles, and is surrounded by six equilateral pentagons, and it is like a cube. For the cube is surrounded by six tetragons, each of which is separated into eight triangles, so that they become in all forty-eight.

3. Theoph., *Phys. Op.* Fr. 17. *Dox.* 492. Favorinus says that he [Pythagoras] was the first to call the heavens a universe and earth round. . . ."

d. The Pythagorean conception of soul and of immortality.

1. Plato, *Phaedo* 86 B-C. Our body, being, as it were, strung together by the warm and the cold, the dry and the

moist, and things of that sort, our soul is a sort of temperament and attunement of these, when they are mingled with one another well and in due proportion. If, then, our soul is an attunement, it is clear that, when the body has been relaxed or strung up out of measure by diseases and other ills, the soul must necessarily perish at once.

2. ARIST., *de Anima* I. 4. 407 a 1. This theory regards the soul as a sort of harmony. Harmony, say its advocates, is a mixture and combination of opposites. . . .

3. HIPP., *loc. cit.* He said that the soul is immortal, and that it changes from one body to another; so he was wont to say that he himself had been born before the Trojan war as Euphorbos, and after that as Hermotimos of Samos, then as Pyrrhos of Delos, fifth as Pythagoras. . . .

4. PLATO, *op. cit.* 62 B. The saying that is uttered in secret rites, to the effect that we men are in a sort of prison, and that one ought not to loose himself from it nor yet to run away, seems to me something great and not easy to see through; but this at least I think is well said, that it is the gods who care for us, and we men are one of the possessions of the gods.

5. EPIPH., *Haer.* III. 8. *Dox.* 390. And Pythagoras said that the soul goes at death into other animals.

6. AET., *op. cit.* IV. 4. *Dox.* 389. Pythagoras, Plato: According to a superficial account the soul is of two parts, the one possessing, the other lacking, reason. . . .

e. Moral theory and ritual.

1. ARIST., *E.N.* II. 1106 b 29. The evil partakes of the nature of the infinite, the good of the finite, as the Pythagoreans conjectured.

2. ———— V. 8. 1132 b 21. Reciprocity seems to some to be absolutely just, as the Pythagoreans say; for these defined the just as that which is reciprocal to another.

3. HEROD., *op. cit.* II. 81 . . . Those that partake of these rites may also not be buried in woollen garments. . . .

4. EPIPH., *loc. cit.* Pythagoras was wont to say that wise men ought not to sacrifice animals to gods, nor yet to eat what had life, or beans, nor drink wine.

5. HIPP., *loc. cit.* And Diodoros of Eretria and Aristoxenos the musician say that Pythagoras had come into Zaratas of Chaldaea. . . . And it is said that Zaratas forbade men to eat beans because he said that at the beginning and composition of all things when the earth was still a whole, the bean arose. And he says that the proof of this is that if one chews a bean to a pulp and exposes it to the sun for a certain time (for the sun will affect it quickly), it gives out the odor of human seed. And he says that there is another and clearer proof: if when a bean is in flower we were to take the bean and its flower, and putting it into a pitcher moisten it and then bury it in the earth, and after a few days dig it up again, we should see in the first place that it had the form of a womb, and examining it closely we should find the head of a child growing with it.

🮱🮱🮱🮱🮱 3

HERACLITUS

FEW PHILOSOPHIES have exerted a more powerful influence than has that of Heraclitus. His speculations upon the cosmos, the processes of events in the cosmos, the theory of perpetual change, and the conception of law which governs change have an enormous intrinsic value and as powerful an effect upon history as had any philosophy of which we have record. In this book of selections, we are primarily concerned with the Heraclitean *natural philosophy* and it is upon this aspect of one of the most brilliant and profound philosophies ever conceived that we shall concentrate our attention. It is not amiss, however, to mention at the outset a few of the ideas other than those directly related to natural philosophy which owe their origin to this extraordinary philosopher of Ephesus.

Heraclitus' theory of "natural law" influences both the physicists' conception of the laws of nature and the Stoic conception of the state and through the latter the conception of *jus naturale*. His conception of the *Logos* or the Word is at the core of Alexandrian speculation and is of particular significance for Philo and Plotinus. Heraclitus separates the *Logos* from the processes which fire undergoes and in doing so begins the differentiation of systems of language from the events to which the words refer (see below, Ch. 6, especially II).

Heraclitus' theory of perpetual change—as Plato expresses it, "Everything flows,"—has been at the basis of the innumerable theories of change and of percepts formulated to account for the world we observe and the processes in it. The theory reappears in areas as widely separated as Plato's philosophy of being and becoming, of knowledge and opinion, Bergson's theory of duration, and T. S. Eliot's *Burnt Norton*. More immediately for our own purposes, Heraclitus' philosophy calls forth the denial of change and motion by the Eleatics and confronts the Pluralists with the problem of "saving appearances" and accounting for change and perception (see above, pp. 23 sq. and below, Chs. 6, 7).

Heraclitus, who died between the years 478 and 470 B.C., was a native of Ephesus, on the coast of Asia Minor.[1] He was a descendant of the royal line of his native city and it is probable that he held temporal and religious powers commensurate with his rank. The priestly duties must have retained a considerable importance even after the rise of democracy had restricted royalty's temporal activities. It seems likely, however, from Heraclitus' attacks upon the mysteries and the sacrifices (see below, B. a. 124-130), that he renounced his priestly privileges. The bitterness of his attack contributed to his reputation as the "weeping philosopher" and it is notable that Heraclitus was no less critical of his predecessors in philosophy (see below, B. a. 16, 17) than of the priests and of his countrymen (see below, B. a. 114).

The habit of mind inculcated by concentration upon spiritual affairs gave to Heraclitus' writings a mystical and esoteric character. This resulted, in the references in antiquity, to the author as "the dark." Some attributed the obscurity of the writing to the author's "spleen." In any case, Diogenes Laertius, in *Lives and Opinions of Eminent Philosophers*, writes that Euripides gave Socrates a small work by Heraclitus and asked him afterwards what he thought of it. Socrates is reported to have answered, "What I have understood is good; and so, I think, is what I have not understood; only the book requires a Delian diver to get at the meaning of it."

We may best get at some of the "meaning of it" by showing

[1] The selections relating to Heraclitus' life and thought begin below, p. 67.

what, latent in Milesian philosophy, is made evident in Heraclitus' speculation.

Implicit in Thales' philosophy is the assumption that the
various manifestations of the underlying "world-stuff" that maintains its identity through change are related to changes in temperature. There is, moreover, in the theory of rarefaction and
condensation held by Anaximenes an emphasis upon the means
by which the change or alteration is brought about. Heraclitus,
who based his philosophy upon Milesian principles, takes fire,
the source of heat, as the substance underlying all change. It is,
however, rather upon the "how," upon the cosmic process by
which fire is transformed, that he concentrates his theory of
evidence.

As has been indicated, the point of departure in Heraclitean-
ism is Milesian. Fire, an infinite mass of substance, uncreated
and eternal, is identical with the universe (see below, B. a. 20).
Empirical observation, the method so thoroughly adopted by
the Milesians, reveals characteristics of the flame that are important for Heraclitus' general theory. Fire, in its combination of
movement in flickering and its apparent identity and permanence,
and in its consumption of fuel and its giving off of ash and
smoke, would appear to be an adequate manifestation of the
principle or substance maintaining its identity despite transformation. But consideration of the process itself and of the order
of the change and transformation causes Heraclitus to move
beyond his predecessors. Fire, in the sun, is condensed into
water. This, in turn, is condensed half into earth, half into
smoke, "fiery storm-cloud," or waterspout. This portion of the
process, Heraclitus calls the "downward way." The "upward
way" begins with the liquefaction of earth into sea and proceeds
through the transformation of the sea into stormcloud or vapor
and, ultimately, into fire. The sun is a concave bowl in which
the vapors from the sea are gathered and burned and it is here
that the process is completed (see below, B. a. 21-23, 25, 69;
and B. b). The purely Milesian beginnings of explanation in
Heraclitus' theory are clearly present in the theory of process,
for it is obvious that he regards as explained what may be referred to common experience. The "upward way," for example,

suggests the use of images and pictorial thinking, in that the transformation of earth into water would fit into the common supposition that springs rising from the earth or streams flowing from the mountainside represent a change of earth to water. Unity in the system referred to is the type of explanation under which the image is subsumed.

More important, Heraclitus conceives the "upward way" and the "downward way" to be identical in nature and simultaneous in process (see below, B. a. 69). For, while there is transformation of fire into water and water into earth and while the contraries are destructive of each other (see below, B. a. 25), the two processes balance each other. There is, then, "measure." For example, for each portion of water transformed into earth, in the "downward way," there is an equal transformation of earth into water in the "upward way." Just as in fire there is an equilibrium of the fuel consumed and the ash and smoke given off, with the maintenance of a steady flame, so in the universe there is equilibrium or balance maintained by the "tension" of the opposing transformations. It follows, therefore, that balance or equilibrium or rhythm is essential. Although such balance may be delayed, as, for instance, during the summer when fire is dominant, the balance eventually must be even (see below, B. a. 29). Heraclitus' balance is analogous to the physical law of the conservation of matter. For the reason that the balance must be maintained by the eternal motion of the process and by the tension or conflict with the opposing movement upward and downward, Heraclitus insists that strife is essential to harmony or balance. When, therefore, he applies his principles to the world at large, strife is considered to be the father of all things (see below, B. a. 43, 44, 46). This view is consistently held with reference to the objects about us: The harp or lyre is what it is because of the equilibrium produced by the tension of strings working against the strength of the frame; the bow is what it is because of a similar conflict or tension of the two opposing forces produced by the hands pulling simultaneously away from and towards the bowman; the river is what it is because the filling compensates the emptying, for if one overbalances, the river no longer exists as such but becomes, in the one case, a lake, in the other, a dry channel (see below, B. a. 41, 42, 45; cf. 50, 52, 58, 67).

Reality, it is clear, is like the stream or the fire, in constant motion and flux. "All things are flowing," including the percipient being (see below, B. a. 81). Implicit in Heraclitus' theory is what later philosophy developed into "natural law" for it is clear that if all is in change and flux, the one exception to the generalization will be the law of change itself. In a sense, Heraclitus interprets his system in this way, for the law is apart from the objects and events of perception and is identified with *Logos* or wisdom (see below, B. a. 4, 16, 18, 19). Thus a philosophy which ostensibly is grounded upon a gross empiricism—although it is to be noted that a distinction is made among the various modes of perceiving and that seeing and hearing are evidently regarded as the "more accurate" modes—is in fact argued on the basis of what is hidden from the senses or perceptions (see below, B. a. 3-6, 10, 15, 16, 18, 45, 91, 92). It is clear that for Heraclitus "hidden harmony is better than apparent harmony" and "nature loves to hide."

It is no less evident, however, that for Heraclitus the law is always exemplified in the objects and events of our perceptual experience. For Heraclitus, the processes of flux and change are not illusory. Change is real and the concrete exemplifications of process indicate that the law and its manifestations are for him one and the same. Heraclitus thinks in terms of concrete images which have not yet become the abstract symbols or ideas of later speculation.

Wisdom is at once the unity of all things, the measure and the harmony, but it is pure fire as well. With reservations, it is Zeus (see below, B. a. 19). However, not only is it the universal substance, the source from which things come; but it is also the principle that directs the universe: "The primitive essence forms all things out of itself, by its own power, according to the law inherent in it." [2]

Fire or wisdom is, in this secondary sense, regarded in a

---

[2] Edward Zeller, *A History of Greek Philosophy.* The quotation is from the English translation of Vol. II, *The Pre-Socratic Philosophy* by S. F. Alleyne (London, Longmans, Green, and Co., Inc., 1881), Vol. I, p. 40.

manner analogous to mind. Again, it is probable that this analogy is based upon simple empirical observation, upon the assumption that consciousness in animal life is associated with warmth, since at death the body is cold. This assumption is borne out in Heraclitus' theories concerning man, considered as a microcosm. Man, as part of the cosmos, is dependent for life and consciousness upon the fire of the universe. Subject to the constant flux and change of the earth, water, and fire which compose him, man breathes in the rational and conscious fire from without (see below, B. c). During sleep, the apertures of sense through which consciousness enters in the form of fire are closed and contact with fire is lost. At such times, the exhalations from water cause the fire to burn low. The balance must be restored, as it must be restored in the macrocosm. If the measure or balance is not restored, death results through the destruction of the fire by water. Heraclitus offers rules by which the balance may be maintained or improved (see below, B. a. 68), the most important being the dicta forbidding drink (see below, B. a. 72, 76).

A. LIFE

D.L., *Lives* IX. 1. Heraclitus was the son of Bloson, or, as some say, of Heraceon, and a citizen of Ephesus. He flourished about the 69th Olympiad (505-500 B.C.). . . . 5. There is a book of his extant . . . and he deposited this book in the temple of Artemis . . . having written it intentionally in an obscure style, in order that only those who were able men might comprehend it, and that it might not be exposed to ridicule at the hands of the common people. . . .

B. THOUGHT

a. The fragments.[3]

1. It is wise, listening not to me but to the Law, to acknowledge that all things are one.

[3] Translated by Richmond Lattimore in Matthew Thompson McClure's *The Early Philosophers of Greece* (New York, Appleton-Century-Crofts, 1935), pp. 119-128. The arrangement of the fragments is that of Ingram Bywater in *Heracliti Ephesii Reliquiae* (Oxford, Oxford University Press, 1877).

2. But although this Law holds forever, men fail to understand it as much when they hear it for the first time as before they have heard it. For while all things take place in accordance with this Law, yet men are like the inexperienced when they make trial of such words and actions as I set forth, classifying each thing according to its nature, and telling the way of it. But other men do not know what they do when awake, even as they forget what they do when asleep.

3. Fools when they hear are like deaf men; it is of them that the saying bears witness, "though present they are not there."

4. Eyes and ears are bad witnesses for men, if they have souls that are alien to them [do not understand their language].

5. Many do not think about the things they experience, nor do they know the things they learn; but they think they do.

6. Knowing neither how to listen nor how to speak.

7. You will not find the unexpected unless you expect it; for it is hard to find, and difficult.

8. They who seek for gold dig up much earth and find little gold.

9. Dispute.

10. Nature loves to hide.

11. The lord to whom belongs the oracle at Delphi neither speaks out nor hides his meaning, but gives a sign.

12. And the Sibyl with raving mouth uttering things mirthless, unadorned, unsweetened, reaches with her voice over a thousand years because of the god in her.

13. The things that can be seen, heard, learned, shall I put them foremost?

14. . . . bringing forth untrustworthy witnesses to support what is untrustworthy.

15. Eyes are more accurate witnesses than ears.

16. Learning of many things does not teach one to have understanding; else it would have taught Hesiod and Pythagoras, and also Xenophanes and Hecataeus.

17. Pythagoras the son of Mnesarchus practised enquiry beyond all men; and selecting these writings he called them his own wisdom; which was only a knowledge of many things, and bad art.

18. Of all men whose accounts I have listened to, not one has got far enough to know that wisdom is divided from all [other] things.

19. Wisdom is a single thing. It is to understand the mind by which all things are steered through all things.

20. This world that is the same for all, neither any god nor any man shaped it, but it ever was and is and shall be everliving Fire that kindles by measures and goes out by measures.

21. The changed states of Fire are, first, sea; half of sea is earth, and half is stormcloud.

22. All things are exchanged for Fire and Fire for all things, as goods for gold and gold for goods.

23. It [the earth] is poured about as sea water, and is measured in the same proportion as it was before it became earth.

24. Fire is want and satiety.

25. Fire lives the death of Air, and Air the death of Fire; Water lives the death of Earth, and Earth of Water.[4]

26. Fire advancing upon all things shall judge them and convict them.

27. How could one escape the notice of what never sets?

28. It is the thunderbolt that steers all things.

[4] Reading H. Ritter and L. Preller, *Historia Philosophiæ Græcæ* (Gotha 1898), p. 37.

29. The sun shall not transgress his measures; if he does, the Erinnyes, the supporters of justice, will find him out.

30. The boundary between dawn and evening is the Bear, and over against the Bear is the confine of bright Zeus.

31. If there were no sun, it would be night [for all the other stars could do].

32. The sun is new every day.

33. [Heraclitus and Democritus bear witness that Thales studied the stars, etc.]

34. . . . the seasons that bear all things.

35. Hesiod is the teacher of many. They believe that he knew a great many things, that man, who did not know day and night! They are one.

36. God is day, he is night; winter and summer, war and peace, satiety and hunger; he changes form even as Fire when mixed with various incenses is named according to the pleasant perfume of each.

37. If all things turned into smoke, the nostrils would distinguish them.

38. Souls smell in Hades.

39. Cold things grow warm, what is warm chills; the moist dries, the dry dampens.

40. It scatters and comes together, approaches and goes away.

41. You could not step twice in the same rivers; for other and yet other waters are ever flowing on.[5]

42. Other things enter the same rivers, and other waters pour in upon them.

43. [And Heraclitus blames Homer for saying: "Would that

[5] Ed. note: I have retained Arthur Fairbanks' reading from The First Philosophers of Greece (London, Routledge & Kegan Paul, Ltd., 1898).

strife were to vanish from among gods and men." For then everything would vanish.] For there could be no harmony without high and deep tones, no animals without male and female; and these are opposites.

44. War is the father and king of all things; he has shown some to be gods and some mortals, he has made some slaves and others free.

45. Men do not understand how what is divided is consistent with itself; it is a harmony of tensions like that of the bow and the lyre.

46. Opposition is good; the fairest harmony comes out of differents; everything originates in strife.

47. Hidden harmony is better than apparent harmony.

48. Let us not make guesses at random about the greatest things.

49. Men who love wisdom must enquire into very many things.

50. The way of the carding-comb, both straight and crooked, is one and the same.

51. Asses would rather have straw than gold.

52. Sea water is the purest and foulest. For fish it is drinkable and life-preserving, for men it is undrinkable and deadly.

53. Swine wash themselves in filth, domestic fowls in dust.

54. . . . to delight in muck.

55. Every beast is driven to pasture with blows.

56. The harmony of the world is of tensions, like that of the bow and the lyre.

57-58. And good and evil are the same. Thus physicians, cutting and cauterizing and torturing sick men in every way, yet complain that they do not get as much pay as they deserve from the sick men; for what they do is good for those diseases.

59. You should combine things whole and not whole, what is drawn together and what is drawn apart, the harmonious and the discordant; from all one, and from one all.

60. They would not have known the name of justice had not these things [unjust actions] occurred.

61. All things are fair and good and right to God; but men think of some as wrong and others as right.

62. One must know that war is common to all, and that strife is justice; and all things both come to pass and perish through strife.

63. For they are absolutely destined. . . .

64. All things we see when awake are death, and all we see when asleep are sleep.

65. The one thing which alone is wise is willing and unwilling to be called by the name of Zeus.

66. The name of the bow (βιός) is life (βίος), but its work is death.

67. Immortals are mortal, mortals immortal, each living the death and dying the life of the other.

68. It is death for souls to become water, and it is death for water to become earth; but water has its origin from earth, and souls from water.

69. The way up and the way down are one and the same.

70. The beginning and the end of a circle's circumference are common.

71. You will not find the limits of the soul, though you take every road; so deep is the tale of it.

72. It is pleasure for souls to become wet.

73. A man when he is drunk is led by an ungrown boy, stumbling, not knowing whither he is going, having a wet soul.

74-76. A dry soul is the wisest and best.

77. Man, like a night light, is kindled and put out.

78. The living and the dead, the waking and sleeping, the young and the old, these are the same; the former are moved about and become the latter, the latter in turn become the former.

79. A lifetime is a child playing at draughts; the power of a king is a child's.

80. I have sought myself out.

81. In the same rivers we step and we do not step. We are and are not.[6]

82. It is a hardship to toil for the same masters and be ruled by them.

83. By changing it rests.

84. Even a potion clots if it is not stirred.

85. Corpses should be cast out sooner than dung.

86. Being born they wish to live and have their fate; or rather to rest; and they leave behind children, who in turn will meet their fate.

87. In thirty years a man can be a grandfather.

91. Thinking is common to all. Those who speak intelligently must be strong in what is common to all, as much as a city is strong in its law, and even more. For all human laws are fostered by the one law, which is divine; for it is as strong as it wishes to be, and is sufficient for all things, and outlives them.

92. Therefore we ought to follow what is common; but the many live as if they had each a wisdom of his own.

93. They are at variance with that with which they are most constantly associated.

6 Fairbanks' reading.

94. For the waking there is one world, and it is common; but when men sleep they turn aside each one into a world of his own.

95. We should not act and speak as if we were asleep.

97. A man is called silly by a god, just as a child is by a man.

98. The wisest of men shows like an ape beside God, in wisdom, beauty, and everything else.

99. The fairest ape is ugly compared with anything of another kind, and the fairest pot is ugly compared with any maiden.

100. The people must fight for its law as it does for its wall.

101. Greater deaths get greater needs.

102. Gods and men honor those who are slain in battle.

103. One should put out insolence sooner than a fire.

104. It would not be better if men were to get all they wish for. Disease makes health pleasant and good; hunger, satiety; and weariness, rest.

105. It is hard to fight desire; what it wants it buys with the soul.

108. It is better to hide ignorance; but it is an effort to do it in relaxation and over the wine.

110. And it is law to obey the counsel of one.

111. What mind or wit is in them? They follow after the poets and take the mob as a teacher, not knowing that many are bad and few good. For the best of them fix upon one thing above all others, that is, everlasting fame among men, but the greater part are satisfied the way beasts are.

112. In Priene lived Bias the son of Teutamas, who is worth more than the rest.

113. One man is ten thousand to me, if he be noble.

114. It would be right for all the Ephesians above age to

strangle themselves and leave the city to those below age; for they cast out Hermodorus, the best man among them, saying: "Let no man among us be the best; if there is one, let it be elsewhere and among others."

115. Dogs bark at the man they do not know.

116. Because of lack of faith [divine things] are not known.

117. A witling is always fluttered at every word.

118. The most esteemed of them knows only semblances; and surely justice will overtake the fabricators of lies and the false witnesses.

119. Homer deserves to be thrown out of the lists and whipped, and so does Archilochus.

120. One day is equal to any other day.

121. A man's character is his destiny.

122. There await men when they die such things as they do not expect, or think of.

123. Before [the god's] presence they must arise and become vigilant guards over the living and the dead.

124. Night-wanderers, Magians, Bacchanals, Lenaeans, keepers of mysteries. . . .

125. For the mysteries recognized by men are celebrated in an unholy fashion.

126. And they pray to these statues like a man chattering to his own house, knowing nothing of gods or heroes or what they are.

127. For if it were not to Dionysus that they held the procession and chanted the ode with the phallic symbols, their actions would be most shameless; for Dionysus, in whose honor they revel and keep the Lenaean festival, is the same as Hades.

128. [Few men are completely purified.]

129. Purgings. [*See the next fragment.*]

130. They are purified by defilement with blood, as if one were to step into mud and wash it off with mud.

b. Fire, the cosmos, the heavenly bodies, and meteorological phenomena.

D.L., *op. cit.* 4. 9. 9-12. Coming to his particular tenets, we may state them as follows: fire is the element, all things are exchange for fire and come into being by rarefaction and condensation; but of this he gives no clear explanation. All things come into being by conflict of opposites, and the sum of things flows like a stream. Further, all that is is limited and forms one world. And it is alternately born from fire and again resolved into fire in fixed cycles to all eternity, and this is determined by destiny. Of the opposites that which tends to birth or creation is called war and strife, and that which tends to destruction by fire is called concord and peace.

Change he called a pathway up and down, and this determines the birth of the world. For fire by contracting turns into moisture, and this condensing turns into water; water again when congealed turns into earth. This process he calls the downward path. Then again earth is liquefied, and thus gives rise to water, and from water the rest of the series is derived. He reduces nearly everything to exhalation from the sea. This process is the upward path.

Exhalations arise from earth as well as from sea; those from sea are bright and pure, those from earth dark. Fire is fed by the bright exhalations, the moist element by the others.

He does not make clear the nature of the surrounding element. He says, however, that there are in it bowls with their concavities turned toward us, in which the bright exhalations collect and produce flames. These are the heavenly bodies.

The flame of the sun is the brightest and hottest; and other stars are further from the earth and for that reason give it less light and heat. The moon, which is nearer to the earth, traverses a region which is not pure. The sun, however, moves in a clear and untroubled region, and keeps a proportionate distance from us. That is why it gives us more heat and light. Eclipses of the sun and moon occur when the bowls are turned upwards; the monthly phases of the moon are due to the bowl turning round in its place little by little.

Day and night, months, seasons and years, rains and winds and other similar phenomena are accounted for by the various exhalations. Thus the bright exhalation, set aflame in the hollow orb of the sun, produces day, the opposite exhalation when it has got the mastery causes night; the increase of warmth due to the bright exhalation produces summer, whereas the preponderance of moisture due to the dark exhalation brings about winter. His explanations of other phenomena are in harmony with this.

He gives no account of the nature of the earth, nor even of the bowls.

These, then, were his opinions.

c. Macrocosm and microcosm.

SEXT. EMP., *Adv. Math.* 7. 129. The natural philosopher is of the opinion that what surrounds us is rational and endowed with consciousness. According to Heraclitus, we become intelligent when we get this divine reason by breathing it in, and in sleep we are forgetful, but on waking we gain our senses again. For in sleep since the openings of the senses are closed, the mind in us is separated from what is akin to it in what surrounds us, and its connection through openings is only preserved like a sort of root (from which the rest may spring again); and being cut off it loses its former power of memory; but when we wake it looks through the openings of the senses, as though little doors, and entering into connection with what surrounds us it regains [assumes] the power of reason.

▣▣▣▣▣ 4

THE ELEATIC SCHOOL

HERACLITUS DERIVES his philosophy from the Milesians and proceeds to a conception of the universe and its components in constant motion and flux. This process of change is exemplified in all phenomena, the most striking instances of which are those of the bow, the lyre, and the river. Derivative from the philosophy of Miletus as well, but in the most striking contrast to Heraclitean speculation, are the philosophies of Xenophanes, Parmenides, Zeno and Melissus. They discover in Milesian philosophy implications which lead to the denial that either change or its specific manifestations can occur. These philosophers are called Eleatic, after the Greek colony of Elea, in Italy, in which they were resident. Of their teachings, Aristotle wrote that they "expressed the opinion about the universe that it is one in its essential nature" (see below, p. 79).

As Aristotle suggests, the expression of this general philosophical position of the Eleatics is given in varied form. Xenophanes approaches the problem of the universe as "one" from a theological point of view and in the language of a religious teacher. Parmenides' approach is that of a metaphysician and in order to maintain his position, he uses the method of dialectic (see above, p. 28, 5). Zeno defends the Eleatic philosophy of Parmenides by the negative method, demonstrating the impossibility of supporting the contrary view that there is space, diversity, one and many, and motion. Zeno refines Parmenides' dialectical procedure. Melissus' arguments are more affirmative in their support of Parmenides' philosophy of *it is* than are Zeno's paradoxes and are among the most interesting of the attacks upon pluralism.

\ristotle's comments on the Eleatic philosophers.

ARIST., *Met*. I. 5. 986 b 10; b 23. There are some who have expressed the opinion about the universe that it is one in its essential nature, but they have not expressed this opinion after the same manner nor in an orderly or natural way.—Xenophanes first taught the unity of these things (Parmenides is said to have been his pupil), but he did not make anything clear, nor did he seem to have grasped either of these two kinds of unity, but looking up into the broad heavens he said: The unity is god. These are to be dismissed, as we have said, from the present investigation, two of them entirely as being rather more crude, Xenophanes and Melissus; but Parmenides seems to speak in some places with more insight.

I. XENOPHANES

Since their author was a wandering poet and a maker of satires and elegies, Xenophanes' writings are more closely related to religion and to conduct than to philosophy. Two fragments [1] of his writings seem clearly to indicate the reasons for that emphasis. These portions of his writings (see below, I. B. a. 8, 22) may be assumed to relate to the conquest of Ionia, the land of which Xenophanes was native, by the Persians under Harpagos. The fragments indicate that Xenophanes was twenty-five years of age at the time of the defeat of the Ionians and his birth would, therefore, have occurred in 565 B.C. After this invasion, Xenophanes wandered sixty-seven years over Hellas. Tradition suggests, however, that he lived in Elea, in Italy, a colony to which the Phocaeans emigrated after the Persian conquest. The extent and duration of his wanderings indicate clearly that it is an affinity of spirit rather than an identity of habitat

[1] The selections from Xenophanes' life and thought begin below, p. 81.

that causes Xenophanes to be allied with Parmenides, Zeno, and Melissus as an Eleatic. It is, however, not too strained an inference to conclude that to the Persian conquest is owing much of the emphasis placed by Xenophanes upon the maintenance of good morals and upon the eradication of anthropomorphic conceptions of the gods. It may be inferred, perhaps, not only that those driven from Ionia desired to hear of old customs, but that Xenophanes, with the fervor of a reformer and religious teacher, attempted to impress upon his auditors the need to abandon certain luxurious practices in living, the prevalence of which had weakened the Greeks and aided the Persians in their conquest (see below, I. B. a. 3). Xenophanes scorns the excesses of perfumery copied from the Lydians. He decries the extravagant interest of the Greeks in athletics and insists that wisdom is preferable to physical strength (see below, I. B. a. 2). Rules of etiquette are touched upon, with the admonition that too much drinking is to be avoided (see below, I. B. a. 1).

The most important part of Xenophanes' writings for philosophy is to be found in the attacks upon the traditional views of the gods. In a manner similar to that of Euripides, Xenophanes decries the attribution of all manner of vice and crime to the deities. This is the motive for his criticism of the writings of Homer and Hesiod (see below, I. B. a. 11). The attribution of depravity to gods follows from the anthropomorphic conception of deity. Men create gods in their own images, just as animals would construct deities with animal characteristics, had they the ability to draw (see below, I. B. a. 11, 14, 15). It is in the elaboration of an alternative theory of the nature of god that Xenophanes reveals at once the didactic reason for his attack upon anthropomorphism and the Eleatic characteristics of his thought. Mindful, no doubt, of the conquest that had forced the Ionians to leave their native land and perhaps aware, too, that the vanquished usually attribute their defeat to failures to observe ritual or to evil fortune rather than to their own deficiencies, Xenophanes seems to insist that men must depend upon their own efforts and not upon the assistance of deities who, as he points out, incorporate such contrary characteristics and who vary so greatly among peoples. It is not fitting that god

"move from one place to another" (see below, I. B. a. 26), presumably at the beck and call of any man or any prayer.
Once Xenophanes has denied motion to god, however, he proceeds to
indicate that common opinion has erred not only in the attribution of motion to god but also in the attribution of sensory
organs. For Xenophanes, god is remote from toil (see below,
I. B. a. 25), all-perceiving, but without sensory organs (see
below, I. B. a. 23, 24).

The Milesians had insisted that the material substances
which they chose as explanatory principles to account for the
cosmos maintain their identity throughout and in despite of
change. These "causes" were also regarded as divine. Xenophanes
calls the ruler of the universe "god" and insists that deity is
homogeneous and unchanging. Aristotle (see above, p. 79)
interpreted Xenophanes' philosophy as a pantheism and with
this inference there has been general agreement. If the inference
be accepted, it follows that the universe is homogeneous and
not subject to alteration. Movement and change would then
appear to be illusions similar to those which produce the conception of deity. Implicit in the assumption that god is homogeneous and identical with the universe is the set of inferences
shortly to be drawn, namely, that changes in the universe must
be denied reality. Substance can undergo no changes or transformations, since it could not be different in one part than in
another, and no alteration could occur.

However, the ease with which Xenophanes postulates a new
sun every day (see below, I. B. b. 1) suggest how little capable
he was of working out the implications of his own theory.

A. LIFE

D.L., *Lives*, IX. 18. Xenophanes, a native of Colophon, the
son of Dexius, or, according to Apollodorus, of Orthomenes, is
praised by Timon, whose words at all events are: "Xenophanes,
not over-proud, perverter of Homer, castigator." He was banished
from his native city and lived at Zancle in Sicily (and having
joined the colony planted at Elea taught there). . . . According
to some he was no man's pupil, according to others he was a

pupil of Boton of Athens, or, as some say, of Archelaus. Sotion makes him a contemporary of Anaximander. . . . He used to recite his own poems. . . .

B. THOUGHT

a. The fragments.[2]

1. For now the floor is clean, the hands of all and the cups are clean; one puts on the woven garlands, another passes around the fragrant ointment in a vase; the mixing bowl stands full of good cheer, and more wine, mild and of delicate bouquet, is at hand in jars, which says it will never fail. In the midst frankincense sends forth its sacred fragrance, and there is water, cold, and sweet, and pure; the yellow loaves are near at hand, and the table of honor is loaded with cheese and rich honey. The altar in the midst is thickly covered with flowers on every side; singing and mirth fill the house. Men making merry should first hymn the god with propitious stanzas and pure words; and when they have poured out libations and prayed for power to do the right (since this lies nearest at hand), then it is no unfitting thing to drink as much as will not prevent your walking home without a slave, if you are not very old. And one ought to praise that man who, when he has drunk, unfolds noble things as his memory and his toil for virtue suggest; but there is nothing praiseworthy in discussing battles of Titans or of Giants or Centaurs, fictions of former ages, nor in plotting violent revolutions. But it is good always to pay careful respect to the gods.

2. But if one wins a victory by swiftness of foot, or in the pentathlon, where the grove of Zeus lies by Pisas' stream at Olympia, or as a wrestler, or in painful boxing, or in that severe contest called the pancration, he would be more glorious in the eyes of the citizens, he would win a front seat at assemblies, and would be entertained by the city at the public table, and he

---

[2] The fragments are given in H. Diels' arrangement in *Die Fragmente der Vorsokratiker*, 3rd ed. (Berlin, Wiedmannsche Buchhandlung, 1906). The Greek text followed is Theodore Bergk's *Anthologia Lyrica sive Lyricorum Graecorum Veterum. . . . ,* 4th ed. by Edward Hiller (Leipzig, B. G. Teubner, 1904).

would receive a gift which would be a keepsake for him. If he won by means of horses he would get all these things although he did not deserve them, as I deserve them, for our wisdom is better than the strength of men or of horses. This is indeed a very wrong custom, nor is it right to prefer strength to excellent wisdom. For if there should be in the city a man good at boxing, or in the pentathlon, or in wrestling, or in swiftness of foot, which is honored more than strength (among the contests men enter into at the games), the city would not on that account be any better governed. Small joy would it be to any city in this case if a citizen conquers at the games on the banks of the Pisas, for this does not fill with wealth its secret chambers.

3. Having learned profitless luxuries from the Lydians, while as yet they had no experience of hateful tyranny, they proceeded into the market-place, no less than a thousand in number all told, with purple garments completely covering them, boastful, proud of their comely locks, anointed with unguents of rich perfume.

4. Nor would any one first pour the wine into the cup to mix it, but water first and the wine above it.

5. For sending the thigh-bone of a goat, thou didst receive the rich leg of a fatted bull, an honorable present to a man, the fame whereof shall come to all Greece, and shall not cease so long as there is a race of Greek bards.

6. The Lydians were the first people who minted coins.

7. Now, however, I come to another topic, and I will show the way. . . . They say that once upon a time when a hound was badly treated a passer-by [Pythagoras] pitied him and said, "Stop beating him, for it is the soul of a dear friend; I recognized him on hearing his voice."

8. Already now sixty-seven years my thoughts have been tossed restlessly up and down Greece, but then it was twenty and five years from my birth, if I know how to speak the truth about these things.

9. Much more feeble than an aged man.

10. From the beginning, according to Homer, since all have learned from him.

11. Homer and Hesiod attributed to the gods all things which are disreputable and worthy of blame when done by men; and they told of them many lawless deeds, stealing, adultery, and deception of each other.

12. They have sung of many lawless deeds on the part of the gods, stealing, adultery, and deception of each other.

13. (Homer antedated Hesiod.)

14. But mortals suppose that the gods are born (as they themselves are), and that they wear man's clothing and have human voice and body.

15. But if cattle or lions had hands, so as to paint with their hands and produce works of art as men do, they would paint their gods and give them bodies in form like their own—horses like horses, cattle like cattle.

16. Ethiopians make their gods black and snub-nosed, Thracians red-haired and with blue eyes.

17. Bacchic wands of fir stand about the firmly built house.

18. In the beginning the gods did not reveal all things clearly to mortals, but by searching men in the course of time find them out better.

19. . . .

20. (Epimenides lived 154 years.) [3]

21. (Simonides . . . a skinflint.) [4]

22. The following are fit topics for conversation for men reclining on a soft couch by the fire in the winter season, when

---

[3] Translation by Richmond Lattimore in Matthew Thompson McClure's *The Early Philosophers of Greece* (New York, Appleton-Century-Crofts, 1935).
[4] *Ibid.*

after a meal they are drinking sweet wine and eating a little pulse: Who are you, and what is your family? What is your age, my friend? How old were you when the Medes invaded this land?

23. God is one, supreme among gods and men, and not like mortals in body or in mind.

24. The whole [of god] sees, the whole perceives, the whole hears.

25. But without effort he sets in motion all things by mind and thought.

26. It [i.e., being] always abides in the same place, not moved at all, nor is it fitting that it should move from one place to another.

27. For all things come from earth, and all things end by becoming earth.

28. The upper limit of earth at our feet is visible and touches the air, but below it reaches to infinity.

29. All things that come into being and grow are earth and water.

30. The sea is the source of water and the source of wind; for neither would blasts of wind arise in the clouds and blow out from within them, except for the great sea, nor would the streams of rivers nor the rain-water in the sky exist but for the sea; but the great sea is the begetter of clouds and winds and rivers.

31. The sun hanging above the earth and warming it.

32. She whom men call Iris [rainbow], this also is by nature cloud, violet and red and pale green to behold.

33. For we are all sprung from earth and water.

34. Accordingly, there has not been a man, nor will there be, who knows distinctly what I say about the gods or in regard to all things, for even if one chances for the most part to say what

is true, still he would not know; but every one thinks he knows [i.e., All are free to guess].

35. These things have seemed to me to resemble the truth.

36. As many things as they have made plain for mortals to see!

37. Holy water trickles down in thy grottoes.

38. If the god had not made light-colored honey, I should have said that a fig was far sweeter.

b. Xenophanes on the phenomena of the heavens.

1. Hipp., *Phil.* 1. 14. *Dox.* 565. The sun is formed each day from small fiery particles which are gathered together; the earth is infinite and is not surrounded by air or by sky; an infinite number of suns and moons exist, and all things come from earth.

2. Aet., *Plac.* 2. 13. *Dox.* 343. The stars are formed of burning cloud; these are extinguished each day, but they are kindled again at night, like coals; for their risings and settings are really kindlings and extinguishings. 20. 348. The sun is composed of fiery particles collected from the moist exhalation and massed together, or of burning clouds. 24. 354. Eclipses occur by extinction of the sun; and the sun is born anew at its risings. 24. 355. Xenophanes held that there are many suns and moons according to the different regions and sections and zones of the earth; and that at some fitting time the disk of the sun comes into a region of the earth not inhabited by us, and so it suffers eclipse as though it had gone into a hole; he adds that the sun goes on for an infinite distance, but it seems to turn around by reason of the great distance. 25. 356. The moon is a compressed cloud. 28. 358. It shines by its own light. 29. 360. The moon disappears each month because it is extinguished. 3. 2. 367. Comets are groups or motions of burning clouds. 3. 368. Lightnings take place when clouds shine in motion. 4. 371. The phenomena of the heavens come from the warmth of the sun as the principal cause. For when the moisture is drawn up from the sea, the sweet water separated by reason of its lightness becomes mist and passes into

clouds, and falls as rain when compressed, and the winds scatter it; for he writes expressly (see above, I. B. a. 30): "The sea is the source of water."

c. The earth, the sea, fossils, man.

HIPP., loc. cit. Xenophanes believes that once the earth was mingled with the sea, but in the course of time it became freed from moisture; and his proofs are such as these: that shells are found in the midst of the land and among the mountains, that in the quarries of Syracuse the imprints of a fish and of seals had been found, and in Paros the imprint of an anchovy at some depth in the stone, and in Melite shallow impressions of all sorts of sea products. He says that these imprints were made when everything long ago was covered with mud, and then the imprint dried in the mud. Farther he says that all men will be destroyed when the earth sinks into the sea and becomes mud, and that the race will begin anew from the beginning; and this transformation takes place for all worlds.

II. PARMENIDES

The far-reaching and profound implications of Eleatic philosophy suggested but unexamined by Xenophanes are made explicit by Parmenides, who was not encumbered either by a theological bent or by a moral mission. Parmenides was the son of Pyres and a native of Elea.[5] Plato, in the Theaetetus, characterizes Parmenides as "a man to be reverenced and at the same time feared" (see below, II. B. b. 2). The dates of Parmenides' life have never been satisfactorily established but he is said by Plato to have conversed with Socrates. This statement would fix the date of his visit to Athens ca. 451-449 B.C. Parmenides is said by Diogenes Laertius to have flourished in the years 504-500 B.C. Tradition has it that he was brought to philosophy by the Pythagorean, Ameinias; that he erected a statue to Diochrates,

[5] The selections relating to Parmenides' life and thought begin below, p. 91.

another Pythagorean; and that he gave laws to Elea, which the natives of that city swore each year to uphold.

Parmenides makes no concession in his philosophy to those who interpret the appearance of change to reveal the cosmos as it is. His is a direct attack upon what became for Greek philosophy in the Pluralists' speculation the effort to "save appearances" and the target for his attack is Heraclitus. He declares that his desire is to restrain those for whom "to be and not to be are thought the same and not the same, and the way of all things turns back against itself" (see below, II. B. a. 6). What *is*, for Parmenides, is neither a conflict of contraries nor is it explicable in terms of eternal flux and change. For classical philosophy, the issue becomes one between *being* and *becoming*. For Parmenides, this issue is expressed in terms of the strict dichotomy: "either *it is* or *it is not*." [6]

The problem from which Parmenides starts in Heraclitus' system is implicit in the philosophy of the Milesians. The attempt to discover the material substance or "world stuff" that maintains its identity despite change carries with it the implication that all objects of our experience are that substance in one or the other of its transformations. For example, water would be, for Anaximenes, air in a particular state of condensation (see above, Ch. 1, III. B. b. 2). Despite its further condensation into earth or stones or its rarefaction into fire, these particular forms, presented to us by the senses as various substances, are in reality but one substance, air.

If now we ask why air appears to be stones or earth or fire, Parmenides' answer to our question suggests that such appearance is due to the difference between the senses and thought. Parmenides adopts an hypothesis prevalent among the Greeks that thought is similar to or identical with what is known— "Thinking and the thing for the sake of which we think are the same" (see below, II. B. a. 8).

[6] See John Burnet, *Early Greek Philosophy*, 4th ed. (London, A. & C. Black, Ltd., 1930), Ch. 4, particularly p. 178: Parmenides "says simply, *What is, is.*" *Loc. cit.*, fn. 4: "We must not render τὸ ἐόν by 'being' . . . It is 'what is'. . . . As to (τὸ) εἶναι it does not occur, and hardly could occur at this date."

The senses present us with variants. Thought reveals what the stones are or what the air is because thought seeks the common, the universal, and the invariant. Heraclitus' attempt to solve the problem of reality, using an hypothesis that emphasizes the reality of the particular concrete manifestation of change, never solves a primary difficulty. The particular concrete manifestations evidence to the senses qualities contrary to the qualities attributed to the substance of which they are a particular manifestation. Water is cold and wet; fire is hot and dry. The senses take these differences to be real. But these qualitative distinctions of fire and water may only be adequately designated by thought through reference to the common; for example, in Anaximenes' philosophy, to air. In such a reference, it is clear that they are not air. But just in so far as they are not air, it follows, since air is the material of which all is composed, that they are in that sense non-existent.

Parmenides does not believe that earth, air, fire, or water is the material substance of which the universe is composed. *It is—* the *being* of later speculation—is that concrete substance. Having selected it, Parmenides proceeds to insist that anything that is not *it is* is non-existent. Throughout, he argues logically in this form: If x is white and y is brown and x is *it is,* then y is either identical with *it is* or it is non-existent; y would be identical with x only if difference were denied and the common or universal, which is the object of thought, were insisted upon. To put the matter more generally still, suppose that *per impossibile* there existed two different kinds of *it is* or *being,* x and y. Then if x is a kind of *it is,* not-x or y would be a kind of *it is not* or *non-being.* For example, if x is a chair, then x represents many ways of not existing, as for example, in the fashion of a table or a desk. If we try to express the difference between x and y, therefore, in the form x is not-y, all we have said is that x is a way of not existing and no positive difference has been expressed or is expressible.

With this logical conclusion as a premise, Parmenides proceeds dialectically to destroy the possibility of generation, destruction, change, and motion. Since *it is* is the common and the invariant, it cannot have come into existence nor could it be destroyed. Parmenides' dialectical method is one of repeated dichotomies: *It is* could not have come into existence, since to do so it must have come either from *it is not* (*non-being*) or from *it is* (*being*). It could not have come from *it is not*, since *it is not* is non-existent. It could not have come from *it is*, in any meaningful sense of the term, since *it is* itself is the existent and the common, and generation or change must mean transformation from one state into another. Similar dialectical argument denies divisibility (see below, II. B. a. 8). Parmenides' argument is not, however, carried on in a purely metaphysical manner, for, as has been remarked, he conceives *it is* to be a concrete substance. He proceeds to think pictorially and in concrete images. *It is* or *being* is homogeneous throughout and is compared to the mass of a rounded sphere, "finite on all sides, like the bulk of a well-rounded sphere, equally balanced from the center in every direction. . . ." It is probable that Parmenides chose the example to demonstrate the analogy between *it is,* as the limit at which apparent difference disappears, and the sphere, as the limit toward which by a repeated division of surfaces all other geometrical figures approach. Since, therefore, *it is* is spatially extended and *it is* is all that exists, there is no empty space. In Parmenides' world, motion is, therefore, impossible.

Considerable controversy centers around Parmenides' *The Way of Opinion.* Parmenides himself undertakes the second portion of his poem with the avowed purpose of ceasing "to give . . . the veritable account and thought concerning truth . . ." (see below, II. B. a. 8) and giving the opinions of mortals. The implication seems to be that Parmenides leaves the realm of pure philosophy to put his thoughts into language comprehensible to the multitude. Aristotle (see below, II. B. b. 4) seeing clearly, however, that in *The Way of Truth* Parmenides has destroyed the possibility of change and motion, urges that *The Way of Opinion* is the author's attempt to account for phenomena. The general implication of Aristotle's comment is that no system could be defended unless it explained empirical data. On the assumption that *The Way of Opinion* is an attempt to "save appearances," Aristotle holds that Parmenides has recourse to two explanatory causal principles, fire and earth. More recent interpretation, particularly that of Burnet, attributes *The Way of Opinion* to Parmenides' desire to acquaint his disciples with an opposing Pythagorean philosophy, presumably better to prepare them for the task of refuting the arguments of the adherents to the opposed doctrine.

A. LIFE

D.L., *op. cit.* IX. 21. Parmenides, a native of Elea, son of Pyres, was a pupil of Xenophanes (Theophrastus in his *Epitome* makes him a pupil of Anaximander). Parmenides, however, though he was instructed by Xenophanes was no follower of his. According to Sotion he also associated with Ameinias the Pythagorean . . . 23. He flourished in the 69th Olympiad (504-500 B.C.). . . . Parmenides is said to have served his native city as a legislator; so we learn from Speusippus in his book *On Philosophers.*

B. THOUGHT

a. The fragments.[7]

1. The horses that draw my chariot have borne me as far as ever my heart might desire, since they have brought me and set me in the famous way of the goddess, which alone carries through all cities the man who knows. Along this way I was borne; for upon it the wise horses drew me, straining at the chariot, and maidens pointed out the road.

And the axle kindling in the nave gave out a sound like the noise of a pipe—for it was sped by two whirling wheels, one on either side—when the daughters of Helius left the abode of Night and hastened to send me into the daylight, with their hands drawing the veils away from their faces.

There lie the gates of the ways to night and day, and a lintel guards them and threshold of marble; the towering portals are stopped with great doors, and requiting *Dicé* [Justice] holds the keys that fit them.

[7] Translated by Richmond Lattimore, *op. cit.,* pp. 145-149. The fragments follow H. Diels' arrangement in *Die Fragmente der Vorsokratiker,* 3rd ed. (Berlin, Wiedmannsche Buchhandlung, 1906).

Yet the maidens beguiling her with soft words shrewdly persuaded her to lift with all speed the fastened bar away from the gates. These as they swung back one after another on the posts rich in bronze, fitted in the sockets and set with nails and clamps, opened a wide space between the doors; and straight through by this way the maidens guided my chariot and horses. And the goddess received me graciously and took my right hand in her hand and addressing me spoke in this wise: O youth, who come to my house companioned by immortal charioteers, with the chariot that has brought you, welcome; for it is no evil lot, but righteousness and justice, that has sent you along this way, far as it is from the trodden path of man. You must learn all, both the untremulous heart of well-rounded truth, and the opinions of mortals, in which there is no true belief. Yet it is necessary that you learn these also, how they ought to have judged the things that appeared to them, as you pass through all things.

But do you keep your mind away from this way of inquiry, nor let the habit of long experience force you to direct along it an aimless eye, a shrill ear and tongue; but examine by reason this much-contested refutation that comes from me. Only one way is left to tell of . . .

THE WAY OF TRUTH

2. Look steadily with the mind upon things afar off as if they were near at hand; for you shall not sever what is from its hold upon what is, since it neither scatters itself throughout the world nor gathers itself together.

3. It is no matter to me whence I take my beginning; for to that point I shall return once more.

4. Come now, you must hear what I say and remember it, as I tell you of the only ways of inquiry that can be thought of. One, according to which there is [*that which is*] and it is impossible for it not to be, is the way of Peitho [Persuasion], for it follows Truth; and one is that according to which *it is not* and there is necessity for it not to be; and this I tell you is a way which is utterly obscure. For you could never learn what is not; that is impossible; nor could you describe it.

5. For the same thing can be thought as can be.

6. It must be that that, which may be spoken of and thought of, is what *is;* for it is possible for it to be, but it is impossible for nothing to be. This I bid you think on. I restrain you from that first way of seeking, and also from this one, which mortals, knowing nothing and torn two ways, fabricate; for helplessness residing in their hearts controls the errant thought, and they are carried about like men deaf and blind, all amazed, herds without discrimination, by whom to be and not to be are thought the same and not the same, and the way of all things turns back against itself.

7. For this shall never be proved, that the things that are not are; but do you force back your thought from this way of seeking.

8. There is one way left for us to tell of, that *it is;* many signs in this way point to this, that what *is* is without beginning, indestructible, entire, single, unshakable, endless; neither *has* it been nor *shall* it be, since not it *is;* all alike, single, solid. For what birth could you seek for it? Whence and how could it have grown? I will not let you say or think that it was from what is not; for it cannot be said or thought that anything is not. What need made it arise at one time rather than another, if it arose out of nothing and grew thence? So it must either be entirely, or not at all.

Nor will the power of faith ever allow that anything grows out of what is not except what is not; wherefore Justice has not loosened the chains to allow it either to take its being or to perish, but ever she holds it. And the decision of the matter rests herein: *either it is* or *it is not;* and so it is decided, of necessity, to give up one way as inconceivable and unnameable—for it is no true way—and to admit that the other is actual and a true way. How then could that which *is* be about to be? How could it come into being? For if it has come to pass or is about to be, then it is not. So becoming is put out of the question, and destruction is inconceivable. Nor is it divisible, since it is all alike; nor is there more of it in one place and less in another, which

would keep it from being continuous; but it is all full of what
is. So it is all consistent. For what is is contiguous with what is.

But it lies motionless in the limit of mighty bonds, without
beginning and without surcease, since beginning and destruction have been removed far away, and true belief has thrust them
aside. Being the same and remaining in the same place it likewise lies within itself and so remains locked in the same position; for *Anangké* (Necessity), being the stronger, holds it in the
bonds of its limitation which confine it all about. Hence that
which is is not allowed to be infinite; for it is in need of nothing,
but if it were infinite it would be in need of everything.

Thinking and the thing for the sake of which we think are
the same; for without that which is, in regard to which it is uttered, you will not find yourself able to think; for neither is there
nor shall there be anything beyond that which is, since Destiny
has bound it so that it is whole and motionless; and thus these
are only names that mortals have made thinking them to be true:
creation and destruction, being and not being, change of place
and alteration of shining color.

So, since there is a limit at its extremity, it is finite on all
sides, like the bulk of a well-rounded sphere, equally balanced
from the center in every direction; for there is no need for it to
be greater or smaller in one place than another; for there is
nothing that is not, which could prevent its coming together,
nor is it possible for what is to be greater or less in any place
than what is, since it is all inviolate; for [the center] which is
equidistant from every side, is just as much within the limits.

THE WAY OF OPINION

Hereupon I cease to give you the veritable account and
thought concerning truth; hereafter learn the opinions of mortals,
following the beguiling order of my words. For they have settled
in their minds to name two forms, one of which they should not
name; and therein they go astray. They have set them apart as
antithetical in shape and given them special marks that they
do not share with each other; to one the airy blaze of flame, which
is mild and very light and everywhere the same as itself, but
not the same as the other; which is in turn the very opposite of

it, flameless night, close and heavy of make. Of these I tell you in the apparent order, so that no mind of mortal may ever surpass you.

9. Now that all things have been termed Light and Darkness and the names that accord with the powers of each have been given to these and these others, everything is full at the same time of Light and obscure Darkness, of both in equal degree. For neither has aught to do with the other.

10. And you shall know the substance of the sky, and all the signs in the sky, and the bright activities of the pure torch of the candid sun, and whence they came; and you shall learn the wandering motions of the round-faced moon, and her substance, and you shall know likewise the sky circling these about, whence it took its being, and how Necessity, guiding it, constrained it to keep the limits of the stars.

11. . . . How the earth and the sun and the moon, and the sky common to all things and the Galaxy, and uttermost Olympus and the hot strength of the stars came into being.

12. Now the narrower rings are filled with unmixed fire, and those next to them with darkness, but through this gushes a division of fire; and in the center of these is the daemon that governs all things; for she controls the work of bitter child-bearing, and mingling in love, driving the female into the arms of the male, and then in turn the male to the female.

13. First of all the Gods she devised Eros.

14. Shining by night about the earth with light stolen from afar.

15. . . . Ever glancing towards the rays of the sun.

16. For thought comes to men with just that mixture of variable organs which it happens to have at the time; for that which has power of thought is for all men in any case the same thing, namely, the substance of their bodies; and this thought is that which is preponderant.

17. Boys are conceived on the right side, girls on the left.

18. So, according to the way of opinion, these things have come into being and now are, and so hereafter having been fostered they shall perish. And to each of these things men have given a distinguishing name, to stand for it.

b. Interpretations of Parmenides' philosophy.

1. ARIST., op. cit. I. 5. 986 b 18 et seq.—but Parmenides seems to speak in some places with greater care. For believing that not-being does not exist in addition to being, of necessity he thinks that being is one and that there is nothing else,—and being compelled to account for phenomena, and assuming that things are one from the standpoint of reason, plural from the standpoint of sense, he again asserts that there are two causes and two first principles, heat and cold, or, as he calls them, fire and earth; of these he regards heat as being, its opposite as not-being.

2. PLATO, Theaet. 183 E. Parmenides seems to me, in the words of Homer, a man to be reverenced and at the same time feared. For when I was a mere youth and he a very old man, I conversed with him, and he seemed to me to have an exceedingly wonderful depth of mind. Ibid. 180 D. I almost forgot, Theodoros, that there were others who asserted opinions the very opposite of these: "the all is alone, unmoved; to this all names apply," and the other emphatic statements in opposition to those referred to, which the school of Melissus and Parmenides make, to the effect that all things are one, and that the all stands by itself in itself, not having space in which it is moved.

3. HIPP., op. cit. 11. Dox. 564. Parmenides supposes that the all is one and eternal, and without beginning and spheroidal in form; but even he does not escape the opinion of the many, for he speaks of fire and earth as the first principles of the all, of earth as matter, and of fire as agent and cause, and he says that the earth will come to an end, but in what way he does not say.

He says that the all is eternal, and not generated, and spherical, and homogeneous, not having place in itself, and unmoved and limited.

4. ARIST., *Phys.* I. 3. 186 a 4. To those proceeding after this impossible manner things seem to be one, and it is not difficult to refute them from their own statements. For both of them reason in a fallacious manner, both Parmenides and Melissus; for they make false assumptions, and at the same time their course of reasoning is not logical—And the same sort of arguments are used by Parmenides—and the refutation consists in showing both that he makes mistakes of fact and that he does not draw his conclusions correctly. He makes a mistake in assuming that being is to be spoken of absolutely, speaking of it thus many times; and he draws the false conclusion that, in case only whites are considered, white meaning one thing, none the less there are many whites and not one; since neither in the succession of things nor in the argument will whiteness be one. For what is predicated of white will not be the same as what is predicated of the object which is white, and nothing except white will be separated from the object; since there is no other ground of separation except the fact that the white is different from the object in which the white exists. But Parmenides had not yet arrived at the knowledge of this.

c. The heavenly bodies.

AET., *op. cit.* 2. 7. *Dox.* 335. Parmenides taught that there were crowns encircling one another in close succession, one of rarefied matter, another of dense, and between these other mixed crowns of light and darkness; and that which surrounded all was solid like a wall, and under this was a crown of fire; and the center of all the crowns was solid, and around it was a circle of fire; and of the mixed crowns the one nearest the center was the source of motion and generation for all, and this "the goddess who directs the helm and holds the keys," he calls "justice and necessity."

III. ZENO

To Zeno, son of Teleutagoras and disciple of Parmenides [8] (see below, III. A), fell the task of defending the teachings of the great Eleatic, Parmenides (see below, III. B. a). A powerful advocacy of the theory, *it is* or *being*, was needed. Parmenides' philosophy runs counter to what men take to be the basic facts got immediately by perception and what experience—unexamined, perhaps—teaches men is the nature of the cosmos. The recurrent efforts in the history of philosophy to provide solutions to Zeno's paradoxes suggest that the advocacy of Parmenides' theory could have fallen into no abler hands.

Zeno was born *ca.* 495-490 B.C. He was a favorite of Parmenides. According to Strabo, Zeno promoted law and order in Elea. Tradition attaches to his name an heroic effort to avoid giving incriminating evidence against friends. Rather than implicate them, Zeno is said to have bitten off his tongue.

Plato tells us (see below, III. B. a) that Zeno formulated his paradoxes for the avowed purpose of supporting Parmenides' theory of the "one." This support is further indicated in fragment 4, in which the Parmenidean argument against the possibility of empty space is maintained by showing that to suppose *it is* or *being* to be other than a *plenum* involves the further supposition that space has an end or limit, that limited space is in another space, and so on *ad infinitum*. This is perhaps the first historical example of a distrust of an infinite regress. The remaining paradoxes concern themselves with multiplicity, in respect to magnitude and to motion.

Restatements of two or three of Zeno's arguments will suffice to demonstrate his method. The problem of the moving arrow (see below, III. B. d. 1) may be stated as follows: A body must either be moving in a place where it is or where it is not. It cannot be moving in a place where it is or it would not be there. It cannot be moving in a place where it is not for it is not there. Therefore the flying arrow cannot be moving. Stated in another way, Zeno's argument involves the assumption that the flying arrow is at rest at any point in its trajectory. But this can be

[8] The selection relating to Zeno's life is below, p. 100.

said of every point in the trajectory and what is at rest at every point does not move at all. The solution to the paradox is impossible for philosophy until mathematics, by the development of the differential calculus could deal with the general problem of velocity at a point. Once the mathematics is developed, the paradox of the flying arrow may be considered as one involving a definite velocity for the arrow at every point of its trajectory.

Concerning magnitude, we may take as an example a restatement of fragment 3 (see below, III. B. b. 3). A line xy is either divisible or it is indivisible. It is divisible if a point not corresponding either to x or to y can be inserted between the end points x and y. Zeno's method of argument would be as follows: If the line is indivisible, the argument of Parmenides is admitted, for *it is* or *being* has no parts. If the line is divisible, it is divisible into a finite number of parts or into an infinite number of parts. Both possibilities must be tested. If the line is divisible into a finite number of parts only, when that number is reached, the parts have no length and the division disappears, since otherwise the division could progress. If the line is divisible into an infinite number of parts, the parts must have either no length or some length. If the parts have no length, and yet by definition the line has an infinite number of parts, an impossibility results since no number would add up to anything. If the parts have some length and the infinite division has ended, the line can be made to grow and to grow as long as we like by adding part to part since our supply of parts can never be exhausted.

The most famous of Zeno's paradoxes is that of Achilles and the Tortoise (see below, III. B. d. 3). Achilles running swiftly cannot catch the tortoise running slowly, for he will have to come to the end of an infinite series and an infinite series has no end. For example, if the distance be divided according to the law of $\frac{1}{2}$, $\frac{1}{4}$, $\frac{1}{8}$, $\frac{1}{16}$ ... $\frac{1}{2}^n$, before he can reach the tortoise he must have passed through the last term. But the series has no last term. Therefore he can never come up to the tortoise.

A solution is offered as follows: Suppose we deny the compulsion of the major premise.[9] If there is no last term, why does

[9] The solution offered is that of H. B. Smith in *How the Mind Falls into Error* (New York, Harper & Row, Publishers, Inc., 1923), p. 23.

Achilles have to pass through the last term in order to come up to the tortoise? This classifies Zeno's problem as a fallacy, as a case of contradiction in definition. It might also be classified as the fallacious use of all in the collective and in the distributive sense.[10] Achilles in order to catch the tortoise has to go through every term of an infinite series in the sense that you can name no term through which he does not have to pass. But he does not have to go through them all collectively because the series, being open at one end, does not constitute a collection. There is no such thing as an infinite collection.

A. LIFE

D.L., op. cit. IX. 25. Zeno was a citizen of Elea. Apollodorus in his Chronology says that he was the son of Teleutagoras by birth, but of Parmenides by adoption. . . . Zeno, then, was all through a pupil of Parmenides and his bosom friend. . . . Aristotle says that Zeno was the inventor of dialectic, as Empedocles was of rhetoric. . . . He, wishing to put an end to the power of Nearches, the tyrant . . . was arrested. . . . And when he was examined, as to his accomplices, and as to the arms which he was taking to Lipara, he named all the friends of the tyrant as his accomplices, wishing to make him feel himself alone. . . . He was asked by the tyrant if there was anyone else. And he replied, "Yes, you, the destruction of the city." . . . And at last he bit off his tongue and spat it at him; and the citizens immediately rushed forward, and slew the tyrant with stones. . . .

B. THOUGHT

a. Plato on the purpose of Zeno's arguments.

PLATO, Parmen. 128 C. In truth, these writings are a kind of support of the doctrine of Parmenides against those who endeavor

---

[10] The statement of the problem is that of E. A. Singer, Jr., who gives the argument concerning principles which apply collectively and distributively in Mind as Behavior (Columbus, Ohio, R. G. Adams and Co., 1924), pp. 67-68.

to ridicule it, by saying that if "one" exists, it would follow that such an assertion would suffer many things of a laughable kind, and contrary to itself. This writing therefore contradicts those who assert that "the many" exists; and it gives in return these and many other reasons; as it intends to show that the hypothesis, which (asserts) the existence of "the many" would suffer things still more laughable than (would) the assumption of "the one," if it is sufficiently worked out.

b. The fragments of Zeno's speculation on the one and the many.

1. SIMP., *Phys.* 30 r. 140, 27. If being did not have magnitude, it would not exist at all. If anything exists, it is necessary that each thing should have some magnitude and thickness, and that one part of it should be separated from another. The same argument applies to the thing that is in front of it, for that also will have magnitude and will have something in front of it. The same may be said of each thing once for all, for there will be no such thing as last, nor will one thing differ from another. So if there is a multiplicity of things, it is necessary that these should be great and small—small enough not to have any magnitude, and great enough to be infinite.

2. ———— 30 r. 138, 30. For if anything were added to another thing, it could not make it any greater; for since greatness does not exist, it is impossible to increase the greatness of a thing by adding to it. So that which is added would be nothing. If when something is taken away that which is left is no less, and if it becomes no greater by receiving additions, evidently that which has been added or taken away is nothing.

3. ———— 30 r. 140, 27. If there is a multiplicity of things, it is necessary that these should be just as many as exist, and not more nor fewer. If there are just as many as there are, then the number would be finite. If there is a multiplicity at all the number is infinite, for there are always others between any two, and yet others between each pair of these. So the number of things is infinite.

4. ARIST., *Met.* I. 1001 b. 7. If the absolute unit is indivisible,

it would, according to Zeno's axiom, be nothing at all. For that which neither makes anything larger by its addition, nor makes anything smaller by its subtraction, is not one of the things that are, since it is clear that what is must be a magnitude, and, if a magnitude, corporeal, for the corporeal has being in all dimensions. Other things, such as the surface and the line, when added in one way make things larger, when added in another way do not; but the point and the unit do not make things larger however added.

c. Zeno's argument concerning space.

If there is such a thing as space, it will be in something, for all being is in something, and that which is in something is in some space. So this space will be in a space, and so on *ad infinitum*. Accordingly, there is no such thing as space.

d. Zeno's paradoxes of motion.[11]

THE ARROW IN FLIGHT

1. If, Zeno says, everything is at rest when it is in a space equal to itself, and the moving body is always in the present moment in a space equal to itself, then the moving arrow is still. Therefore the arrow in flight is stationary.

THE RACE COURSE

2. Motion does not exist because the moving body must go half the distance before it goes the whole distance.[12]

ACHILLES AND THE TORTOISE

3. The slow runner will never be overtaken by the swiftest, for it is necessary that the pursuer should first reach the point from which the pursued started, so that necessarily the slower is always somewhat in advance. This argument is the same as the preceding, the only difference being that the distance is not divided each time into halves.

[11] The paradoxes of motion are given in Aristotle's *Physics* VI. 9. 239 b 5 sq. and VIII. 8. 263 a 5 sq.

[12] Cf. Aristotle, *Physics* VIII. 8. 263 a 5: The same method should also be adopted in replying to those who ask, in the terms of Zeno's argument, whether we admit that before any distance can be traversed half the distance must be traversed, that these half-distances are infinite in number, and that it is impossible to traverse distances infinite in number.

THE STADIUM

4. With reference to equal bodies moving in opposite directions past equal bodies in the stadium with equal speed, some from the end of the stadium, others from the middle, Zeno thinks half the time equal to twice the time.[13]

THE GRAINS OF MILLET

5. Simp., *Phys.* 255 r. Aristotle accordingly solves the problem of Zeno the Eleatic, which he propounded to Protagoras the Sophist.[14] "Tell me, Protagoras," said he, "does one grain of millet make a noise when it falls, or does the ten-thousandth part of a grain?" On receiving the answer that it does not, he went on: "Does a measure of millet grains make a noise when it falls, or not?" He answered, "It does make a noise." "Well," said Zeno, "does not the statement about the measure of millet apply to the one grain and the ten-thousandth part of a grain?" He assented, and Zeno continued, "Are not the statements as to the noise the same in regard to each? For as are the things that make a noise, so are the noises. Since this is the case, if the measure of millet makes a noise, the one grain and the ten-thousandth part of a grain make a noise."

IV. MELISSUS OF SAMOS

As was remarked in the Introduction to the Eleatic School, Melissus, the last of the three generations of philosophers called

---

[13] John Burnet, *op. cit.*, reconstructs the paradox as follows, p. 319: Half the time may be equal to double the time. Let us suppose three rows of bodies, one of which (A) is at rest while the other two (B, C) are moving with equal velocity in opposite directions (Fig. 1). By the time they are all in the same part of the course, B will have passed twice as many of the bodies in C as A (Fig. 2).

	Fig. 1			Fig. 2
A	o o o o		A	o o o o
B	o o o o		B	o o o o
C	o o o o		C	o o o o

Therefore the time which it takes to pass C is twice as long as the time it takes to pass A. But the time which B and C take to reach the position of A is the same. Therefore double the time is equal to the half.

[14] Aristotle, *Physics* VIII. 5. 250 a 20.

"Eleatic," provides more affirmative arguments in support of Parmenides' *it is* or *being* than we find in Zeno's paradoxes. Moreover, Melissus' speculations [15] concerning the great Eleatic's thought influenced succeeding philosophers to a far lesser degree than did Zeno's and, in fact, evoked from Aristotle the comment that his arguments were "wearisome." It is important, however, to note that problems of eternity and time are raised by the Samian's arguments and that his thinking upon Parmenidean philosophy directs our attention to the pluralistic interpretation of natural philosophy as it was to be formulated by the Atomists. (For the philosophy of the Atomists, Leucippus and Democritus, see below, Ch. 5, III and IV. B.) It was Melissus who, as Zeller points out,[16] "first maintained the unlimitedness of the One Being."

We know little of Melissus' life. He was the son of Ithagenes and his birthplace was Samos. Parmenides is said to have been his teacher. Plutarch, in the *Life of Pericles,* writes of Melissus that he was a general of the Samians and that it was he who commanded the Samians in the battle in which Pericles was defeated.[17]

As were Zeno's arguments, Melissus' philosophical speculations were intended to defend and strengthen the theory of *being* or *it is* formulated by Parmenides. Zeno and Melissus differ, however, in their approaches to that defence. Zeno's method is dialectical. It is primarily intended to show that the opponents of the Parmenidean philosophy are themselves entangled in difficulties, a point which Zeno makes with great skill by adopting the premises with which the opponents of *it is* begin. Melissus, on the other hand, offers a positive argument for the validity of the Parmenidean philosophy. As Simplicius remarks [18] Melissus makes "use of the axioms of the physicists." In general, Melissus tries to present his arguments by reference to the relation be-

[15] The selections from Melissus' philosophy begin below, p. 106.

[16] E. Zeller, *A History of Greek Philosophy.* The quotation is from the English translation of Vol. 1, 1. III, *The Pre-Socratic Philosophy,* by S. F. Alleyne (London, Longmans, Green, and Co., Inc., 1881), p. 534.

[17] The selections relating to Melissus' life begin below, p. 106.

[18] Simplicius, *Physics* 30 r 139.

tween the more usual philosophical approaches to the explanation of the universe and the Eleatic point of view.

Melissus maintains that *it is* or *being* is infinite in magnitude (see below, III, B. a. 3), in sharp contrast to the arguments put forward by Parmenides and Zeno (see above, p. 94; and III. B. b. 4). Melissus evidently draws the inference from his beliefs that what *is* could only be limited by empty space (see below, IV. B. a. 5, 7); that there is no motion (*ibid.*, 7); and that there is no change (*ibid.*).

Melissus completes his argument in the assertion that *it is* or *being* is eternal; that, because it is infinite, it has neither beginning nor end in either spatial or temporal terms; that it is homogeneous; and—because it is changeless, motionless, and without conditions—there is no need to assume that it originates or ends, or that it moves in space (see below, IV. B. a. 7).

Aristotle is severe in his criticism of Melissus (see below, IV. B. b. 1, 2). Not only does he find the arguments "wearisome," but he believes that what Melissus argues is illogically presented. Aristotle asserts that Melissus believes that "what is generated has a beginning, and that what has a beginning is generated" are equivalent statements. John Burnet writes [19] that this "somewhat pedantic" objection charges a man with performing a "false conversion," whereas Melissus "knew nothing about the rules of conversion." Had he known the rules of formal logic, Burnet writes, Melissus could easily have corrected the reasoning without changing the system.

In any case, it is clear that Melissus made one highly significant contribution to the history of philosophy. This is implicit in IV. B. a. 8 in which he maintains that "if a multiplicity of things exist, it is necessary that they should be such as the one is." Many historians have argued that this statement is an anticipation of the pluralist philosophy of the Atomists. (For the Atomist philosophy, see below, Ch. 6.) Burnet argues [20] in fact that this is not only the formula of Atomism but that in

[19] John Burnet, *op. cit.*, p. 328.
[20] John Burnet, *Greek Philosophy: Part I Thales to Plato* (London, Macmillan and Co., Ltd., 1928), p. 86.

rejecting it because he denied empty space, Melissus "prepared the way for the atomic theory by making it necessary for Leukippos to affirm the existence of the Void."

A. LIFE

1. D.L., *op. cit.* IX. 4. Melissus was a Samian, and the son of Ithagenes. He was a pupil of Parmenides; but he also had converse with Heraclitus, when he recommended him to the Ephesians, who were unacquainted with him. . . . He was a man greatly occupied with political affairs, and held in great esteem among his fellow citizens; on which account he was elected admiral. And he was admired still more on account of his private virtues. . . . Apollodorus states that he flourished about the 84th Olympiad (444-440 B.C.).

2. AET., *op. cit.* I. 3. *Dox.* 285. Melissus of Miletus, son of Ithagenes, became his (Parmenides) companion, but he did not preserve in its purity the doctrine that was transmitted to him. . . .

3. EPIPH., *Haer.* III. 12. *Dox.* 590. Melissus of Samos, son of Ithagenes, said that the all is one in kind, but that nothing is fixed in its nature, for all things are potentially destructible.

4. PLUT., *Peri.* For Melissus, (the son of Ithagenes, a great Philosopher) being at the time general of the Samians: perceiving that few ships were left behind at the siege of the city, and that the captains also that had the charge of them were no very expert men of war, persuaded his citizens to make a sally upon them. Whereupon they fought a battell, and the Samians overcame. . . . Aristotle writeth that Pericles self was once overcome in a battell by sea by Melissus.[21]

B. THOUGHT

a. The fragments.

1. If nothing is, how could this be spoken of as though something is? And if anything is, either it has come into being, or

[21] Sir Thomas North's translation of *Plutarch's Lives.*

else it has always been. If it came into being, it sprung either from being or from not-being; but it is impossible that any such thing should have sprung from not-being (for nothing else that is could have sprung from it, much less pure being).

2. Since then it did not come into being but *is*, it always was and always will be, and has neither beginning nor end, but is infinite. For if it had come into existence it would have had a beginning (for that which once came into existence would have a beginning) and an end (for that which once came into existence would come to an end); if it neither had a beginning nor came to an end, it always was and always will be; it has not beginning or end; but it is impossible that anything which is not the whole should always exist.

3. But as it always exists, so it is necessary also that it be always infinite in magnitude.

4. Nothing which has beginning and end is either eternal or infinite.

5. If it were not one, it would be bounded by something else.

6. And if it is infinite, it is one; for if being were two, both parts could not be infinite, but each would be limited by the other. But being is infinite; there could not be several beings; accordingly being is one.

7. So then the all is eternal and infinite and homogeneous; and it could neither perish nor become greater nor change its arrangement nor suffer pain or distress. If it experienced any of these things it would no longer be one; for if it becomes different, it is necessary that being should not be homogeneous, but that which was before must perish, and that which was not must come into existence. If then the all should become different by a single hair in ten thousand years, it would perish in the whole of time.

And it is impossible for its order to change, for the order existing before does not perish, nor does another which did not exist come into being; and since nothing is added to it or subtracted from it or made different, how could any of the things that are change their order? But if anything became different, its order would already have been changed.

Nor does it suffer pain, for the all could not be pained; it would be impossible for anything suffering pain always to be; nor does it have power equal to the power of what is healthy. It would not be homogeneous if it suffered pain; it would suffer pain whenever anything was added or taken away, and it would no longer be homogeneous. Nor could what is healthy suffer a pang of pain, for both the healthy and *being* would perish, and not-being would come into existence. The same reasoning that applies to pain also applies to distress.

Nor is there any void, for the void is nothing, and that which is nothing could not be.

Nor does it move, for it has nowhere to go to, since it is full; for if there were a void it could go into the void, but since there is no void it has nowhere to go. It could not be rare and dense, for it is not possible for the rare to be as full as the dense, but the rare is already more empty than the dense.

This is the test of what is full and what is not full: if it has room for anything, or admits anything into it, it is not full; if it does not have room for anything, or admit anything into it, it is full.

If no void exists it must be full; if then it is full it does not move.

8. This argument is the strongest proof that being is one only. And the proofs are as follows: For if a multiplicity of things existed it would be necessary that these things should be just such as I say the one is. For if earth exists, and water and air and iron and gold and fire and the living and the dead and black and white, and everything else which men say is real,—if these things exist and we see and hear them correctly, it is necessary that each thing should be such as we first determined, namely, it should not change its character or become different, but should always be each thing what it is. Now we say that we see and hear and understand correctly; but it seems to us that hot becomes cold and cold hot, that hard becomes soft and soft hard, that the

living being dies and life comes from what is not living; and
that all these things become different, and what they are is not
like what they were. It seems to us that iron, being hard to the
touch, wastes away because of rust, and so does gold, and rock,
and whatever else seems to be strong, so that we conclude that
we do not see or know things that are. And earth and rock arise
from water. These things then do not harmonise with each other.
Though we said that many things are eternal, and have forms
and strength, it seems that they all become different and change
their character each time they are seen. Evidently we do not
see correctly, nor is the appearance of multiplicity correct; for
they would not change their character if they were real, but
would remain each thing as it seemed, for nothing is nobler than
that which is real. But if they change their character, being
perishes and not-being comes into existence. So then if a multiplicity of things exist, it is necessary that they should be such
as the one is.

9. If being exists it must be one, and being one it is necessary
that it should not itself have body; and if it should have thickness,
it would have parts and would no longer be a unity.

10. If being is separated it moves; and that which moves
could not exist simultaneously.

b. Aristotle's criticism of Melissus' philosophy.

1. Arist., *Phys.* 1. 3. 186 a 6. Both Melissus and Parmenides
argue fallaciously, and they make false assumptions and their
reasonings are not logical; but the argument of Melissus is the
more wearisome, for it sets no problem, but granted one strange
thing, others follow; and there is no difficulty in this. The error
in the reasoning of Melissus is plain, for he thinks that if everything which has come into being has a beginning, he can assume
that that which has not come into being does not have a beginning. This, then, is strange, that he should think that everything
has a beginning except time, and this does not, and that simple
generation has no beginning but change alone begins, as though
change as a whole did not come into being. Even if the all is a

unity, why then should it not move? Why should not the whole be moved even as a part of it which is a unity, namely water, is moved in itself? Then why should there not be change? It is not possible that being should be one in form, but only in its source.

2. ARIST., *Soph. El.* 5. 163 b 3. The same is true of syllogisms, as for instance in the case of Melissus' argument that the all is infinite; in this he assumes that the all is not generated (for nothing is generated from not-being), and that that which is generated, is generated from a beginning. If then the all was not generated, it does not have a beginning, so it is infinite. It is not necessary to assent to this, for even if everything which is generated has a beginning, it does not follow that if anything has a beginning it was generated, as a man with a fever is warm, but one who is warm may not have a fever.

3. —— 6. 164 b 35. Or again, as Melissus assumes in his argument that generation and having a beginning are the same thing, or that that which is generated from equals has the same size. The two statements, that what is generated has a beginning, and that what has a beginning is generated, he deems equivalent, so that the generated and the limited are both the same in that they have each a beginning. Because what is generated has a beginning, he postulates that what has a beginning is generated, as though both that which is generated and that which is finite were the same in having a beginning.

5

THE PLURALISTS

THE PHILOSOPHIES of Empedocles, Anaxagoras, and the Atomists, Leucippus and Democritus, are differing systems of thought, each with its own intrinsic value. But each begins as an effort to avoid the dilemma with which the opposing theories of Heraclitus and the Eleatic philosophers presented their successors. Heraclitus, concentrating upon the orderly process of change and its exemplifications in concrete phenomena, provides an approach to an explanation of the constant variation and mutability of the world of experience. Primarily, Heraclitus, in accounting for the periodicity of the seasons, the recurrence of life and death and the phenomena of generation and corruption, faces up to the "hard facts" of the world, the "fact" observed that this or that bow releases an arrow and that this or that river flows. Parmenides and Zeno, concentrating upon the identity of *it is* or *being*, deny its change. Thought or reason demands fixity and universality, as opposed to change or flux or explicit concentration upon "facts" as explanatory of reality. How Heraclitus' fire transforms itself into other elements is, however, left unanswered. Why appearances seem real and why "facts" and phenomena affect us are questions dismissed by Parmenides and Zeno with compelling logic. Yet, they dismiss these problems with little effort to satisfy the mind's craving for some relating of *being* to becoming or, at least, to the appearance of becoming.

Empedocles, Anaxagoras, and the Atomists do not accept the absolute dichotomy between *being* and change. Logically, their position may be indicated by saying that the Pluralists refused to accept the alternative "*either* being *or* becoming." They subject previous thought to a close analysis and demonstrate that all of the possibilities had not been exhausted by their predecessors.

I. EMPEDOCLES

Empedocles,[1] son of Meton and a native of Agrigentum, is the first philosopher to attempt the reconciliation of Eleatic and Heraclitean philosophy. Zeller puts the dates of Empedocles' life *ca.* 494-434 B.C. Of an aristocratic family, Empedocles opposed tyranny and refused the crown of his native town. Forced to leave Agrigentum for political reasons, tradition had it that Empedocles leapt, after a feast, into the crater of Mt. Etna. Empedocles was not only a philosopher but a magician and religious teacher. He is said, for example, to have forbidden the winds to enter Agrigentum and to have halted them by stretching asses' skins across the hollows through which the winds ordinarily passed. On his own evidence, he was a healer of the sick, one who recalled the dead to life and a believer in the transmigration of the soul (see below, I. B. a. 24, 369, 383).

As a starting point for his thought, Empedocles adopts the implications of Parmenides' philosophy of *being*. The coming into existence of *being* or its destruction cannot be maintained (see below, I. B. a. 45, 48). Nevertheless, while the acceptance of Parmenides' *being* means the denial of origin and destruction, changes of location that do not affect the nature of substance but merely its distribution are admissible. Such mechanical processes are accepted by Empedocles in "mixture and separation" (see below, I. B. a. 36, 60). By mixture, what gives the appearance of origin, growth, or becoming takes place. Decay, destruction, and death are accounted for by separation. This, however, leads Empedocles to reinterpret *being* in a most

[1] See below, p. 115 for Empedocles' life. The selections from Empedocles' poem begin below, p. 116.

important sense, for if *being* is homogeneous throughout, the mixture and separation will not produce an adequate explanation of change. Empedocles, therefore, seeks the necessary and sufficient "roots" or "elements" to which, as *being*, all phenomena will reduce but which are themselves irreducible (see above, p. 4). These "roots" or "elements" are *being*—immortal, indestructible, and qualitatively unchangeable. They are identified by Empedocles with earth, air, fire, and water (see below, I. B. a. 33). Earth, air, fire, and water are the ultimate elements from which the universe is compounded (see below, I. B. a. 87). Empedocles is the first philosopher to introduce them as the four elements. Aristotle indicates, however, that Empedocles followed Parmenides' *On Opinion* and employs but two elements, the division being fire on one side and earth, air, and water on the other (see below, I. B. b. 3). Empedocles' analyses of the characteristics of each element are cursory.

It is necessary for Empedocles more specifically to explain change as it is brought about by the mixture and separation of the qualitatively unchangeable "roots" or elements. Since no qualitative change can occur in the element, there can be no such transformation of one element into another as occurs in Heraclitus' account of process. The elements are mixed, always retaining their qualitative differences, through the interpenetration of the protrusions of one element into the pores or interstices of another element: "But these [elements] are the same; and penetrating through each other they become one thing in one place and another in another, while ever they remain alike (i.e., the same)" (see below, I. B. a. 87). Separation is the withdrawal of what was intermingled. In what manner such mixture and separation could take place in a world in which empty space is specifically denied and in which the elements are by definition indivisible is not revealed. To answer the question that inevitably arises concerning the relation of the qualitatively changeless elements to the infinity of qualitatively different phenomena of the world, Empedocles offers the analogy of the artist mixing paints (see below, I. B. a. 121). He points out that some mixtures occur more easily than others (see below, I. B. a.

284), and the analogy seems to be based on the generalization that the more closely correspondent the pores of one body are to the protrusions or emanations of another body, the more susceptible the two are of mixture. This theory is likewise utilized to explain sensation and perception, the assumption being that objects are perceived through the presence of elements in us identical or similar to elements in the things perceived (cf. I. B. a. 169-195 and I. B. a. 287-333).

A factor implicit in the Milesian philosophy is made explicit in Empedocles' theory of change. Anaximenes, for example, tacitly assumes that changes in temperature transform air into its varied phenomenal states. Empedocles concludes of the four "roots," since they constitute *being* and involve no change or movement within themselves, that they cannot contain within themselves the force or impulse causing the beginning or continuation of the mixture and separation. Processes require an "efficient cause" or "moving force." Empedocles' solution to the problem is an argument derived from the observation of man and other living creatures. Love is the force that attracts men to men, Strife the force that repels. Love and Strife are applied as principles—"efficient causes" by means of which *being* and *becoming* achieve their roles in the processes of cosmic change and *stasis*—to the universe at large and are interpreted as the causes of change. As Empedocles observes the microcosm, so he interprets the macrocosm: Love causes the mixture of the elements, Strife causes their separation (see below, I. B. c. 2; and I. B. a. 60, 66, 74, 96, 110). Heraclitus' conception of eternal process is interpreted by Empedocles in terms of stages or phases of change and ceasing from change. The result is that the operation of the forces of Love and Strife produces a process or "immovable circle" (see below, I. B. a. 66) in the cosmos. In the first phase of the process, the elements or roots are in a complete mixture, owing to the effects of Love in bringing them together or uniting them. As Strife enters, the elements are separated, causing the second phase of the process. With Strife dominant, the elements are completely separated and the third phase occurs. As Love enters, the uniting or coming together of the mixture takes place. By this process of separation and mixture the physical universe comes into existence (see below, I. B. a. 96). Life is possible in the second and fourth phases of the mixture and separation, Love bringing separate parts and organs of men and animals together, but, at first, pure chance prevailed and organs united with each other indiscriminately. A theory of the "survival of the fittest" is implied: those forms which were the result of the proper placing and distributing of the organs survived (see below, I. B. a. 244), an argument which Empedocles holds even though "all things have understanding and their share of intelligence" (see below, I. B. a. 222).

A. LIFE

D.L., *Lives* VIII. 51. Empedocles was . . . the son of Meton and the grandson of Empedocles, and was a native of Agrigentum. . . . Aristotle and Heraclides both affirm that he died at the age of sixty. . . . 54. That he belonged to Agrigentum in Sicily he himself testifies at the beginning of his *Purifications*. . . . (See below, I. B. a. 1, 352 sq.) 55. Theophrastus affirms that he was an admirer of Parmenides and imitated him in his verses. . . . 58. Satyrus in his *Lives* says that he was also a physician and an excellent orator: At all events Gorgias of Leontini, a man pre-eminent in oratory and the author of a treatise on the art, had been his pupil. . . . Empedocles performed magic feats. . . . This man was held in high esteem on many accounts. . . . Once, when the etesian gales were blowing violently, so as to injure the crops, he ordered some asses to be flayed, and some bladders to be made of their hides, and these he placed on the hills and high places to catch the wind. . . . 69. . . . He set out on his way to Etna; then, when he had reached it, he plunged into the fiery craters and disappeared, his intention being to confirm the report that he had become a god. Afterwards the truth was known, because one of his slippers was thrown up in the flames. . . . 77. His poems *On Nature* and *Purifications* run to 5000 lines, his *Discourse on Medicine* to 600. . . .

B. Thought

a. The fragments.[2]

BOOK I

1. And do thou hear me, Pausanias, son of wise Anchites.

2. For scant means of acquiring knowledge are scattered among the members of the body; and many are the evils that break in to blunt the edge of studious thought. And gazing on a little portion of life that is not life, swift to meet their fate, they rise and are borne away like smoke, persuaded only of that on which each one chances as he is driven this way and that, but the whole he vainly boasts he has found. Thus these things are neither seen nor heard distinctly by men, nor comprehended by the mind. And thou, now that thou hast withdrawn hither, shalt learn no more than what mortal mind has seen.

11. But, ye gods, avert the madness of those men from my tongue, and from lips that are holy cause a pure stream to flow. And thee I pray, much-wooed white-armed maiden Muse, in what things it is right for beings of a day to hear, do thou, and Piety, driving obedient car, conduct me on. Nor yet shall the flowers of honor well esteemed compel me to pluck them from mortal hands, on condition that I speak boldly more than is holy and only then sit on the heights of wisdom.

19. But come, examine by every means each thing how it is clear, neither putting greater faith in anything seen than in what is heard, nor in a thundering sound more than in the clear assertions of the tongue, nor keep from trusting any of the other members in which there lies means of knowledge, but know each thing in the way in which it is clear.

24. Cures for evils whatever there are, and protection against old age shalt thou learn, since for thee alone will I accomplish all these things. Thou shalt break the power of untiring gales which rising against the earth blow down the crops and destroy

---

[2] The order of the fragments and the enumeration of the lines follows H. Stein's *Empedoclis Agrigentini Fragmenta* (London, A. Marcum, 1852).

them; and, again, whenever thou wilt, thou shalt bring their blasts back; and thou shalt bring seasonable drought out of dark storm for men, and out of summer drought thou shalt bring streams pouring down from heaven to nurture the trees; and thou shalt lead out of Hades the spirit of a man that is dead.

33. Hear first the four roots of all things: bright Zeus, life-giving Hera (air), and Aidoneus (earth), and Nestis who moistens the springs of men with her tears.

36. And a second thing I will tell thee: There is no origination of anything that is mortal, nor yet any end in baneful death; but only mixture and separation of what is mixed, but men call this "origination."

40. But when light is mingled with air in human form, or in form like the race of wild beasts or of plants or of birds, then men say that these things have come into being; and when they are separated, they call them evil fate; this is the established practice, and I myself also call it so in accordance with the custom.

45. Fools! for they have no far-reaching studious thoughts who think that what was not before comes into being or that anything dies and perishes utterly.

48. For from what does not exist at all it is impossible that anything come into being, and it is neither possible nor perceivable that being should perish completely; for things will always stand wherever one in each case shall put them.

51. A man of wise mind could not divine such things as these, that so long as men live what indeed they call life, so long they exist and share what is evil and what is excellent, but before they are formed and after they are dissolved, they are really nothing at all.

55. But for base men it is indeed possible to withhold belief from strong proofs; but do thou learn as the pledges of our Muse bid thee, and lay open her word to the very core.

58. Joining one heading to another in discussion, not com-

pleting one path (of discourse) . . . for it is right to say what
is excellent twice and even thrice.

60. Twofold is the truth I shall speak; for at one time there
grew to be one alone out of many, and at another time, however, it separated so that there were many out of the one. Twofold is the coming into being, twofold the passing away, of
perishable things; for the latter (i.e., passing away) the combining of all things both begets and destroys, and the former
(i.e., coming into being), which was nurtured again out of
parts that were being separated, is itself scattered.

66. And these [elements] never cease changing place continually, now being all united by Love into one, now each
borne apart by the hatred engendered of Strife, until they are
brought together in the unity of the all, and become subject to
it. Thus inasmuch as one has been wont to arise out of many
and again with the separation of the one the many arise, so
things are continually coming into being and there is no fixed
age for them; and farther inasmuch as they [the elements] never
cease changing place continually, so they always exist within
an immovable circle.

74. But come, hear my words, for truly learning causes the
mind to grow. For as I said before in declaring the ends of
my words: Twofold is the truth I shall speak; for at one time
there grew to be the one alone out of many, and at another
time it separated so that there were many out of the one; fire
and water and earth and boundless height of air, and baneful
Strife apart from these, balancing each of them, and Love
among them, their equal in length and breadth. 81. Upon her
do thou gaze with thy mind, nor yet sit dazed in thine eyes; for
she is wont to be implanted in men's members, and through her
they have thoughts of love and accomplish deeds of union, and
call her by the name of Delight, and Aphrodite; no mortal man
has discerned her with them [the elements] as she moves on
her way. But do thou listen to the undeceiving course of my
words. . . .

87. For these [elements] are equal, all of them, and of like

ancient race; and one holds one office, another another, and
each has his own nature. . . . For nothing is added to them,
nor yet does anything pass away from them; for if they were
continually perishing they would no longer exist. . . . Neither
is any part of this all empty, nor over full. For how should anything cause this all to increase, and whence should it come? And
whither should they [the elements] perish, since no place is
empty of them? And in their turn they prevail as the cycle comes
round, and they disappear before each other, and they increase
each in its allotted turn. But these [elements] are the same; and
penetrating through each other they become one thing in one
place and another in another, while ever they remain alike (i. e.,
the same).

96. But come, gaze on the things that bear farther witness
to my former words, if in what was said before there be anything defective in form. Behold the sun, warm and bright on all
sides, and whatever is immortal and is bathed in its bright ray,
and behold the raincloud, dark and cold on all sides; from the
earth there proceed the foundations of things and solid bodies.
In Strife all things are, endued with form and separate from each
other, but they come together in Love and are desired by each
other. 104. For from these [elements] come all things that are
or have been or shall be; from these there grew up trees and
men and women, wild beasts and birds and water-nourished
fishes, and the very gods, long-lived, highest in honor.

110. For they two (Love and Strife) were before and shall
be, nor yet, I think, will there ever be an unutterably long time
without them both.

121. And as when painters are preparing elaborate votive
offerings—men well taught by wisdom in their art—they take
many-colored pigments to work with, and blend together har-
moniously more of one and less of another till they produce
likenesses of all things; so let not error overcome thy mind to
make thee think there is any other source of mortal things that
have likewise come into distinct existence in unspeakable numbers; but know these [elements], for thou didst hear from a god
the account of them.

130. But come, I will tell thee now the first principle of the sun, even the sources of all things now visible, earth and billowy sea and damp mist and Titan æther (i.e., air) binding all things in its embrace.

135. Then neither is the bright orb of the sun greeted, nor yet either the shaggy might of earth or sea; thus, then, in the firm vessel of harmony is fixed God, a sphere, round, rejoicing in complete solitude.

139. But when mighty Strife was nurtured in its members and leaped up to honor at the completion of the time, which has been driven on by them both in turn under a mighty oath. . . .

142. For the limbs of the god were made to tremble, all of them in turn.

143. For all the heavy (he put) by itself, the light by itself.

144. Without affection and not mixed together.

145. Heaped together in greatness.

146. If there were no limit to the depths of the earth and the abundant air, as is poured out in foolish words from the mouths of many mortals who see but little of the all.

149. Swift-darting sun and kindly moon.

150. But gathered together it advances around the great heavens.

151. It shines back to Olympus with untroubled face.

152. The kindly light has a brief period of shining.

153. As sunlight striking the broad circle of the moon.

154. A borrowed light, circular in form, it revolves about the earth, as if following the track of a chariot.

156. For she beholds opposite to her the sacred circle of her lord.

157. And she scatters his rays into the sky above, and

spreads darkness over as much of the earth as the breadth of the gleaming-eyed moon.

160. And night the earth makes by coming in front of the lights.

161. Of night, solitary, blind-eyed.

162. And many fires burn beneath the earth.

163. (The sea) with its stupid race of fertile fishes.

164. Salt is made solid when struck by the rays of the sun.

165. The sea is the sweat of the earth.

166. But air sinks down beneath the earth with its long roots. . . . For thus it happened to be running at that time, but oftentimes otherwise.

168. (Fire darting) swiftly upwards.

169. But now I shall go back over the course of my verses, which I set out in order before, drawing my present discourse from that discourse. When Strife reached the lowest depth of the eddy and Love comes to be in the midst of the whirl, then all these things come together at this point so as to be one alone, yet not immediately, but joining together at their pleasure, one from one place, another from another. And as they were joining together Strife departed to the utmost boundary. But many things remained unmixed, alternating with those that were mixed, even as many as Strife, remaining aloft, still retained; for not yet had it entirely departed to the utmost boundaries of the circle, but some of its members were remaining within, and others had gone outside. 180. But, just as far as it is constantly rushing forth, just so far there ever kept coming in a gentle immortal stream of perfect Love; and all at once what before I learned were immortal were coming into being as mortal things, what before were unmixed as mixed, changing their courses. And as they [the elements] were mingled together there flowed forth the myriad species of mortal things, patterned in every sort of form, a wonder to behold.

186. For all things are united, themselves with parts of themselves—the beaming sun and earth and sky and sea—whatever things are friendly but have separated in mortal things. And so, in the same way, whatever things are the more adapted for mixing, these are loved by each other and made alike by Aphrodite. But whatever things are hostile are separated as far as possible from each other, both in their origin and in their mixing and in the forms impressed on them, absolutely unwonted to unite and very baneful, at the suggestion of Strife, since it has wrought their birth.

195. In this way, by the good favor of Tyche, all things have power of thought.

196. And in so far as what was least dense came together as they fell.

197. For water is increased by water, primeval fire by fire, and earth causes its own substance to increase, and air, air.

199. And the kindly earth in its broad hollows received two out of the eight parts of bright Nestis, and four of Hephaistos, and they became white bones, fitted together marvellously by the glues of Harmony.

203. And the earth met with these in almost equal amounts, with Hephaistos and Ombros and bright-shining Aether (i. e., air), being anchored in the perfect harbors of Cypris; either a little more earth, or a little less with more of the others. From these arose blood and various kinds of flesh.

208. . . . glueing barley-meal together with water.

209. (Water) tenacious Love.

BOOK II
210. And if your faith be at all lacking in regard to these [elements], how from water and earth and air and sun (fire) when they are mixed, arose such colors and forms of mortal things, as many as now have arisen under the uniting power of Aphrodite. . . .

214. How both tall trees and fishes of the sea arose.

215. And thus then Cypris, when she had moistened the earth with water, breathed air on it and gave it to swift fire to be hardened.

217. And all these things which were within were made dense, while those without were made rare, meeting with such moisture in the hands of Cypris.

219. And thus tall trees bear fruit (*lit.*, eggs), first of all olives.

220. Wherefore late-born pomegranates and luxuriant apples. . . .

221. Wine is water that has fermented in the wood beneath the bark.

222. For if thou shalt fix them in all thy close-knit mind and watch over them graciously with pure attention, all these things shall surely be thine for ever, and many others shalt thou possess from them. For these themselves shall cause each to grow into its own character, whatever is the nature of each. But if thou shalt reach out for things of another sort, as is the manner of men, there exist countless evils to blunt your studious thoughts; soon these latter shall cease to live as time goes on, desiring as they do to arrive at the longed-for generation of themselves. For know that all things have understanding and their share of intelligence.

232. Favor hates Necessity, hard to endure.

233. This is in the heavy-backed shells found in the sea, of limpets and purple-fish and stone-covered tortoises . . . there shalt thou see earth lying uppermost on the surface.

236. Hair and leaves and thick feathers of birds are the same thing in origin, and reptiles' scales, too, on strong limbs.

238. But on hedgehogs, sharp-pointed hair bristles on their backs.

240. Out of which divine Aphrodite wrought eyes untiring.

241. Aphrodite fashioning them curiously with bonds of love.

242. When they first grew together in the hands of Aphrodite.

243. The liver well supplied with blood.

244. Where many heads grew up without necks, and arms were wandering about naked, bereft of shoulders, and eyes roamed about alone with no foreheads.

247. This is indeed remarkable in the mass of human members; at one time all the limbs which form the body, united into one by Love, grow vigorously in the prime of life; but yet at another time, separated by evil Strife, they wander each in different directions along the breakers of the sea of life. Just so it is with plants and with fishes dwelling in watery halls, and beasts whose lair is in the mountains, and birds borne on wings.

254. But as divinity was mingled yet more with divinity, these things kept coming together in whatever way each might chance, and many others also in addition to these continually came into being.

257. Many creatures arose with double faces and double breasts, offspring of oxen with human faces, and again there sprang up children of men with oxen's heads; creatures, too, in which were mixed some parts from men and some of the nature of women, furnished with sterile members.

261. Cattle of trailing gait, with undivided hoofs.

262. But come now, hear of these things; how fire separating caused the hidden offspring of men and weeping women to arise, for it is no tale apart from our subject, or witless. In the first place there sprang up out of the earth forms grown into one whole, having a share of both, of water and of fire. These in truth fire caused to grow up, desiring to reach its like; but they showed as yet no lovely body formed out of the members, nor voice nor limb such as is natural to men.

270. But the nature of the members (of the child?) is divided, part in the man's, part in the woman's (body).

271. But desire also came upon him, having been united with . . . by sight.

273. It was poured out in the pure parts, and some meeting with cold became females.

275. The separated harbors of Aphrodite.

276. In its warmer parts the womb is productive of the male, and on this account men are dark and more muscular and more hairy.

279. As when fig-juice curdles and binds white milk.

280. On the tenth day of the eighth month came the white discharge.

281. Knowing that there are exhalations from all things which came into existence.

282. Thus sweet was snatching sweet, and bitter darted to bitter, and sharp went to sharp, and hot coupled with hot.

284. Water combines better with wine, but it is unwilling to combine with oil.

286. The bloom of the scarlet dye mingles with shining linen.

287. So all beings breathe in and out; all have bloodless tubes of flesh spread over the outside of the body, and at the openings of these the outer layers of skin are pierced all over with close-set ducts, so that the blood remains within, while a facile opening is cut for the air to pass through. Then whenever the soft blood speeds away from these, the air speeds bubbling in with impetuous wave, and whenever the blood leaps back the air is breathed out; as when a girl, playing with a klepsydra of shining brass, takes in her fair hand the narrow opening of the tube and dips it in the soft mass of silvery water, the water does not at once flow into the vessel, but the body of air within pressing on the close-set holes checks it till she uncovers the compressed stream; but then when the air gives way

the determined amount of water enters. 302. And so in the same way when the water occupies the depths of the bronze vessel, as long as the narrow opening and passage is blocked up by human flesh, the air outside striving eagerly to enter holds back the water inside behind the gates of the resounding tube, keeping control of its end, until she lets go with her hand. 306. Then, on the other hand, the very opposite takes place to what happened before; the determined amount of water runs off as the air enters. Thus in the same way when the soft blood, surging violently through the members, rushes back into the interior, a swift stream of air comes in with hurrying wave, and whenever it (the blood) leaps back, the air is breathed out again in equal quantity.

313. With its nostrils seeking out the fragments of animals' limbs, <as many as the delicate exhalation from their feet was leaving behind in the wood>.

314. So, then, all things have obtained their share of breathing and of smelling.

315. (The ear) an offshoot of flesh.

316. And as when one with a journey through a stormy night in prospect provides himself with a lamp and lights it at the bright-shining fire—with lanterns that drive back every sort of wind, for they scatter the breath of the winds as they blow—and the light darting out, inasmuch as it is finer (than the winds), shines across the threshold with untiring rays; so then elemental fire, shut up in membranes, it entraps in fine coverings to be the round pupil, and the coverings protect it against the deep water which flows about it, but the fire darting forth, inasmuch as it is finer. . . .

326. There is one vision coming from both (eyes).

327. (The heart) lies in seas of blood which darts in opposite directions, and there most of all intelligence centers for men; for blood about the heart is intelligence in the case of men.

330. For men's wisdom increases with reference to what lies before them.

331. In so far as they change and become different, to this extent other sorts of things are ever present for them to think about.

333. For it is by earth that we see earth, and by water water, and by air glorious air; so, too, by fire we see destroying fire, and love by love, and strife by baneful strife. For out of these (elements) all things are fitted together and their form is fixed, and by these men think and feel both pleasure and pain.

BOOK III

338. Would that in behalf of perishable beings thou, immortal Muse, mightest take thought at all for our thought to come by reason of our cares! Hear me now and be present again by my side, Calliopeia, as I utter noble discourse about the blessed gods.

342. Blessed is he who has acquired a wealth of divine wisdom, but miserable he in whom there rests a dim opinion concerning the gods.

344. It is not possible to draw near (to god) even with the eyes, or to take hold of him with our hands, which in truth is the best highway of persuasion into the mind of man; for he has no human head fitted to a body, nor do two shoots branch out from the trunk, nor has he feet, nor swift legs, nor hairy parts, but he is sacred and ineffable mind alone, darting through the whole world with swift thoughts.

ON PURIFICATIONS

352. O friends, ye who inhabit the great city of sacred Akragas up to the acropolis, whose care is good deeds, who harbor strangers deserving of respect, who know not how to do baseness, hail! I go about among you an immortal god, no longer a mortal, honored by all, as is fitting, crowned with fillets and luxuriant garlands. With these on my head, so soon as I come to flourishing cities I am reverenced by men and by women; and they follow after me in countless numbers, inquiring of me what is the way to gain, some in want of oracles, others of help in diseases, long time in truth pierced with grievous

pains, they seek to hear from me keen-edged account of all sorts of things.

364. But why do I lay weight on these things, as though I were doing some great thing, if I be superior to mortal, perishing men?

366. Friends, I know indeed when truth lies in the discourses that I utter; but truly the entrance of assurance into the mind of man is difficult and hindered by jealousy.

369. There is an utterance of Necessity, an ancient decree of the gods, eternal, sealed fast with broad oaths: whenever any one defiles his body sinfully with bloody gore or perjures himself in regard to wrong-doing, one of those spirits who are heir to long life, thrice ten thousand seasons shall he wander apart from the blessed, being born meantime in all sorts of mortal forms, changing one bitter path of life for another. For mighty Air pursues him Seaward, and Sea spews him forth on the threshold of Earth, and Earth casts him into the rays of the unwearying Sun, and Sun into the eddies of Air; one receives him from the other, and all hate him. One of these now am I too, a fugitive from the gods and a wanderer, at the mercy of raging Strife.

383. For before this I was born once a boy, and a maiden, and a plant, and a bird, and a darting fish in the sea. 385. And I wept and shrieked on beholding the unwonted land where are Murder and Wrath, and other species of Fates, and wasting diseases, and putrefaction and fluxes.

388. In darkness they roam over the meadow of Ate.

389. Deprived of life.

390. From what honor and how great a degree of blessedness have I fallen here on the earth to consort with mortal beings!

392. We enter beneath this over-roofed cave.

393. Where were Chthonie and far-seeing Heliope (i. e., Earth and Sun?), bloody Contention and Harmony of sedate

face, Beauty and Ugliness, Speed and Loitering, lovely Truth and dark-eyed Obscurity, Birth and Death, and Sleep and Waking, Motion and Stability, many-crowned Greatness and Lowness, and Silence and Voice.

400. Alas, ye wretched, ye unblessed race of mortal beings, of what strifes and of what groans were ye born!

402. She wraps about them a strange garment of flesh.

403. Man-surrounding earth.

404. For from being living he made them assume the form of death by a change. . . .

405. Nor had they any god Ares, nor Cydoimos (Uproar), nor king Zeus, nor Cronos, nor Poseidon, but queen Cypris. Her they worshipped with hallowed offerings, with painted figures, and perfumes of skilfully made odor, and sacrifices of unmixed myrrh and fragrant frankincense, casting on the ground libations from tawny bees. And her altar was not moistened with pure blood of bulls, but it was the greatest defilement among men, to deprive animals of life and to eat their goodly bodies.

415. And there was among them a man of unusual knowledge, and master especially of all sorts of wise deeds, who in truth possessed greatest wealth of mind; for whenever he reached out with all his mind, easily he beheld each one of all the things that are, even for ten and twenty generations of men.

421. For all were gentle and obedient toward men, both animals and birds, and they burned with kindly love; and trees grew with leaves and fruit ever on them, burdened with abundant fruit all the year.

425. This is now lawful for some and unlawful for others, but what is lawful for all extends on continuously through the wide-ruling air and the boundless light.

427. Will ye not cease from evil slaughter? See ye not that ye are devouring each other in heedlessness of mind?

430. A father takes up his dear son who has changed his form and slays him with a prayer, so great is his folly! They are borne along beseeching the sacrificer; but he does not hear their cries of reproach, but slays them and makes ready the evil feast. Then in the same manner son takes father and daughters, their mother, and devour the dear flesh when they have deprived them of life.

436. Alas that no ruthless day destroyed me before I devised base deeds of devouring with the lips!

438. Among beasts they become lions haunting the mountains, whose couch is the ground, and among fair-foliaged trees they become laurels.

440. Refrain entirely from laurel leaves.

441. Miserable men, wholly miserable, restrain your hands from beans.

442. Compounding the water from five springs in unyielding brass, cleanse the hands.

444. Fast from evil.

445. Accordingly ye are frantic with evils hard to bear, nor ever shall ye ease your soul from bitter woes.

447. But at last are they prophets and hymn-writers and physicians and chieftains among men dwelling on the earth; and from this they grow to be gods, receiving the greatest honors, sharing the same hearth with the other immortals, their table companions, free from human woes, beyond the power of death and harm.

b. Aristotle's comments on Empedocles' natural philosophy.

1. ARIST., *de Caelo* III. 2. 302 a 28. Empedocles says that fire and earth and associated elements are elements of bodies, and that all things are composed of these.

2. ────── *de Gen. et Corr.* I. 1. 314 b 7. Wherefore Em-

pedocles speaks after this manner, saying that nothing comes into being, but there is only mixture and separation of the mixed.

3. ——— *Met.*, I. 4. 915 a 21. And Empedocles makes more use of causes than Anaxagoras, but not indeed sufficiently; nor does he find in them what has been agreed upon. At any rate love for him is often a separating cause and strife a uniting cause. For whenever the all is separated into the elements by strife, fire and each of the other elements are collected into one; and again, whenever they all are brought together into one by love, parts are necessarily separated again from each thing. Empedocles moreover differed from those who went before, in that he discriminated this cause and introduced it, not making the cause of motion one, but different and opposite. Further, he first described the four elements spoken of as in the form of matter; but he did not use them as four but only as two, fire by itself, and the rest opposed to fire as being one in nature, earth and air and water.

4. ——— I. 8. 989 a 20. And the same thing is true if one asserts that these are more numerous than one, as Empedocles says that matter is four substances. For it is necessary that the same peculiar results should hold good with reference to him. For we see the elements arising from each other inasmuch as fire and earth do not continue the same substance (for so it is said of them in the verses on nature); and with reference to the cause of their motion, whether it is necessary to assume one or two, we must think that he certainly did not speak either in a correct or praiseworthy manner.

c. The order of becoming.

1. AET., *Plac.* II. 6. *Dox.* 334. Empedocles: The aether was first separated, and secondly fire, and then earth, from which, as it was compressed tightly by the force of its rotation, water gushed forth; and from this the air arose as vapor, and the heavens arose from the aether, the sun from the fire, and bodies on the earth were compressed out of the others.

2. PLUT., *Strom.* 10. *Dox.* 582. Empedocles of Agrigentum:

The elements are four—fire, water, aether, earth. And the cause of these is Love and Strife. From the first mixture of the elements he says that the air was separated and poured around in a circle; and after the air the fire ran off, and not having any other place to go to, it ran up from under the ice that was around the air. And there are two hemispheres moving in a circle around the earth, the one of pure fire, the other of air and a little fire mixed, which he thinks is night. And motion began as a result of the weight of the fire when it was collected.

d. Theory of perception.

THEOPH., *de Sen. 7. Dox.* 500. Empedocles speaks in like manner concerning all the senses, and says that we perceive by a fitting into the pores of each sense. So they are not able to discern one another's objects, for the pores of some are too wide and of others too narrow for the object of sensation, so that some things go right through untouched, and others are unable to enter completely. And he attempts to describe what vision is; and he says that what is in the eye is fire and water and what surrounds it is earth and air, through which light being fine enters, as the light in lanterns. Pores of fire and water are set alternately, and the fire-pores recognize white objects, the water-pores black objects; for the colors harmonize with the pores. And the colors move into vision by means of effluences. And they are not composed alike . . . and some of opposite elements; for some the fire is within and for others it is on the outside, so some animals see better in the daytime and others at night; those that have less fire see better by day, for the light inside them is balanced by the light outside them; and those that have less water see better at night, for what is lacking is made up for them. And in the opposite case the contrary is true; for those that have the more fire are dim-sighted, since the fire increasing plasters up and covers the pores of water in the daytime; and for those that have water in excess, the same thing happens at night; for the fire is covered up by the water. . . . Until in the case of some the water is separated by the outside light, and in the case of others the fire by the air; for the cure of each is its opposite. That which is composed of both in equal parts is the best tempered and most excellent vision. This, approximately, is what he says concerning vision. And hearing is the result of noises coming from outside. For when (the air) is set in motion by a sound, there is an echo within; for the hearing is as it were a bell echoing within, and the ear he calls an "offshoot of flesh": and the air when it is set in motion strikes on something hard and makes an echo. And smell is connected with breathing, so those have the keenest smell whose breath moves most quickly; and the strongest odor arises as an effluence from fine and light bodies. But he makes no careful discrimination with reference to taste and touch separately, either how or by what means they take place, except the general statement that sensation takes place by a fitting into the pores; and pleasure is due to likenesses in the elements and in their mixture, and pain to the opposite. And he speaks similarly concerning thought and ignorance: Thinking is by what is like, and not perceiving is by what is unlike, since thought is the same thing as, or something like, sensation. For recounting how we recognize each thing by each, he said at length: Now out of these [elements] all things are fitted together and their form is fixed, and by these men think and feel pleasure and pain. So it is by blood especially that we think; for in this specially are mingled <all> the elements of things. And those in whom equal and like parts have been mixed, not too far apart, nor yet small parts, nor exceeding great, these have the most intelligence and the most accurate senses; and those who approximate to this come next; and those who have the opposite qualities are the most lacking in intelligence. And those in whom the elements are scattered and rarefied, are torpid and easily fatigued; and those in whom the elements are small and thrown close together, move so rapidly and meet with so many things that they accomplish but little by reason of the swiftness of the motion of the blood. And those in whom there is a well-tempered mixture in some one part, are wise at this point; so some are good orators, others good artisans, according as the mixture is in the hands or in the tongue; and the same is true of the other powers.

II. ANAXAGORAS

Anaxagoras, as does Empedocles, accepts the Eleatic conclusions concerning *being* but attempts to introduce motion
and change into the world. Born *ca.* 500 B.C., the son of
Hegesiboulos and native of Klazomenae in Thrace, Anaxagoras
was the first philosopher to make his home in Athens.[3] There, as
a friend of Pericles, Anaxagoras attracted the attention of men
of scientific interests. In 434 B.C., the philosopher was tried for
impiety, the charge being that he taught that the sun was a hot
stone and the moon was earth. It is probable that the suit had
political implications and that it was brought to embarrass
Anaxagoras' patron, Pericles. Forced to leave Athens, Anaxagoras
lived in Lampsakos, where he established a school and where
an altar was erected in his memory. He is described by Aristotle
as "older in years, younger in works than Empedocles." (See below, Ch. 7, p. 254 for Socrates' statement concerning the charges
made against Anaxagoras.)

Anaxagoras denies "coming into being" and "perishing."
With Empedocles, he believes that change is the result of mixture and separation (see below, II. B. b. 17; cf. 5, 11). Thus far,
Empedocles and Anaxagoras are agreed but Empedocles' selection of the four qualitatively unchangeable elements, earth, air,
fire, and water, as ultimate *being* is not acceptable to Anaxagoras.
For Anaxagoras, *being* is an infinity of "seeds" or "germs." It
would naturally be regarded as a scientific retrogression to
multiply the number of elements, once they had been reduced
to four, since science from Milesian times had sought simplicity
and unity. There must be, therefore, strong reasons for such a
change. Anaxagoras gives us a clue to his reasons: "Things in one
universe are not divided from each other, nor yet are they cut
off with an axe, neither hot from cold, nor cold from hot" (see
below, II. B. b. 8). When Empedocles has explained some "new"
phenomenon or situation in the world as the result of the mix-

[3] The selections relating to Anaxagoras' life and thought begin below,
p. 138.

ture of the four qualitatively unchanged elements, the "new" situation or phenomenon must be in itself unreal, since Empedocles in his own words has accepted the Eleatic doctrine: "Fools! for they have no far-reaching studious thoughts who think that what was not before comes into being or anything dies or perishes utterly" (see above, I. B. a. 45). Since the four qualitatively unchanged elements will not account for the infinite variety and differentiation of the world of experience, the alternative, if qualitative distinction in elements are to be maintained, is to assume that qualitative distinctions are ultimate. Since there is an infinity of qualitative distinctions in the world, there must be on this hypothesis ultimate substances, "seeds," or "germs infinite in number, in no way like each other" (see below, II. B. b. 4).[4]

Since the seeds are infinite and qualitatively distinct, what for Empedocles would be a novel and ultimately inexplicable situation or phenomenon is for Anaxagoras proof that the "new" (i. e., qualitatively differentiated) is the ultimate. To establish this position, Anaxagoras contends that "In all things there is a portion of everything—" (see below, II. B. b. 4, 11) and "that in all the objects that are compound there existed many things of all sorts, and germs of all objects, having all sorts of forms and color and tastes." On these grounds, the Eleatic assumption of the indestructibility and uncreatedness of *being* may be accepted, for phenomena may be explained without resort to the addition or subtraction of qualities. This view is maintained in Anaxagoras' statement, "For how could hair come from what is not hair? Or flesh from what is not flesh?" (see below, II. B. b. 10). The "coming into being" of hair or flesh is explicable on

---

[4] Cf. E. Zeller, *A History of Greek Philosophy*, Vol. II, English Translation, *The Pre-Socratic Philosophy*, translated by S. F. Alleyne (London, Longmans, Green, and Co., 1881), p. 330: "Anaxagoras . . . supposes all the qualities and differences of derived things already inherent in the primitive matter, and therefore conceives the original substances as unlimited in kind, as well as in number. . . ." See, also, *ibid*, p. 336: ". . . The substances of which things consist, are in this, their qualitative determinateness, underived and imperishable; and since there are innumerable things, of which no two are perfectly alike, he says that there are innumerable seeds, not one of which resembles another." See above, Introduction, pp. 23 sq., for the general problem.

the ground that hair and flesh, as well as eyes, teeth, bone, etc., are contained in food. The names we apply to things are determined by the preponderance of certain seeds in them (cf. below, II. B. d. 1).

That all things contain a portion of everything seems a paradoxical position, but Anaxagoras, having learned perhaps from Zeno the possibilities of infinite divisibility, is making an application of his theory of *being* to material things in much the same way that the Pythagoreans applied their geometrical hypotheses to physical things. At any rate, one may perhaps clarify Anaxagoras' position by an analogy to the points on a line: If you take away a portion of a straight line, there still remains an infinity of points. Anaxagoras argues, similarly, that if you separate a material fragment of any thing, you have left an infinity of seeds and an infinity of each kind.

Anaxagoras' universe, before separation, was an infinite mass, in which "nothing was clear and distinct" (see below, II. B. b. 1), "not even was any color clear and distinct" (see below, II. B. b. 4). This mass corresponds to Anaximander's infinite, spoken of in terms of undifferentiated *being*. Motion must be introduced into the mass to account for change, since the ultimate substances are not self-moved. To account for motion, Empedocles had introduced Love and Strife. Anaxagoras likewise argues from his observation of man and selects mind or *Nous* as the cause of motion. *Nous* is material but it is the purest and most rarefied of things. It is apart from all else for "things mingled with it would prevent it from having power over anything in the same way that it does now that it is alone by itself" (see below, II. B. b. 12). As an efficient cause, *Nous* sets up a rotary motion in the undifferentiated mass of *being* and separation occurs. The separation involves no increase or decrease in the "seeds" (see below, II. B. b. 5). Air and aether (see below, II. B. b. 2) are first separated off from the mass by the swiftness of the rotary motion initiated by mind (see below, II. B. b. 9). Air, all that is cold, dark, and dense, moves to the center. Aether, all that is warm, light, and rare, moves to the periphery (see below, II. B. b. 15, II. B. d. 3). Condensation produces water, earth and stones (see below, II. B. b. 16).

Thus far, *Nous* has been utilized solely to initiate the rotation necessary for the separation of the mass of *being*. Moreover, it is clear that Anaxagoras is content to explain phenomena by the rotation and by the further method of condensation and rarefaction. It is on this ground that Aristotle and Plato (see below, II. B. c. 1-3) [5] criticize the conception of *Nous*, Aristotle pointing out that Anaxagoras uses it merely as a *deus ex machina* when other means of explanation fail him. Despite the authority of antiquity, it may be indicated, however, that other hypotheses are implicit in Anaxagoras' *Nous*. That it should function as mind and still be material is in the tradition of Anaxagoras' predecessors. It is clear, however, that Anaxagoras differentiates it as much as possible from the other material substances in the universe. It is homogeneous, omniscient, omnipotent, and has a specific function in ruling over all that has life. It is important to notice, too, that *Nous* arranges all things in order. *Nous* makes distinct the things set in motion. It is not necessary to personify Anaxagoras' conception of *Nous* in order to assume that the philosopher believed that this efficient cause makes comprehensible the mass of *being* and that it does this by giving order or structure to *being*.

A more difficult issue is raised once it is seen that *Nous* not only arranges things in order and makes them distinct in doing so, but that it does so with reference to ends (see below, II. B. b. 12). It may be granted that Anaxagoras' procedure is not wholly consistent. The philosopher separates *Nous* from all else. Anaxagoras tells us that "in all things there is a portion of everything except mind; and there are things in which there is mind also" (see below, II. B. b. 11). It is probable that the statement is intended by Anaxagoras to distinguish the animate from the inanimate. But the basic issue is one which becomes significant once Socrates attacks natural philosophy (see below, Ch. 7, A. 16). Socrates evidently believes that explanatory principles must include such as will permit teleological explanation. While Anaxagoras implies that the order and structure of the cosmos is arranged by *Nous* with relation to ends, Socrates is prepared

[5] See also, below, Ch. 7, A. 16 for extended quotation of a passage relating to Anaxagoras in Plato's *Phaedo*.

to deny that the earlier philosopher does more than use a mechanical principal in an eccentric fashion. For Socrates, philosophy must include explanation in terms of "the best" or "the good" as the end, which implies that the "seeds" of Anaxagoras would at most be mere conditions for the critical explanation in terms of purposes. It is highly probable, however, that Anaxagoras had evolved a theory of "material teleology" and would have been little perturbed by either Plato's or Aristotle's strictures on his philosophy, based as they were upon the original Socratic denial of adequacy to the theories underlying natural philosophies.[6]

Anaxagoras assumed that perception is caused by differences between the perceiving substance and the perceived objects (see below, II. B. e. 1).

A. LIFE

1. STRABO, *Geog.* XIV. 1. 36. Anaxagoras, the natural philosopher, an illustrious man and associate of Anaximenes, the Milesian, was a Clazomenian.

2. D.L., *op. cit.* VII. 1. Anaxagoras, the son of Hegesibulus, . . . was a citizen of Clazomenæ. He was a pupil of Anaximenes, and was the first philosopher who attributed mind to matter. . . . 3. It is said, that at the time of the passage of the Hellespont by Xerxes, he was twenty years old and that he lived to the age of seventy-two. Apollodorus in his *Chronology* says that he was born in the 70th Olympiad (500-497 B.C.) and that he died in the first year of the 88th Olympiad (428 B.C.). He began to study philosophy at Athens in the archonship of Callias, (480 B.C.) (i.e., when Calliades was archon) when he was twenty . . . and they say he remained at Athens thirty years. . . .

3. PLUT., *Lives* (*Life of Nicias*) XXXII. And Diopheites brought in a bill providing for the public impeachment of such

---

[6] Werner Jaeger, *The Theology of the Early Greek Philosophers* (Oxford, Oxford University Press, 1947), p. 163.

as did not believe in gods, or who taught doctrines regarding the heavens, directing suspicions against Pericles by means of Anaxagoras. . . . Well, then, . . . he (Pericles) begged off, by shedding copious tears at the trial, as Aeschines says, and by entreating the jurors; and he feared for Anaxagoras so much that he sent him away from the city.

4. D.L., *op. cit.* II. 14. At length he retired to Lampsacus and died there. And it is said, that when the governors of the city asked him what he would like to have done for him, he replied, "That they would allow the children to play every year during the month in which he died." And this custom is kept up even now. . . .

5. Plut., *Lives* (*Life of Nicias*) XXIII. The first man to put in writing the clearest and boldest of all doctrines about the changing phases of the moon was Anaxagoras. But he was no ancient authority, nor was his doctrine of high repute. It was still under the seal of secrecy. . . .

B. Thought

a. Aristotle describes Anaxagoras' philosophy.

1. Arist., *Met.* I. 3. 984 a 11. Anaxagoras of Clazomenæ, who preceded him (Empedocles) in point of age and followed him in his works, says that the first principles are infinite in number; for nearly all things being made up of like parts (*homoeomeries*), as for instance fire and water, he says, arise and perish only by composition and separation, and there is no other arising and perishing, but they abide eternal.

2. ———, *de Caelo* III. 3. 302. a 31. Anaxagoras says the opposite to Empedocles, for he calls the *homoeomeries* elements (I mean such as flesh and bone and each of those things), and air and fire he calls mixtures of these and of all the other "seeds"; for each of these things is made of the invisible homoeomeries all heaped together. Wherefore all things arise out of these things; for he calls fire and aether the same.

b. The fragments.[7]

1. All things were together, infinite both in number and in smallness; for the small was also infinite. And when they were all together, nothing was clear and distinct because of their smallness; for air and aether comprehended all things, both being infinite; for these are present in everything, and are greatest both as to number and as to greatness.

2. For air and aether are separated from the surrounding mass; and the surrounding [mass] is infinite in quantity.

3. For neither is there a least in what is small, but there is always a less. For being is not non-being. But there is always a greater than what it great. And it is equal to the small in number; but with reference to itself each thing is both small and great.

4. And since these things are so, it is necessary to think that in all the objects that are compound there existed many things of all sorts, and germs of all objects, having all sorts of forms and colors and tastes. And men were constituted, and the other animals, as many as have life. And the men have inhabited cities and works constructed as among us, and they have sun and moon and other things as among us; and the earth brings forth for them many things of all sorts, of which they carry the most serviceable into the house and use them. These things then I have said concerning the separation, that not only among us would the separation take place, but elsewhere too. But before these were separated, when all things were together, not even was any color clear and distinct; for the mixture of all things prevented it, the mixture of moist and dry, of the warm and the cold, and of the bright and the dark (since much earth was present), and of germs infinite in number, in no way like each other; for none of the other things at all resembles the one the other. Since these things are so, we must suppose that all things are in the entire mass.

[7] H. Diels' arrangement in *Die Fragmente der Vorsokratiker*, 3rd ed. (Berlin, Wiedmannsche Buchhandlung, 1906).

5. When they are thus distinguished, it is necessary to recognize that they all must be no fewer and no more. For it is impossible that more than all should exist, but all are always equal.

6. And since the portions of the great and the small are equal in number, thus also all things would be in everything. Nor yet is it possible for them to exist apart, but all things include a portion of everything. Since it is not possible for the least to exist, nothing could be separated, nor yet could it come into being of itself, but as they were in the beginning so they are now, all things together. And there are many things in all things, and of those that are separated there are things equal in number in the greater and the lesser.

7. . . . One cannot know therefore the number of things separated either in theory or in practice.

8. Things in the one universe are not divided from each other, nor yet are they cut off with an axe, neither hot from cold, nor cold from hot.

9. So these things rotate and are separated by force and swiftness. And the swiftness produces force; and their swiftness is in no way like the swiftness of the things now existing among men, but it is certainly many times as swift.

10. For how could hair come from what is not hair? Or flesh from what is not flesh?

11. In all things there is a portion of everything except [*Nous*] mind; and there are things in which there is mind also.

12. Other things include a portion of everything, but mind is infinite and self-powerful and mixed with nothing, but it exists alone itself by itself. For if it were not by itself, but were mixed with anything else, it would include parts of all things, if it were mixed with anything; for a portion of everything exists in everything, as has been said by me before, and things mingled with it would prevent it from having power over anything in the same way that it does now that it is alone by itself. For it is the

most rarefied of all things and the purest, and it has all knowledge in regard to everything and the greatest power; over all that has life, both greater and less, mind rules. And mind ruled the rotation of the whole, so that it set it in rotation in the beginning. First it began the rotation from a small beginning, then more and more was included in the motion, and yet more will be included. Both the mixed and the separated and distinct, all things mind recognized. And whatever things were to be, and whatever things were, as many as are now, and whatever things shall be, all these mind arranged in order; and it arranged that rotation, according to which now rotate stars and sun and moon and air and aether, now that they are separated. Rotation itself caused the separation, and the dense is separated from the rare, the warm from the cold, the bright from the dark, the dry from the moist. And there are many portions of many things. Nothing is absolutely separated nor distinct, one thing from another, except mind. All mind is of like character, both the greater and the smaller. But nothing different is like anything else, but in whatever object there are the most, each single object is and was most distinctly these things.

13. And when mind began to set things in motion, there was separation from everything that was in motion, and however much mind set in motion, all this was made distinct. The rotation of the things that were moved and made distinct caused them to be yet more distinct.

14. But mind, which always is, especially now also is where all other things are, in the surrounding mass, and in the things that were separated, and in the things that are being separated.

15. The dense, the moist, the cold, the dark, collected where now is the earth; the rare, the warm, the dry, the bright, departed toward the farther part of the aether.

16. Earth is condensed out of these things that are separated. For water is separated from the clouds, and earth from the water; and from the earth stones are condensed by cold; and these are separated farther from water.

17. The Greeks do not rightly use the terms "coming into being" and "perishing." For nothing comes into being nor yet does anything perish, but there is mixture and separation of things that are. So they would do right in calling the coming into being "mixture," and the perishing "separation."

18. The sun puts its brightness into the moon.[8]

19. And the glimmer of the sun reflected in the clouds we call Iris [i.e., the rainbow]. It is a sign of storm; for the water flowing about the cloud creates a wind or causes the shedding of rain.

20. As the Dog-Star ascends men begin to reap; as it sets they begin plowing and harrowing. The Dog-Star is hidden for forty days and forty nights.

21. By reason of their [the senses] feebleness, we are not able to discern the truth.

21a. Apparent things are a view of the unseen.

21b. We can make use of them the lower animals by means of experience, memory, wisdom, and skill.

22. What is called birds' milk is the white in the egg.

c. *Plato and Aristotle comment on Anaxagoras'*
conception of Mind or Nous.

1. PLATO, *Phaedo* 97 B. Then I heard some one who had a book of Anaxagoras . . . out of which he read that mind was the disposer and cause of all, and I was quite delighted at the notion of this. . . . 98 C. As I proceeded, I found my philosopher altogether forsaking mind or any other principle of order, but having recourse to air, and ether, and water, and other eccentricities. . . .[9]

---

[8] This and the following fragments are in Richmond Lattimore's translation, from Matthew Thompson McClure's *The Early Philosophers of Greece* (New York, Appleton-Century-Crofts, 1935), p. 193.

[9] See below, Ch. 7, A. 16 for a more extensive quotation from Plato's *Phaedo* on Anaxagoras' theory of mind.

2. ARIST., *Met.* I. 3. 984 b 8. Besides these and similar causes, inasmuch as they are not such as to generate the nature of things, they (again compelled, as we said, by the truth itself) sought the first principle which lay nearest. For perhaps neither fire nor earth nor any other such things should fittingly be or be thought a cause why some things exist and others arise; nor is it well to assign any such matter to its voluntary motion or to chance. Moreover one who said that as mind exists in animals, so it exists in nature as the cause of the universe and of all order, appeared as a sober man in contrast with those before who spoke rashly.

3. ———— I. 4. 985 a 18. Anaxagoras uses mind as a device by which to construct the universe, and when he is at a loss for the cause why anything necessarily is, then he drags this in, but in other cases he assigns any other cause rather than mind for what comes into being.

d. Anaxagoras on the principles and the process.

1. ARIST., *Phys.* I. 4. 187 a 36. They thought that (what arose) arose necessarily out of things that are and their attributes, and, because the masses were so small, out of what we cannot perceive. Wherefore they say that everything was mixed in everything because they saw everything arising out of everything; and different things appeared and were called different from each other according to what is present in greatest number in the mixture of the infinites; for the whole is not purely white or black or sweet or flesh or bone, but the nature of the thing seems to be that of which it has the most.

2. THEOPH., *Phys. Op.* Fr. 4. *Dox.* 479. Theophrastus says that the teaching of Anaxagoras is much like that of Anaximander; for Anaxagoras says that in the separation of the infinite, things that are akin come together, and whatever gold there is in the all becomes gold, and whatever earth becomes earth, and in like manner each of the other things, not as though they came into being, but as though they were existing before. And Anaxagoras postulated intelligence (*Nous*) as the cause of motion and of coming into being, and when this caused separa-

tion, worlds were produced and other objects sprang forth. He might seem, he says, to make the material causes of things taking place thus infinite, but the cause of motion and of coming into being one. But if one were to assume that the mixture of all things is one nature undefined in form and in amount, which he seems to mean, it follows that he speaks of two first principles, the nature of the infinite and intelligence, so that he appears to treat all the material elements in much the same manner as Anaximander.

3. HIPP., *Phil.* 8. *Dox.* 561. After him came Anaxagoras of Clazomenæ, son of Hegesiboulos. He said that the first principle of the all is mind and matter, mind the active first principle, and matter the passive. For when all things were together, mind entered and disposed them. The material first principles are infinite, and the smaller ones of these he calls infinite. And all things partake of motion when they are moved by mind and like things come together. And objects in the heavens have been ordered by their circular motion. The dense and the moist and the dark and the cold and all heavy things come together into the midst, and the earth consists of these when they are solidified; but the opposite to these, the warm, the bright, the dry, and the light move out beyond the aether. The earth is flat in form, and keeps its place in the heavens because of its size and because there is no void; and on this account the air by its strength holds up the earth, which rides on the air. And the sea arose from the moisture on the earth, both of the waters which have fallen after being evaporated, and of the rivers that flow down into it. And the rivers get their substance from the clouds and from the waters that are in the earth. For the earth is hollow and has water in the hollow places. And the Nile increases in summer because waters flow down into it from snows at the north.

Sun and moon and all the stars are fiery stones that are borne about by the revolution of the aether. And sun and moon and certain other bodies moving with them, but invisible to us, are below the stars. Men do not feel the warmth of the stars, because they are so far away from the earth; and they are not warm in the same way that the sun is, because they are in a colder region. The moon is below the sun and nearer us. The sun is larger than the Peloponnesos. The moon does not have its own light, but light from the sun. The revolution of the stars takes them beneath the earth. The moon is eclipsed when the earth goes in front of it, and sometimes when the bodies beneath the moon go in front of it; and the sun is eclipsed when the new moon goes in front of it. And the solstices are occasioned because the sun and the moon are thrust aside by the air. And the moon changes its course frequently because it is not able to master the cold. He first determined the matter of the moon's phases. He said the moon is made of earth and has plains and valleys in it. The milky way is a reflection of the light of the stars which do not get their light from the sun. The stars which move across the heavens, darting down like sparks, are due to the motion of the sphere.

And winds arise when the air is rarefied by the sun, and when objects are set on fire and moving towards the sphere are borne away. Thunders and lightnings arise from heat striking the clouds. Earthquakes arise from the air above striking that which is beneath the earth; for when this is set in motion, the earth which rides on it is tossed about by it. And animals arose in the first place from moisture, and afterwards one from another; and males arise when the seed that is separated from the right side becomes attached to the right side of the womb, and females when the opposite is the case.

e. Anaxagoras' theories of perception and intelligence.

1. THEOPH., *de Sen.* 27. *Dox.* 507. Anaxagoras held that sensation takes place by opposite qualities; for like is not affected by like. And he attempts to enumerate things one by one. For seeing is a reflection in the pupil, and objects are not reflected in the like, but in the opposite. And for many creatures there is a difference of color in the daytime, and for others at night, so that at that time they are sharpsighted. But in general the night is more of the same color as the eyes. And the reflection takes place in the daytime, since light is the cause of reflection; but that color which prevails the more is reflected in its opposite.

In the same manner both touch and taste discern; for what is equally warm or equally cold does not produce warm or cold when it approaches its like, nor yet do men recognize sweet or bitter by these qualities in themselves, but they perceive the cold by the warm, the drinkable water by the salt, the sweet by the bitter, according as each quality is absent; for all things are existing in us. So also smell and hearing take place, the one in connection with breathing, the other by the penetration of sound into the brain; for the surrounding bone against which the sound strikes is hollow. And every sensation is attended with pain, which would seem to follow from the fundamental thesis; for every unlike thing by touching produces distress. And this is evident both in the duration and in the excessive intensity of the sensations. For both bright colors and very loud sounds occasion pain, and men are not able to bear them for any long time. And the larger animals have the more acute sensations, for sensation is simply a matter of size. For animals that have large, pure, and bright eyes see large things afar off, but of those that have small eyes the opposite is true. And the same holds true of hearing. For large ears hear large sounds afar off, smaller ones escape their notice, and small ears hear small sounds near at hand. And the same is true of smell: for the thin air has the stronger odor, since warm and rarefied air has an odor. And when a large animal breathes, it draws in the thick with the rarefied, but the small animal only the rarefied, so that large animals have a better sense of smell. For an odor near at hand is stronger than one far off, because that is thicker, and what is scattered is weakened. It comes about to this, large animals do not perceive the thin air, and small animals do not perceive the thick air.

2. ARIST., *de Part. Anim.* 687 a 8. Anaxagoras . . . asserts that it is his possession of hands that makes man the most intelligent of the animals; but surely the reasonable point of view is that it is because he is the most intelligent animal that he has got hands. . . .[10]

[10] Aristotle, *Parts of Animals*, translated by A. L. Peck (Cambridge, Harvard University Press, 1937), p. 371.

THE ATOMISTS

The classical hypothesis of a universe explicable in terms of atoms and void exerted an enormous influence upon later science and philosophy. The Greek atomist philosophy is important, however, not alone because of its historical influences but also because, as a philosophical system, it is so completely the working out of the many motives which led men to philosophize from the time of Thales in Miletus to the period of Sophist and Socratic speculation in Athens.

No system of speculation followed more rigorously than did Atomism the requirement implicit in Milesian speculation that the explanatory principles employed be reduced to a minimum and that, to the degree possible at the time, these "causes" be validated in the examination of phenomena. In their elaboration of Anaximenes' hypothesis that quantitative differentiations explain qualitative diversity (see above, p. 35); in the denial of the ultimacy of qualitative differentiations so brilliantly put forward by Anaxagoras; in their reinterpretation of Parmenides' *it is* or *being* in terms of atoms irreducible as physical entities; and in their assertion that *it is not* or non-being is, as space or place, in all these aspects of speculation, the Atomist philosophers produced a brilliant and profound refinement of natural philosophy. Nor is it unimportant to notice that in Atomist thinking, early Greek speculation upon the cosmos becomes a philosophy from which the "eagle of Zeus" has been exiled. There are here no traces—such as remain in the Pluralist philosophies of entities such as Empedocles' Love and Hate or Anaxagoras' Mind, which evoke memories of cosmic teleology (see above, p. 25).

With reference to Leucippus, the founder of Atomism, tradition is vague. There is certainty concerning neither the dates of his life nor his actual contribution to philosophy.[11] He is said to have been born in Abdera, the birthplace, *ca.* 460 B.C., of his

[11] The selections relating to Leucippus' life and thought begin below, p. 152.

disciple Democritus. The development of the Atomists' philosophy is commonly attributed to Democritus,[12] who was reputed to have been the most learned man of his time.

The problem for the Atomists is to account for phenomena and "to save appearances," while yet maintaining the validity of Parmenides' postulate of *it is* or *being*. The Atomists' theories may be clarified by comparison to and contrast with those held by Empedocles and Anaxagoras. In spite of Empedocles' assumption that *being* consists of four qualitatively changeless elements, his explanation of change by mixture through the interpenetration of the elements easily leads to the assumption that such change may occur only if the elements be subdivided into parts or particles. The Atomists assume that such a division of *being* is logically necessary. Consequently, *being* is defined in terms of infinite atoms, which are neither created nor destroyed. Atoms are not subject to change. They are homogeneous and contain no spaces. They vary infinitely in size below the level at which the specific atom is perceptible. Unlike such mathematical entities as Zeno conceives (see above, Ch. 4, III. B. b. 4), the physical bodies called atoms are not divisible.

In their assumption that *being* is an infinity of atoms, Leucippus and Democritus propound a theory similar to that of Anaxagoras, who had recognized the necessity for infinite seeds or germs to explain the infinite variety of phenomena. However, the seeds or germs of Anaxagoras' philosophy vary infinitely in quality. In contrast, atoms are qualitatively homogeneous. Qualitative differentiations observed in the world are explained by the Atomists in quantitative terms. In their reduction of qualitative differentiations to quantitative principles, the Atomists carry to a logical conclusion the motive underlying Anaximenes' hypothesis of rarefaction and condensation (see above, p. 24).

To account for the interpenetration of the elements, Empedocles postulated pores or interstices, but denied the existence of empty space. The Atomists, assuming that the atoms vary not

[12] The selections relating to Democritus' life begin below, p. 154. The fragments of Democritus' philosophy begin below, p. 156 and The Golden Maxims at p. 200.

only in shape but in order and in position (see below, IV. B. 37, 38, 45), insist that void or *non-being* is as real as the *plenum* or *being* (see below, IV. B. 38). Since atoms are said to possess an inherent velocity, their movement in empty space results i collision, union, separation, variation in position, and change order. Upon the combination and separation of atoms in spa depend the observable characteristics of the world. Since such combinations and separations of atoms occur by necessity (see below, III. 2), the phenomenal characteristics of the universe at a given time will be the spatial distribution of the atoms. Generation or "coming into being" is explicable, on the Atomists' hypothesis, by the union of atoms; destruction or "passing out of being" by the subtraction of atoms (see below, IV. B. 58). Change, then, is the redistribution of atoms in space (see below, IV. B. 37).

The economy and explicitness of the Atomists' system may be further illustrated by specific reference to Democritus' philosophy. The weight of the composite bodies is in proportion to the density of the atoms of which it is constructed. Larger bodies may, therefore, be lighter than smaller ones if the former contain more void (see below, IV. B. 60). Worlds originate as a result of the collision of atoms in the void. "Lighter" atoms are driven "upward." A vortex is produced by the resulting collisions, since like atoms join with like (see below, IV. B. 43; IV. B. a. 164). The inclusiveness of the system and the economy of the principles used are further demonstrated in the Atomists' hypotheses concerning life and death, the relation of the soul to the body, and the nature of "secondary qualities." Like the body, the soul is composed of atoms. The atoms composing the soul are, however, the most mobile (see below, IV. B. 101). Life is attributable to the presence of these swiftly moving atoms which alternate with the less mobile somatic atoms. The dispersion of the "soul" atoms brings death, a constantly impending danger, owing to the fineness and mobility of the "soul" atoms. The dispersion of the soul is prevented by breathing in the surrounding air, which is likewise composed of the mobile atoms (see below, IV. B. 106). With reference to tastes, Democritus assigned "a shape to each quality." Sour tastes, for example, are caused by "very large, rough shapes, with many angles and no curves" (cf. IV. B. 49, 77, 129; IV. B. a. 11, 166 for the general theory of perception and secondary qualities). It is notable, however, that to this "realist" interpretation of "secondary qualities," the Atomists added the dictum that "Sweet is by convention" (see below, Ch. 6, pp. 213 sq., for the contrasting Sophist view).

In its historical development in classical times, Atomism underwent radical alterations. Perhaps the most important consequences for the history of philosophy arose from speculation concerning the need for adding weight as a dimension of atoms. The doxographical tradition attributes this change to Epicurus (see below, IV. B. 47; cf. IV. B. 50). The weight of the atoms caused them to fall "downward" in straight lines. Since the atoms move by their inherent velocity, are governed by necessity, and originally are separated one from another, the doxographers assumed that no atom could overtake any other atom. As a result, the collisions essential to the formation of composite bodies, including worlds, could not occur. According to tradition, Epicurus solved the difficulty by introducing into the atoms "an inherent declination" (see below, IV. B. 50) to ensure the necessary collision and entanglement. It was in this "declination" of atoms that Lucretius found the solution to the problem of human freedom in a world subject in all else to mechanical law and necessity. In accepting this one exception to the law of necessity, later Atomism destroyed at once the law of nature governing the universe and the adequacy with which all phenomena had been explained. The earlier Atomism of Leucippus and Democritus remains, despite the inadequacies brought out by its later adherents, a model for future science and philosophy in its economy of principles and in its demand that those principles be tested in all phenomena.

Democritus wrote, too, upon morals and the good life for man. In general, his ethical theory (see below, IV. B. 169) centers upon cheerfulness, self-restraint, and the need for reason to dominate the passions (see The Golden Maxims, IV. B. a. 1 sq.). There is little more than a formal relation between the Atomists' metaphysics and their ethics, except in the issue of freedom.

III. LEUCIPPUS

LIFE AND THOUGHT

1. D.L., *op. cit.* IX. 28. Leucippus was born at Elea, but some say at Abdera and others at Miletus. He was a pupil of Zeno. . . .

2. Fragment 2. Nothing occurs at random, but everything for a reason . . . and by necessity.[13]

3. D.L., *op. cit.* IX. 31. He declared[14] the All to be unlimited, as already stated; but of the All part is full and part empty, and these he calls elements. Out of them arise the worlds unlimited in number and into them they are dissolved. This is how the worlds are formed. In a given section many atoms of all manner of shapes are carried from the unlimited into the vast empty space. These collect together and form a single vortex, in which they jostle against each other and, circling round in every possible way, separate off, by like atoms joining like. And, the atoms being so numerous that they can no longer revolve in equilibrium, the light ones pass into the empty space outside, as if they were being winnowed; the remainder keep together and, becoming entangled, go on their circuit together, and form a primary spherical system. This parts off like a shell, enclosing within it atoms of all kinds; and, as these are whirled round by virtue of the resistance of the center, the enclosing shell becomes thinner, the adjacent atoms continually combining when they

[13] Translated by Cyril Bailey, *The Greek Atomists and Epicurus, a Study* (London, The Clarendon Press, 1928), p. 85.
[14] Reprinted by permission of the publishers and The Loeb Classical Library from Diogenes Laertius, *Lives of Eminent Philosophers,* translated by R. D. Hicks (Cambridge, Harvard University Press, 1923).

touch the vortex. In this way the earth is formed by portions brought to the center coalescing. And again, even the outer shell grows larger by the influx of atoms from outside, and, as it is carried round in the vortex, adds to itself whatever atoms it touches. And of these some portions are locked together and form a mass, at first damp and miry, but, when they have dried and revolve with the universal vortex, they afterwards take fire and form the substance of the stars.

The orbit of the sun is the outermost, that of the moon nearest the earth; the orbits of the other heavenly bodies lie between these two. All the stars are set on fire by the speed of their motion; the burning of the sun is also helped by the stars; the moon is only slightly kindled. The sun and the moon are eclipsed <when . . . , but the obliquity of the zodiacal circle is due> to the inclination of the earth to the south; the regions of the north are always shrouded in mist, and are extremely cold and frozen. Eclipses of the sun are rare; eclipses of the moon constantly occur, and this because their orbits are unequal. As the world is born, so, too, it grows, decays, and perishes, in virtue of some necessity, the nature of which he does <not> specify.

4. Arist., *de Gen. et Corr.*[15] A. 8. 325 a 23. . . . Leucippus thought he had a theory, which should be consistent with sense-perception and not do away with coming into being or destruction or motion or the multiplicity of things. He agreed so far with appearances, but to those who hold the theory of the One, on the ground that there could be no motion without empty space, he admitted that empty space is not real, and that nothing of what is real is not real: for the real in the strict sense is an absolute *plenum*. But the *plenum* is not one, but there is an infinite number of them, and they are invisible owing to the smallness of their bulk. These move in empty space (for there is empty space), and by the coming together produce coming into being and by their separation destruction.

[15] Translated by Cyril Bailey, *op. cit.*, p. 70.

IV. DEMOCRITUS [16]

A. LIFE

1. D.L., *op. cit.* IX. 34 ff.[17] Democritus was the son of Hegesistratus, though some say of Athenocritus, and others again of Damasippus. He was a native of Abdera or, according to some, of Miletus. He was a pupil of certain Magians and Chaldaeans. For when King Xerxes was entertained by the father of Democritus he left men in charge, as, in fact, is stated by Herodotus; and from these men, while still a boy, he learned theology and astronomy. Afterwards he met Leucippus and, according to some, Anaxagoras, being forty years younger than the latter. . . .

According to Demetrius in his book on *Men of the Same Name* and Antisthenes in his *Successions of Philosophers,* he travelled into Egypt to learn geometry from the priests, and he also went into Persia to visit the Chaldaeans as well as to the Red Sea. Some say that he associated with the Gymnosophists in India and went to Aethiopia. Also that, being the third son, he divided the family property. . . .

Aristoxenus in his *Historical Notes* affirms that Plato wished to burn all the writings of Democritus that he could collect, but that Amyclas and Clinias the Pythagoreans prevented him, saying that there was no advantage in doing so, for already the books were widely circulated. And there is clear evidence for this in the fact that Plato, who mentions almost all the early philosophers, never once alludes to Democritus, not even where it would be necessary to controvert him, obviously because he knew that he would have to match himself against the prince of philosophers, for whom, to be sure, Timon has this meed of praise:

Such is the wise Democritus, the guardian of discourse, keen-witted disputant, among the best I ever read.

[16] The translation of Democritus, except where otherwise noted, is the work of Dr. Gordon H. Clark. Professor Isaac Husik graciously revised a large number of the paragraphs.

[17] Translated by R. D. Hicks, *op. cit.* Reprinted by permission of the publishers and the Loeb Classical Library.

(43) Of the death of Democritus the account given by Hermippus is as follows. When he was now very old and near his end, his sister was vexed that he seemed likely to die during the festival of Thesmophoria and she would be prevented from paying the fitting worship to the goddess. He bade her be of good cheer and ordered hot loaves to be brought to him every day. By applying these to his nostrils he contrived to outlive the festival; and as soon as the three festival days were passed he let his life go from him without pain, having then, according to Hipparchus, attained his one hundred and ninth year. . . .

(44) His opinions are these. The first principles of the universe are atoms and empty space; everything else is merely thought to exist. The worlds are unlimited; they come into being and perish. Nothing can come into being from that which is not nor pass away into that which is not. Further, the atoms are unlimited in size and number, and they are borne along in the whole universe in a vortex, and thereby generate all composite things—fire, water, air, earth; for even these are conglomerations of given atoms. And it is because of their solidity that these atoms are impassive and unalterable. The sun and the moon have been composed by such smooth and spherical masses [i.e., atoms], and so also the soul, which is identical with reason. We see by virtue of the impact of images upon our eyes.

(45) All things happen by virtue of necessity, the vortex being the cause of the creation of all things, and this he calls necessity. The end of action is tranquillity, which is not identical with pleasure, as some by a false interpretation have understood, but a state in which the soul continues calm and strong, undisturbed by any fear or superstition or any other emotion. This he calls well-being and many other names. The qualities of things exist merely by convention; in nature there is nothing but atoms and void space. These, then, are his opinions.[18]

[18] There follows in Diogenes Laertius' account a long list of Democritus' writings. These were arranged by Thrasylus. *Pythagoras, The Great Diacosmos, Geometrica, and Concerning Homer* are perhaps the most important of the works listed.

B. TEACHING

35. ARIST., *de Gen. et Corr.* A. 2. 315 a 34. On the whole, no one gave more than superficial attention to any [of these] problems, except Democritus; and he seems to have thought deeply on them all and is particularly superior in respect to method.

36. ———, *de Part. Anim.* A. 1. 642 a 24. The reason our predecessors did not arrive at this method is that they could not define reality or conceptual being; Democritus was the first to grasp it, not however as necessary to physical investigation, but he was led up to it by the subject matter. In the time of Socrates this method flourished, but the investigation of nature declined, for the philosophers turned to politics and utilitarianism *Met.* M. 4. 1078 b 19. In natural science Democritus grasped the method only slightly, and after a fashion defined hot and cold.

37. SIMP., *de Caelo* p. 293, 33 Heib. A few notes from Aristotle's *On Democritus* will clarify the thought of these men. "Democritus considers the eternal objects to be small substances infinite in number. For these he posits a place infinite in magnitude, and he calls place by such names as void, nothing, and infinite, but each of the substances he calls, something, solid, and existent. He thinks the substances are so small that we cannot perceive them, yet they have all sorts of forms and shapes, and differences in size. Accordingly from these as from elements he generates and combines visible objects and perceptible masses. And they are disturbed and move in the void because of their dissimilarity and the other differences mentioned, and as they move they collide and become entangled in such a fashion as to be near to and touch each other. However this does not in truth give rise to any one single nature, for it is altogether silly that two or more things may ever become one. The coherence up to a certain point of substances he explains by the gripping and intermingling of the bodies, for some of them are scalene in shape, some are barbed, some concave, some convex and others have countless other differences. Accordingly he thinks they cling to each other and cohere until some stronger necessity from the

surroundings approaches, shakes and scatters them." And he speaks of genesis and its contrary, separation, not only with reference to animals, but to plants, and worlds, and, in general, all sensible bodies. If, therefore, genesis is the commingling of atoms, and destruction is their separation, then according to Democritus genesis is also the same as qualitative change.

38. ———, *Phys.* 28, 15. And likewise his friend, Democritus the Abderite, posited as principles the full and the void, of which he called the first Being and the second Non-being. For positing the atoms as the material of things, they [Democritus and Leucippus] produce the other things by their differences. And these are three, proportion, impulsion, and arrangement, which is the same as saying shape, position, and order. For the like is naturally set in motion by the like, and the homogeneous is drawn together, and each of the shapes when it is arranged into a different combination produces another design. Consequently, since the elements are infinite, they could reasonably promise to render an account of all qualities and things, an account both of the cause and the process of anything's generation. Therefore they also claim that only if we assume the elements to be infinite will all things happen according to reason. And they say the number of shapes among the atoms is infinite because there is no more reason for an atom to be of one shape than another. And this is the cause they themselves assign for the infinity of the atoms.

39. PLUT., *Strom.* 7. *Dox.* 581. Democritus the Abderite supposed the universe to be infinite because it had not been fashioned by any Maker. And again he says it is unchangeable, and in general he states in express terms the kind of universe it is: The causes of what now exists have no beginning, but from infinitely preceding time absolutely everything which was, is, and shall be, has been held down by necessity. But he says the sun and the moon came into existence. They had their own motion without having any heat or light but having, on the contrary, a nature similar to earth. Each of them first came into being by a peculiar change of the cosmos, and later when the circle of the sun was enlarged fire was included in it.

40. Hipp., *op. cit.* I. 13. *Dox.* 565. Democritus was an acquaintance of Leucippus. Democritus, son of Damasippus an Abderite, consulted with the Gymnosophists in India and with the priests in Egypt and with the astrologers and wise men in Babylon. Now like Leucippus he says of the elements, solid and void, that the solid really exists and the void does not. And he would say that the realities were always moving in the void; and there are an infinite number of worlds differing in size; in some there is neither sun nor moon, in others they are larger than ours, and in others there are many suns and moons. The distances between the worlds are unequal and in some quarters there are more worlds, in others fewer, and some are growing and others have reached their full size, and others are disintegrating, and in some quarters worlds are coming into being and in others they are ceasing to exist. They are destroyed by colliding with each other. And some worlds are devoid of living beings and all moisture. In our system the earth came into being before the stars, and the moon is nearest the earth, and then the sun, and then the fixed stars. The planets are not equally distant from the earth. The world remains at its maturity until it can no longer receive any [nourishment] from outside. This man ridiculed everything as if all human interests were ridiculous.

41. Arist., *Phys.* T. 4. 203 a 33. Democritus affirms that no element arises from any other. However, their common property, body, differing in its parts by size and shape, is the principle of all things.

42. ――――, *Met.* Z. 13. 1039 a 9. For it is impossible, he says, for one thing to come from two or two from one. For the magnitudes or atoms constitute reality.

43. Dionys., from Eus., *P.E.* XIV. 23, 2.3. Those who spoke of atoms, i. e., certain infinitely numerous, indestructible, and extremely small bodies, and who assumed a void space of unbounded size, say that these atoms move at random in the void and collide with each other by chance because of an irregular momentum, and they catch hold of each other and are entangled because of the variety of shapes. Thus they produce the world

and its contents, or rather, an infinite number of worlds. Epicurus and Democritus accepted this view, but they differed in that the former held all atoms to be minute and imperceptible, while Democritus believed that some atoms were large. But both assert the existence of atoms, so called because of their indestructible hardness.[19] But, for appearances not to contradict us, we ought not to attribute every size to the atoms, though we should admit certain differences in size.

44. HERM., *I.G.P.* 13. *Dox.* 654. Democritus . . . makes the principles Being and Non-being. Being is the full and Non-being the void. And the full produces all things by its impulsion and proportion in the void.

45. ARIST., *Phys.* A. 5. 188 a 22. Democritus asserts the solid and the void exist, of which the former is like Being and the latter like Non-being. Then again [there are differences] in position, shape, and order. The following are their generic contraries: of position, up and down, backwards and forwards; of shape, angular, straight, and round.

46. AET., *op. cit.* I. 3, 16. *Dox.* 285. The well-kneaded [solid] and the void [are principles.] GALEN, *de Elem. sec. Hipp.* VIII. 931. K. What the word *well-kneaded* may mean I do not rightly know because it is not customary with the Greeks to use this word in such a context. For they call a kind of bread well-kneaded but I do not know that they call anything else by that name. Archigenes himself . . . seems to use the word *well-kneaded* for the full.

47. AET., *Plac.* I. 3, 18. *Dox.* 285. For Democritus ascribed two qualities [to the atoms], size and shape. But Epicurus added to these a third, weight; for, he says, the atoms require the impact of weight to move. 12, 6. *Dox.* 311. Democritus says the primary bodies (these, as we have seen, are the solids) do not have weight, but are moved in the infinite by striking each other. And there can be an atom the size of a whole world. CIC., *de Fato.* 20, 46. [Epicurus] said the atom has a declination. First, why?

---

[19] Cf. Epicurus, *Epicurea* I. 55, ed. by H. Usener (Leipzig, Teubner, 1887), pp. 12, 15.

Because they have a certain force of motion which Democritus calls impact, but which you, Epicurus, refer to gravity and weight. SIMP., *Phys.* 42, 10. Democritus says the atoms, naturally immobile, are set in motion by an impact. AET., *op. cit.* I. 23, 3. *Dox.* 319. Democritus declared that there is but one kind of motion, namely through striking.

48. ———— I. 16, 2. *Dox.* 315. Those who believe in atoms say that division stops at the indivisible substances and does not continue to infinity.

49. GALEN., *op. cit.* I. 2. [I. 417. K]. "For by convention color exists, by convention bitter, by convention sweet, but in reality atoms and void," (see below, IV. B. a. 125) says Democritus, believing that from the conjunction of atoms all sensible qualities come into being for us who perceive them, but by nature nothing is white, black, yellow, red, bitter, or sweet; for the phrase "by convention" means the same thing as "by custom," and "for us," not according to the nature of the things themselves, which he calls "in reality" coining the term from "real" which means true. And the complete sense of his argument would be as follows: Men think that there is such a thing as white, black, sweet, or bitter; but in truth the universe is composed of "thing" and "nothing" (cf. IV. B. a. 156). For this is what he himself says, referring to the atoms by the word "thing," to the void by the word "nothing." Since all the atoms are minute bodies, they have no qualities, and the void is a kind of place in which all these bodies, as they move up and down through all time, either become somehow entangled with each other, or collide and rebound, and they separate and mix again with each other by reason of such contacts, and in this way produce all other combinations including our own bodies with their affections and sensations. But the primary bodies he holds to be without qualities, (and some persons, like the disciples of Epicurus, say they are unbreakable because of their hardness, but others make them indivisible because of their smallness, as do the colleagues of Leucippus,) nor can they in any respect undergo those qualitative changes which all men have believed to exist because they are taught by their senses. For example they deny that any of

those bodies can grow warm or cold, and in the same way they can neither become moist nor dry, and still more is it impossible for them to become white or black or in general to assume any other quality by any change whatever.

50. DIOGEN. of Oinoanda, *Fr.* 80. 81 col. 3, 3. If any one should use the argument of Democritus, saying that the atoms have no freedom in their motion because they collide with each other, and all things below apparently move by necessity, we shall reply to him: Then you do not know who you are, and there is a certain freedom in the motion of the atoms, which Democritus did not discover, but Epicurus brought to light, namely an inherent declination as is proved by the phenomena.

51. CIC., *de Nat. Deor.* I. 26, 73. [s 62. A. 5]. What is there in Epicurus' physics which does not come from Democritus? For although he changed some things, as the declination of the atoms which I have just mentioned, none the less for the most part he says the same things, atoms, void, images, infinity of space, and innumerable worlds, their generation and destruction, practically everything on which the explanation of nature depends.

53. PLUT., *Adv. Colot* 3. p. 1108 e. And indeed Epicurus for a long time called himself a Democritean, as many assert including Leonteus, one of Epicurus' chief disciples, who wrote to Lycophron that Democritus was honored by Epicurus because he was the first to grasp a right knowledge of things, and that the treatise as a whole is called Democritean because Democritus was the first to hit upon the principles of nature. And Metrodorus [in his work] *On Philosophy* has said plainly that if Democritus had not led the way, Epicurus could never have attained to wisdom.

56. CIC., *de Fin.* I. 6, 17. He believes in what he calls atoms, that is in bodies indivisible because of their solidity which move in an infinite void which has neither highest, lowest, middle, farthest, nor limit. They collide and stick together and thus all things we see come into being. This motion of the atoms never had a beginning but should be understood to be eternal.

57. PLUT., *Adv. Colot.* 8 p. 1110 f. For what does Democritus say? Substances infinite in number, indivisible, and different from each other, without qualities and unchanging, are scattered about and move in the void. When they approach each other or collide or become entangled, some of these aggregations form water, some fire, some plants, and some men. But all things are really atoms or forms as he calls them, and besides these nothing exists. For there is no generation from non-being nor can there be any generation from things which exist because the atoms on account of their solidity neither change nor suffer any impression. Therefore color does not arise from the uncolored, nor nature or soul from that which is without quality and impassible. ARIST., *Met.* I. 1069 b 22. And as Democritus says, all things were together potentially, but not actually.

58. ARIST. *Phys.* VIII. 265 b 24. And they say motion exists because of the void; for these men also say that nature moves in space. SIMP., *in loc.* 1318, 33. That is, the natural, primary and atomic bodies, for these they would call nature and used to say that by their weight they move through space because the void gives way and offers no resistance; for they said that they are tossed about. And these men explain that this is not only the primary motion of the elements but the only motion; the other motions belong to compounds. For they say that growth and decay, qualitative change, generation and corruption occur by the combining and separating of the primary bodies.

59. SEXT. EMP., *Adv. Math.* VIII 6. The disciples both of Plato and Democritus held that only intelligible objects are real. Democritus thought so because there is no sensible substratum in nature, for the atoms which give rise to things by combining have a nature devoid of all sensible quality; Plato held this view because the sensibles are always in process of becoming, but never really are.

60. ARIST., *de Gen. et Corr.* A. 8. 326 a 9. And Democritus says that each of the indivisibles is heavier according to its excess. *de Caelo* Δ 2. 309 a 1. [In opposition to Plato, those who call the primary objects] solids are better able to say that the

greater is the heavier. But since this does not always appear true, and we see many heavier compounds with less bulk, for example bronze has less bulk than the same weight of wool, some adopt and assert another explanation. For they say the void enveloped in the bodies makes them light and makes it possible for the larger bodies sometimes to be lighter than smaller ones, for they have more void. . . . And this is the way they explain it. But to those who so define matters, we must add, not merely that there be more void if a thing is to be lighter, but that there also be less solid, for if a certain ratio be exceeded, the body will not be lighter. For this reason also they say fire is the lightest of all bodies because it has most void. It will follow, then, that a great deal of gold which has more void than a little fire is lighter, unless it also have many times the amount of solid. b. 34. [And if matter has] a contrary, (310 a) as the proponents of the void and the full maintain, bodies intermediate between the absolutely heavy and light will have no explanation for their being heavier or lighter than each other, or than the bodies absolutely heavy or light. To make this distinction depend on size and smallness seems more artificial than the previous views . . . and there is nothing absolutely light nor anything which ascends except what is left behind [in falling] or is squeezed up, and many small things are heavier than a few large things.

61. SIMP., *de Caelo* 569, 5. Democritus' followers and later Epicurus assert that all the atoms are homogeneous and have weight, but because some are heavier, the lighter ones are thrust aside by the others as they fall and are carried upwards, and thus it is they say, that some things are considered light and some heavy. 712, 27. The Democritean group thinks that all things have weight, but since fire has less weight and is squeezed out by the things ahead of it, it is carried upward, and for this reason it appears light. And they consider that only what is heavy exists, and it is always in motion toward the center. *Contra Democritum*, EPIC., *Ep.* I. 61. [p. 18, 15 Us.] The atoms necessarily have equal speeds when they move through the void which offers no resistance. For neither will the [large and] heavy atoms move more quickly than the small and light, when nothing

obstructs them, nor will the small atoms, all of which have commensurate passageways, move more slowly than the large ones when nothing resists them either.

62. ARIST., *de Caelo* Δ 6. 313 a 21. The impression that all these phenomena [the floating of metal discs etc. on water] are explained by Democritus' theory is erroneous. For he says that the warm particles which move upwards through the water support broad bodies even though they are heavy, but the narrow bodies fall through, for all the resisting particles are too sparse for them. But this ought to occur still more in air, as he himself objects. And his solution of the objection is poor; for he says the rush does not start in one direction, where by "rush" he means the motion of the rising particles.

63. ―――, *de Gen. et Corr.* A. 7. 323 b 10. Democritus in opposition to other philosophers had a peculiar theory of his own. For, he says, agent and patient must be the same and similar. For things that are other and different cannot be affected by each other, but even if several different things actually affect one another, it is not in so far as they are other that this happens but in so far as they are the same.

64. ALEX., *de Mixt.* 2. [II 214, 18 Bruns.] Democritus, therefore, considering that [chemical] "mixture" so-called occurs by the juxtaposition of bodies, which are divided into minute particles and produce the mixture by the positions of the particles alongside of each other, asserts that in truth things are not mixed even in the beginning, but the apparent mixture is a juxtaposition of bodies in minute particles, preserving the proper nature of each, which they had before the mixing. They seem to be mixed because on account of the smallness of the juxtaposed particles our senses cannot perceive any one of them by itself.

65. ARIST., *Phys.* VIII. 252 a 32. But in general, to think that, because something always is or always happens in a given fashion, we have sufficiently explained it, is not to understand the matter aright. By such a principle Democritus reduces the explanation of nature to the statement that, thus it happened

formerly also, and there is no sense in looking for an explanation of what always happens.

66. Cic., *de Fato.* 17, 39. All things so happen by fate that fate produces the force of necessity: of which opinion were Democritus, Heraclitus, Empedocles and [Anaxagoras]. Arist., *de Gen. Anima.* E. 8. 789 b 2. Democritus denies purpose by saying, everything which nature uses reduces to necessity. Aet., *op. cit.* I. 26, 2 (*Dox.* 321; concerning the nature of necessity) Democritus calls it the resistance, motion, and impulsion of the material (cf. IV. B. 83).

67. Simp., *Phys.* 327, 24. Democritus also, where he says "A vortex of all sorts of forms was separated from the universe," (how and through what cause he does not say) seems to produce the world by chance and luck.

68. Arist., *Phys.* B. 4. 195 b 36. For some doubt whether [luck] exists or not; for they say nothing comes by luck, but all things which we say come by chance or luck, have some definite cause. Simp., *Phys.* p. 330, 14. The phrase, "the old theory which eliminates luck," seems to refer to Democritus. For even though he seems to have used luck in the formation of the world, yet in the parts of the world, he says, luck is the cause of nothing, but refers phenomena to other causes, for example, the cause of discovering the treasure was digging, or planting the olive tree, and the reason why the baldheaded man's skull was cracked was that the eagle dropped a tortoise so that the shell might break. For this is how Eudemus tells the story.

69. Arist., *Phys.* B. 4. 196 a 24. And there are some who explain our system and all worlds by chance; for chance gave rise to the vortex or motion which separates and fixes the universe in its present arrangement. . . . . For they affirm that neither animals nor plants exist or come into being by luck, but that nature, or intelligence, or some other such thing is their cause (for it is not any chance thing which grows from a given seed, but from one sort of seed we get olives, from another kind, human beings) but the heavens and the most divine of visible things arose by chance without a cause such as plants and animals have.

70. ———— B. 4. 196 b 5. There are some to whom chance seems to be a cause, but a cause obscured from human understanding as something divine and mysterious. AET., *op. cit.* I. 29, 7. *Dox.* 326 n. Anaxagoras, Democritus, and the Stoics [make luck] a cause hidden from human understanding.

71. ARIST., *Phys.* VIII. 251 b 16. Democritus proves it impossible for all things to have come into being, for time never came into being. SIMP., *Phys.* 1153, 22. Democritus, however, was so persuaded that time is eternal that when he wished to prove that not everything has come into being, he used the fact that time has not come into being as something self-evident.

72. SEXT. EMP., *op. cit.* X. 181. Such a notion of time as "time is an appearance under the forms of day and night" seems to refer to the schools of Epicurus as well as Democritus.

73. THEOPH., *d. Sign.* 52. One may ask why the form of fire is pyramidal. And Democritus says that as its extremities are cooled it is contracted to a small size and finally becomes pointed.

77. PLUT., *Quaest Conv.* VIII. 10, 2. p. 734 f. And Favorinus, . . . taking down an old saying of Democritus, obscured as it were by the smoke of centuries, was able to dust it off and polish it up, assuming that common principle of Democritus, viz: images pass through the pores into the body and, rising [to the head,] cause dreams. These images go to and fro in every direction, springing off implements, clothes, plants, and especially living beings because of their motion and warmth, and they not only have impressed on them the same shape as the bodies (as Epicurus thinks, agreeing with Democritus thus far, but abandoning the argument at this point), but they also assume the appearances of the changes, thoughts, habits, and emotions of each person's soul and so are drawn together. And if with these qualities they strike a person, then like living beings they announce and declare to those who receive them the opinions, arguments, and impulses of those who released them, provided they retain the likenesses articulate and unconfused for impingement. The best results are obtained in calm air, since their motion is then unimpeded and swift. But the air of autumn when the trees shed

their leaves is irregular and blustery. Therefore it twists and distorts the images in various ways dimming and weakening their clearness which is obscured by the slowness of their progress, while on the other hand those which dart forth from things warm and fertile and are quickly conveyed, deliver fresh and significant impressions.

80. Cic., *Ac. Pr.* II. 38, 121.[20] The world is composed of rough and smooth and hooked and bent bodies with void all around.

81. ———— 17, 55. Then you have recourse to those scientists who are most ridiculed in the Academy, from whom you will not even now abstain, and you say Democritus holds innumerable worlds to exist and that some of them are not only similar to each other, but so absolutely and perfectly correspondent in every particular that there is no difference at all between them [and they are innumerable] and so also are men.

82. Simp., *de Cael.* p. 310, 5. "For," says Alexander, "the dissolution and destruction of the world did not result in a cosmic matter which had the potentiality of becoming a world, but it results in another world; and since there is an infinite number of them succeeding one another, it does not follow that the process necessarily leads back to the same world as before." Thus it seemed to the followers of Leucippus and Democritus . . . but the worlds of Democritus, since they change into other worlds which are composed of the same atoms, are the same in kind even if not in number.

83. Sext. Emp., *op. cit.* IX. 113. Consequently the world could not be set in motion by necessity and the vortex, as the school of Democritus asserts.

84. Aet., *op. cit.* II. 4, 9. *Dox.* 331. According to Democritus the world is destroyed when the greater conquers the smaller.

85. ———— 13. [The stars are] stones.

20 Diels, *op. cit.*, has quoted material Cicero attributes to Strato, not Democritus. A line or two above we find the following reported of Democritus.

86. ———— 15. The fixed stars come first, and after them the planets among which are the sun, the morning star, and the moon.

87. ———— 20, 7. According to Democritus [the sun is] a red hot mass or a fiery stone.

88. Luc., *de Rer. Nat.* V. 621 ff. First, it is possible, one would suppose, for things to happen as the divine wisdom of the great Democritus teaches. If so, the nearer the stars are to the earth, the slower do they revolve in the celestial vortex. For its speed diminishes and loses its force as it descends. Therefore the sun little by little falls behind the signs that accompany it; for it is much lower than the fiery stars, and the moon still more so. Since its path is still farther beneath the sky and is near the earth, all the less can it keep pace with the signs. For the weaker the vortex which propels it in its position below the sun, the more can the signs overtake and pass beyond it. Therefore, it seems to return more quickly to the signs because the signs overtake it again.

89. Aet., *op. cit.* II. 23, 7. *Dox.* 353. According to Democritus, [the solstices result from] the vortex' making the sun revolve.

89a. Plut., *de Fac. in Orb. Lun.* 16, p. 929 c. Democritus says when [the moon] stands in a straight line with the illuminating body, it receives and takes in the sun. Consequently it was probable that the moon itself was visible and made the sun visible also.

90. Aet., *op. cit.* II. 25, 9. (*Dox.* 356; on the Moon) 30, 3 (*Dox.* 361; why the moon appears earth-like). According to Democritus, a kind of shadow cast by the high parts on it, for it has hollows and glens.

91. Arist., *Meteor.* A. 8. 345 a 25. (on the Milky Way) Alex., *in loc.* p. 37, 23. Anaxagoras and Democritus say the Milky Way is the light of certain stars. For the sun at night goes under the earth. Hence those stars above the earth which the sun illumines cannot make their own light visible because it is obscured by the rays of the sun; but those which the shadow of the earth darkens so that they are not illuminated by the light of the sun, do show

their own light and this is the Milky Way. Aet., *op. cit.* III. 1. *Dox.* 365. [The Milky Way is] the combined brilliance of many small stars in juxtaposition uniting their light because they are so closely packed.

92. Alex., *in Arist. Meteor.* p. 26, 11. With respect to comets Anaxagoras and Democritus say that the comet is a "conjunction" of the planetary stars, Saturn, Jupiter, Venus, Mars, and Mercury. For these when they come near each other produce an appearance of merging together into one star, the so-called comet. For "conjunction" means their appearance as one which happens when they come together. Sen., *Qu. Nat.* VII. 3, 2. Democritus also, the most acute of all the ancients, said he suspected that there are more planetary stars [than five], but he did not indicate either their number or their names, since they did not then understand the orbits of the five [known] planets. [Note: Alexander, seems to have misunderstood Democritus who guessed that there exist other "planets," i.e., wandering particles, whose conjunction produces comets.]

93. Aet., *op. cit.* III. 3, 11. *Dox.* 369. Democritus held that thunder is produced by an unstable mixture forcing the cloud enclosing it to move downward. Lightning is a clashing together of clouds by which the fire-producing atoms rubbing against each other are assembled through the porous mass into one place and pass out. And the thunderbolt occurs when the motion is forced by the very pure, very fine, very uniform and "closely-packed" fire-producing atoms, as he himself calls them. But heat lightning occurs when very porous mixtures of fire, which are enclosed in porous places and are made into single bodies each with its own surrounding membrane, start downward because of their heterogeneous composition.

94. ——— 10. *Dox.* 377. [The earth] is like a disc in breadth, but hollow in the middle. Eustath. *Corr. I. O.* H. 446 p. 690. Posidonius the Stoic and Dionysius say the inhabited earth is shaped like a sling, but Democritus asserts it is oblong.

95. Aet., *op. cit.* III. 13, 4. *Dox.* 378. Democritus believed that originally the earth roamed about because of its smallness

[rarity?] and lightness, but in time when it became dense and heavy, its position was fixed.

96. ———— 12, 2. *Dox.* 337. Since the south is weaker than the surrounding points, the earth increases in size and leans in that direction; for the northern sections are untempered, whereas the southern are tempered. Hence the world is weighted down in this direction where it abounds in fruits and growth.

97. ARIST., *Meteor.* B. 7. 365 b. Democritus says the earth is full of water, and when it receives an added quantity of rain-water, the water causes it to move. For when there is too much for the bowels of the earth to contain, the water is forced off and produces earthquakes. And when the earth is drained dry and pulls water to the empty places from the fuller sections, the falling water shakes the earth.

98. SEN., *op. cit.* VI. 20. [from Posidonius] Democritus thinks that there are many [causes of earthquakes]. For, he says, the motion is sometimes produced by air, sometimes by water, and sometimes by both. And this takes place as follows: A certain part of the earth is concave and in this place a great mass of water collects. Some of this water is lighter and more fluid than the rest. When this is thrust aside by a weight coming upon it, it is dashed against the earth and causes it to quake. For the water cannot surge without moving that which it hits. . . . . When the water is crowded into one place and cannot be contained in it, it presses against something and forces a way through first by its weight and then by its impetus. For, after being impounded for so long a time, it cannot escape except by a downward motion, nor can it fall straight with moderate force or without shaking the things through which or into which it falls. And if, when it begins to be carried off, it is stopped somewhere, and the force of the stream turns on itself, it is forced back against the earth which contains it, and sets it in motion where it is least stable. And further, the earth, at length almost saturated by the fluid, settles deeper and the foundation itself is weakened. Then that part sinks down, against which the weight of the moving waters presses hardest. And the wind sometimes drives the waves; and

if it blows them vehemently, it moves the part of the earth against which it hurls the water. And at other times thrown together in the subterranean passageways and seeking an exit, the wind puts everything in motion. For the wind penetrates the earth and is both too subtle to be excluded and too powerful to be resisted when rapid and violent.

99. AET., *op. cit.* IV. 1, 4. *Dox.* 385. As the snow in the north melts under the summer sun and flows away, clouds are formed from the vapor. When these are driven south toward Egypt by the monsoons, violent storms arise and fill the lakes, and the Nile.

99a. HIBEH. PAPYR. 16. 62. Grenfell and Hunt, [reconstructed]. There has been the greatest disagreement on the source of salt in the sea. Some say it is the deposit of the first moisture after the waters have mostly evaporated. Others say it is the sweat of the earth. Democritus thinks it is produced in the same way as salt things in the earth, [rock] salt and potassium for example. [Lacuna.] After putrefaction [has ceased,] he says, similars [are gathered] to similars in the fluid as is the case in the universe as a whole, and in this manner the sea came into being and all the briny pools when the things of the same kind were brought together. That the sea is composed of things of the same kind is also clear from other considerations. For neither frankincense, nor sulphur, nor silphium, nor alum, nor bitumen, nor whatever is great and marvellous is produced in many places in the earth. For this reason, then, even if for no other, it is worthwhile to examine why, after making the sea a part of the world, he said, "in the same manner the wonders and rarities of nature occur" on the ground that in earth there are not many distinctions. For him, at any rate, who explains flavors by shapes and derives salt from large and angular atoms, it is not unreasonable that the salinity in the earth should occur in the same manner as in the sea.

100. ARIST., *Meteor.* B. 3. 356 b 4. In discussing the saltness (of the sea) we must also say whether it has always been the same or whether it once did not exist and will in the future cease to exist; for some people think so. Now everyone admits that the

sea came into being if the world as a whole did too, for they make the processes simultaneous. Consequently it is clear that if the universe is eternal, we must hold the same opinion regarding the sea. But the notion that the size of the sea is decreasing, as Democritus says, and will finally disappear, is on a par with Aesop's fables. For he propounded the myth that Charybdis had twice gulped down [some of the sea]. The first time it made the mountains appear, the second time, the islands; and on the final gulp it will make everything dry land. Now it was fitting for Aesop when irritated at the boatman to tell such a myth, but not so appropriate for those who seek the truth. For the cause of the sea's continuing at first, weight as some of them say, . . . will clearly be the cause of its persistence for the rest of time.

101. ARIST., *de Anima* A. 2. 404 a 27. But not entirely like Democritus. For he held that soul and mind are absolutely the same and that appearance is truth. Therefore Homer did well in making "Hector prostrate thinking other thoughts." So he does not use mind as a potentiality for truth, but affirms that soul and mind are the same. 405 a 5. To some it seemed to be fire, for this is the finest and least corporeal of the elements, and further it excels in being moved and in causing motion. And Democritus has spoken very elegantly in explaining each of these phenomena; for soul and mind are the same. And this is that group of the primary, indivisible bodies which produce motion by their minute parts and shape. Now the most mobile of shapes is the sphere, he says; and such is mind and fire. PHILOP., *in loc.* p. 83, 27 H. He said fire was incorporeal, not strictly incorporeal (for none of them said this), but corporeally incorporeal on account of the fineness of its parts.

104. ARIST., *de Anima* A. 3. 406 b 15. Some say the soul moves the body in which it is as it itself is moved, for example when Democritus uses the same idea as Philippus the comic poet who said, Daedalus made the wooden Aphrodite move by pouring in mercury. Democritus speaks in a similar vein when he says, the indivisible spheres are in motion because by nature they can never be still, and so they draw along and set in motion the whole body.

104a. ——— A. 5. 409 a 32. He says [the body] is moved by the soul. . . . If, then, there is a soul in the sentient body as a whole, there will of necessity be two bodies in the same place, since the soul is a body.

105. Aet., op. cit. IV. 4, 6. Dox. 390. Democritus and Epicurus held that the soul has two parts, the rational part seated in the chest, and the non-rational part diffused throughout the whole body. 5, 1. (Dox. 391 n. Theodoret.) For Hippocrates, Democritus, and Plato locate the [Ruler of the soul] in the brain. Philop., de Anima p. 35, 12 Hayd. Democritus asserts [the soul] is neither divisible nor multi-functional, for he believes that thinking is the same as perceiving and that these two functions proceed from a single faculty.

106. Arist., de Resp. 4. 471 b 30. In animals who breathe, says Democritus, breathing prevents the soul's being squeezed out of the body. He said nothing at all, however, to indicate that this was nature's purpose in the arrangement; for like the other scientists he too fails to grasp this type of explanation. Instead, he says the soul is the same as the hot, the primary forms of the spherical atoms. As they are being mixed together by the atmosphere which squeezes them out, breathing comes to the rescue. For in the air there are numerous atoms of the type he calls mind and soul; accordingly by breathing in the air, these enter too, and ward off the expulsion by preventing the dispersion of the soul which is within the living being. Therefore, to live and to die is to inhale and to exhale; for when the pressure of the atmosphere dominates and the atoms can no longer enter to ward off expulsion because breath has ceased, then the animal dies; for death is the loss of such shaped particles from the body because of the atmospheric pressure. But the reason why everyone must die sometime—for death is not just a chance event, but is either natural owing to old age or unnatural because of violence—he has not made clear at all.

108. Luc., op. cit. III. 370. On this point, do not accept the theory of the revered Democritus that the body atoms and soul atoms alternate and so bind our members together.

109. AET., *op. cit.* IV. 7, 4. *Dox.* 393. Democritus and Epicurus hold [the soul] to be destructible, for it is destroyed along with the body.

112. ARIST., *Met.* T. 5. 1009 b 7. Furthermore, appearances to many of the other animals contradict the appearances of the same things to us, and even in the case of each individual a thing does not always seem the same in sensation. Which, then, are true or false is not clear; for one appearance is no more true than another, they are equally true. For this reason Democritus says, either nothing is true or at any rate we cannot distinguish what is. In general, then, they say the sensible appearance is necessarily true because they consider that knowledge is sensation and sensation is a [chemical] alteration.

113. PHILOP., *de Anima* p. 71, 19. (in Ar. A2, 404 a 25 sqq.) If they said mind moves the universe, how could they say that motion is a proper attribute of soul? Yes, he says, for they assumed mind and soul to be the same, just as Democritus did. True we have it nowhere expressly stated by them that mind and soul are the same, but he arrives at this conclusion by a syllogism. For Democritus, he says, evidently had this opinion, for he said plainly that truth and appearance are the same and there is no distinction between truth and the sensible phenomenon; for that which appears and seems to anyone is also true, just as Protagoras said, though if we judge by correct reason, they are different, sensation and imagination dealing with appearance, while mind deals with truth (cf. IV. B. a. 11). If, therefore, mind deals with truth and soul with appearance, and truth and opinion are identical, as Democritus teaches, then mind also is identical with soul. For as mind is related to truth so is soul related to appearance; hence also by alternation, as appearance is to truth so is soul to mind. If then, appearance and truth are the same, so are mind and soul the same.

115. AET., *op. cit.* IV. 10, 5. *Dox.* 399. How many senses are there? Democritus says that the senses are more numerous than the sensibles, but since the sensibles do not correspond [?] to the

number [of senses] we are not aware of the fact.[21] Because they are so fine, the mind cannot perceive them clearly, unless it makes a decided effort.

116. ——— IV. 10, 4. *Dox.* 399. Brutes, sages, and gods have more [than five] senses.

117. ——— IV. 4, 7. *Dox.* 390. Democritus says all things possess a soul of some sort, even corpses, because they clearly always share in a certain warmth and power of sensation, though the greater part disperses in air. ALEX., *Top.* 21, 21. Dead bodies perceive, as Democritus thought.

118. CIC., *Epist.* XV. 16, 1. (To Cassius). For I do not know how it happens that when I write something to you you seem to be present before me, and not in the sense of "phantoms of the imagination" as your new friends say who think that even "rational imagination" is produced by the spectres of Catius. For, lest you forget, the Epicurean, Catius, an Insubrian, who died recently, called those things spectres which Epicurus, and, still more remotely, Democritus called "phantoms." But even if these spectres can strike the eye because they collide with it without your permission, how they can strike the mind I cannot understand. You will have to teach me, when you arrive here safely, whether I can make your spectre strike me whenever I wish to think of you, and not only of you who dwell in my heart of hearts, but whether if I begin to think of the island of Britain, its phantom will fly to my soul.

119. ARIST., *de Sen.* 4. 442 a 29. Democritus and most of the scientists who treat of sensation make a most absurd blunder, for they make all sensible qualities tangible. Now if this were so it is clear that each of the other senses would be a kind of touch.

121. ——— 2. 438 a 5. When Democritus says that it is water [by which we see] he speaks well, but when he thinks that sight is the reflection, not so well. . . . However, in general,

---

[21] Cf. Lucretius, *de Rerum Natura* IV. 800.

it seems nothing much was made clear on the subjects of re-
fraction and reflections. And it is strange that he did not think
of asking why the eye alone can see, but not other things in
which the reflections appears.

122. ————, *de Anima* B. 7. 419 a 15. Democritus was not
correct in thinking that if the space between should become void,
it would be possible to see accurately whether there were an
ant in the sky.

123. ————, *de Gen. et Corr.* A. 2. 316 a 1. Color also does
not exist, he says, for a thing becomes colored by position.

124. AET., *op. cit.* I. 15, 11. *Dox.* 314. Those who say no atom
ever has any color, declare that all sensible qualities arise from
things which have no qualities, but which are apprehended by
reason.

125. ———— 15, 8. *Dox.* 314. Color does not exist by nature.
For the elements have no qualities, neither the solids nor the
void. What is composed of these, however, is colored by arrangement, proportion, and impulsion, that is, order, shape, and position; for appearances arise from these. Of these colors which are
due to appearance, there are four types, white, black, red, and
yellow.

126. ARIST., *de Sen.* 4. 442 b 11. For white is smooth, he
says, and black is rough. But flavors he reduces to shapes.

127. DIONYS. THRAC., *Schol.* p. 482, 13 Hildeg. Epicurus,
Democritus, and the Stoics assert that sound is a body.

128. AET., *op. cit.* IV. 19, 3. (*Dox.* 408; on sound, presumably
from Posidonius). Democritus says that the air, too, is broken
into bodies of similar shapes and rolls about with the fragments
of the sound. For "birds of a feather flock together" and "God always treats similars alike" (see below, IV. B. a. 164). For even
on the seashore the similar pebbles are seen in the same places,
here the spherical pebbles, there the long ones. In sifting also,
the same shapes collect in the same places so that the beans
and the pulse fall apart from each other. But someone might ask

the advocates of this view, how a few fragments of wind completely fill a theatre containing ten thousand men?

129. THEOPH., *de Caus. Plant.* VI. 1. 6. Democritus in assigning a shape to each quality made sweet to consist of fairly large, spherical atoms. To the quality sour he assigned very large, rough shapes with many angles and no curves. The sharp [in taste], as its name implies, he regarded as consisting of atoms sharp in mass, angular, crooked, thin, and unrounded. The pungent needs atoms which are thin, angular, and bent, but rounded also. Salt is angular, fairly large, twisted, although symmetrical. Bitter is rounded and smooth, unsymmetrical and small in size (cf. above, IV. B. 67; below, IV. B. 135).

132. ———— VI. 7, 2. Against Democritus one might raise the objection how a thing's taste could change. It must be in one of three ways: Either the shapes are remodeled so that what was crooked and angular becomes rounded, or, if all the shapes of sour and sharp and sweet are there together, some must be separated out (that is, the eternal realities which are prior to any specific taste as well as those peculiar to a given taste) while others remain, or, in the third place, some must go out and new ones come in. Since they cannot be remodeled (for an atom undergoes no modification), the second and third possibilities remain. But both are irrational, for it is necessary to explain further what causes these effects.

133. ———— *de Odor.* 64. Why indeed does Democritus explain flavors by a reference to taste, but does not similarly explain odors and colors by referring to their underlying senses? For he ought to derive them from the shapes.

135. ————, *de Sen.* 49 ff. *Dox.* 513.[22] Democritus in his account of sense perception does not make it entirely clear whether it is due to contrast or to similarity. For in so far as he ascribes the action of the senses to an alteration, it would seem to depend on contrast; for the like is never altered by the like.

---

[22] The translation is from George Malcolm Stratton's *Theophrastus and the Greek Physiological Psychology Before Aristotle* (New York, George Allen & Unwin Ltd., 1917), pp. 109 et seq. Stratton uses angular brackets, < >, to indicate where translation is non-literal.

On the other hand, sense perception would seem to depend on similarity in so far as he ascribes the perceptive process and, in a word, alteration to the fact that something is acted upon. For things that are not the same cannot be acted upon, he says; but even when things that are different do act, <their action is> not due to their difference but to the presence in them of something identical. Upon such matters as these he may consequently be understood either way. He now undertakes to discuss the <senses> each in turn.

(50) Vision he explains by the reflection <in the eye>, of which he gives a unique account. For the reflection does not arise immediately in the pupil. On the contrary, the air between the eye and the object of sight is compressed by the object and the visual organ, and thus becomes imprinted; since there is always an effluence of some kind arising from everything. Thereupon this imprinted air, because it is solid and is of a hue contrasting <with the pupil>, is reflected in the eyes, which are moist. A dense substance does not receive <this reflection>, but what is moist gives it admission. Moist eyes accordingly have a better power of vision than have hard eyes; provided their outer tunic to be exceedingly fine and close-knit, and the inner <tissues> be to the last degree spongy and free from dense and stubborn flesh, and free too, from thick oily moisture; and provided, also, the ducts connected with the eyes be straight and dry that they may "perfectly conform" to the entering imprints. For each knows best its kindred.

(51) Now in the first place this imprint upon the air is an absurdity. For the substance receiving such an imprint must have a certain consistence and not be "fragile"; even as Democritus himself, in illustrating the character of the "impression," says that "it is as if one were to take a mold in wax." In the second place, an object could make a better imprint upon water <than upon air>, since water is denser. While the theory would require us to see more distinctly <an object in water>, we actually see it less so. In general, why should Democritus assume this *imprint,* when in his discussion of forms he has supposed an *emanation* that conveys the object's form? For these images <due to emanation> would be reflected.

(52) But if such an imprint actually occurs and the air is molded like wax that is squeezed and pressed, how does the reflection <in the eye> come into existence, and what is its character? For the imprint here as in other cases will evidently face the object seen. But since this is so, it is impossible for a reflection facing us to arise unless this imprint is turned around. What would cause this reversal, and what the manner of its operation, ought, however, to be shown; for in no other way could vision come to pass. Moreover when several objects are seen in one and the same place, how can so many imprints be made upon the self-same air? And again, how could we possibly see each other? For the imprints would inevitably clash, since each of them would be facing <the person> from whom it sprung. All of which gives us pause.

(53) Furthermore, why does not each person see himself? For the imprints <from ourselves> would be reflected in our own eyes quite as they are in the eyes of our companions, especially if these imprints directly face us and if the effect here is the same as with an echo,—since Democritus says that <in the case of the echo> the vocal sound is reflected back to him who utters it. Indeed the whole idea of imprints made on the air is extravagant. For we should be forced to believe, from what he says, that all bodies are producing imprints <in the air>, and that great numbers of them are sending <their impressions> across one another's path,—a state of things at once embarrassing to sight and improbable on other grounds. If the impression moreover endures, we ought to see bodies that are out of sight and remote,—if not by night, at all events by day. And yet it would be but fair to assume that these imprints would persist at night, since then the air is so much cooler.

(54) Possibly, however, the reflection in the eye is caused by the sun, in sending light in upon the visual sense in the form of rays,—as Democritus seems to mean. For the idea that the sun "drives the air from itself and, in thus repelling, condenses it," as he says,—this is indefensible; since the sun by its very nature disperses the air. He is unfortunate, too, in regarding visual perception as a function not only of the eyes but of the rest of the body as well; for he says that the eye must contain

emptiness and moisture, in order that it may the more readily receive <impressions> and transmit <them> to the rest of the body. Farther, it is unreasonable to declare that what is "kindred" to the organ of sight is preëminently the object of vision, and yet to explain the reflection <in the eye> by color-contrast, on the ground that colors of the eyes' own hue are not reflected in them. And though he tries to explain how magnitudes and distances are reflected, he does not succeed. Thus Democritus in his endeavor to say something unique with regard to vision has bequeathed us the problem even farther from solution.

(55) His explanation of hearing is very much like others'. For the air, he holds, burst into the <aural> cavity and sets up a commotion. And while it gains entrance to the body in this same manner at every point, yet it enters more fully and freely through the ears because there it traverses the largest empty space, where least it "tarries." In consequence no part of the body perceives <sounds> save this <sensory region>. But once the commotion has been started within, it is "sent broadcast" by reason of its velocity; for sound, he holds, arises as the air is being condensed and is making forcible entry <into the body>. So he explains sensation within the body, just as he explains perception external to it, by contact.

(56) Hearing is keenest, he maintains, when the outer tunic is tough and the ducts are empty and unusually free from moisture and are well-bored in the rest of the body as well as in the head and ears; when, too, the bones are dense and the brain is well-tempered and that which surrounds it is exceedingly dry. For the sound thus enters compact, since it traverses a cavity large and dry and with good orifices, and swiftly the sound is "sent broadcast" impartially through the body and does not again escape.

(57) Such hazy definition is found in other writers as well. Yet it is absurd, while original, to say that sound permeates the entire body, and that when it has entered by the organ of hearing it is spread to every nook and cranny, as though perception here were due not to the ears but to the body entire. For if <the rest of the body> is somehow affected conjointly with the organ of hearing, it by no means follows that the per-

ception depends upon the <body as a whole>. For the <entire body> acts thus in the case of every sense; and not of the senses only, but of the soul as well.

Thus he accounts for sight and hearing. As for our other senses, his treatment hardly differs from that of the mass of writers.

(58) Concerning thought, Democritus says merely that "it arises when the soul's composition is duly proportioned." But if one becomes excessively hot or cold, he says, thinking is transformed; and it was for some such reason, the ancients well believed, that the mind became "deranged." Thus it is clear that he explains thought by the composition of the body,—a view perhaps not unreasonable in one who regards the soul itself as corporeal.

In sum and substance, then, these are the conclusions with regard to perception and thinking, which have come down to us from the earlier investigators.

[PART II. THE OBJECTS OF SENSE]

(59) What may be the intrinsic character and quality of each of the senses' *objects,* the writers other <than Democritus and Plato> fail to state. Of the objects perceived by touch, they discuss the heavy and the light, the warm and the cold, saying that the rare and fine is hot; the dense and thick, cold,—which is the distinction Anaxagoras makes between air and aether. And in general <they explain> weight and lightness by the same <causes>—that is to say, by "tendencies" respectively upward and downward; and they further agree that sound is a movement of the air, and that odor is an emanation. Empedocles discusses the colors also, and holds that white is composed of fire, and black of water. The other investigators confine themselves to the statement that white and black are the fundamental colors and that the rest are derived from these by mixture. For even Anaxagoras treats of the <colors> in only a loose and general way.

(60) Democritus and Plato, however, are the investigators who go into the question most fully, for they define the object of each sense; although <Plato> never robs these objects of their external reality, whereas Democritus reduces them one and all to effects in our sensuous faculty. Where the truth itself lies,

is not the question we are now discussing. Let our aim be rather to report the range of each author's treatment and the precise definitions he gives, stating by way of preface his general method.

Democritus has no uniform account of all <the sensory objects>: some he distinguishes by the size <of their atoms>, others by the shape, and a few by the <atomic> order and position. Plato, on the other hand, refers nearly all of them to effects in us, and to our perceptive faculty. Consequently each of these authors would seem to speak directly counter to his own postulate. (61) For the one of them, who would have sensory objects to be but effects in our perceptive faculty, actually describes a reality resident in the objects themselves; while the other, who attributes the objects' character to their own intrinsic being, ends by ascribing it to the passive change of our perceptive faculty.

Heaviness and lightness, to begin with, Democritus distinguishes in terms of size. For if we were to divide each substance into its <atomic> units, then even though these were to differ in shape, he contends, their reality would have as its standard <of weight> their size. In the case of compounds, on the contrary, a substance that contains more of void is lighter; one that contains less is heavier. This at least is what he says in certain passages. (62) In others, he holds that it is simply its fineness that makes a substance light.

And he speaks in almost the same terms of the hard and of the soft. For him anything is hard that is compact; it is soft if loose; while the different degrees, and so on, <of such qualities are also explained> in accord with this idea. Yet the position and grouping of the void spaces that make substances hard or soft differ in some respects from those that make them heavy or light. Consequently though iron is harder than lead, lead is heavier. For iron is of uneven composition, and its void spaces are many and of large extent, although here and there iron is condensed; but speaking generally it contains more void spaces <than does lead>. But lead, though it had less of the void, is of even and uniform composition throughout; and so, while heavier than iron, lead is softer. (63) Such is his account of the heavy, the light, the hard, and the soft.

As for the other sensory objects, he holds that none has an objective reality, but that one and all are effects in our sensuous faculty as it undergoes alteration,—and that from this faculty arises the inner presentation. For not even of heat or cold is there for him an objective reality; but configuration, in "undergoing a change," effects a qualitative alteration in us also; since what is massed together in anything prevails in it, and what is widely diffused is imperceptible.

Proof that <these sensory qualities> are not objectively real is found in the fact that they do not appear the same to all creatures: what is sweet to us is bitter to others, and to still others it is sour or pungent or astringent; and similarly of the other <sensory qualities>.

(64) Moreover Democritus holds that "men vary in composition" according to their condition and age; whence it is evident that a man's physical state accounts for his inner presentation. So we must in general, according to him, hold this view regarding sensory objects. Nevertheless here too, as elsewhere, he falls back upon <atomic> figures; yet he does not recount the shapes <of the atoms> of all <the sensory objects>, but centers his attention upon those of the tastes and of colors; and even of these, he describes with greater precision the <figures> connected with taste, although he refers the presentation itself to <the sentience of> man.

(65) What is "sour," he holds, is at once "angular" in its <atomic> figure and is "twisted," minute, and thin. By its keenness it swiftly slips in and penetrates everywhere, and by its roughness and "angularity" it draws the parts together and binds them. It also heats the body, in consequence, since it produces emptiness within; for whatever has most of empty space <amongst its atoms> is most heated.

"Sweet" consists of <atomic> figures that are rounded and not too small; wherefore it quite softens the body by its gentle action, and unhastening makes its way throughout. Yet it disturbs the other <savors>, for it slips in among the other <atomic figures> and "leads them from their accustomed ways" and

moistens them. And the <atomic figures> thus moistened and
disturbed in their arrangement flow into the belly, which is most
accessible, since empty space is there in greatest measure.

(66) The "astringent" taste, according to Democritus, is
derived from <atomic> figures that are large and of many
angles and are least rounded. For when these enter our bodies,
they clog and occlude the ducts and prevent <their contents>
from intermingling, and consequently stay the action of the
bowels.

"Bitter" is composed of small, smooth, round <atomic fig-
ures> whose surfaces moreover are furnished with hooks; as a
consequence bitter is sticky and viscous.

The taste derived from large <atoms> that are unrounded,
—some of them are "crooked," yet for the most part they are
regular—this taste is "saline"; <its atoms> therefore are not
provided with "many hooks"; (by "crooked" <atoms> he means
such as overlap and become entangled in one another). <The
saline quality is derived> from large <atoms> because salt
comes to the surface of bodies; while if <its atoms> were small
and were battered against the surrounding <particles>, they
would mingle with the whole; from unrounded <atoms>, because what is saline is rough while the rounded is smooth; from
<atoms> that are not "crooked," because these do not "stick
to one another," and in consequence they "crumble apart."

(67) The "pungent" savor according to him is small, round,
and angular, but not irregular. Having many angles, this taste
heats and melts by reason of its roughness, because it is small,
round, and angular; for the angular too has this character.

In a like manner he accounts for all the other effects of
each <savor> by referring them to figures. But no one of all
these figures is present, he holds, pure and without admixture
of the others; on the contrary, there is a multitude of them in
each savor, and the self-same taste includes figures that are
smooth, rough, round, sharp, and so on. The preponderant figure, however, exerts the most influence upon the faculty of
sense and determines the <savor's> effect; and, moreover, the
condition in which it finds <us influences the result>. For it
makes a great difference <what our condition is>, inasmuch as

the same substance at times causes opposite feeling, and opposite substances cause the same feeling. (68) Such is Democritus's account of tastes.

In the first place, it might seem odd not to assign causes to all <sensory qualities> according to a uniform principle, but to explain heaviness and lightness, softness and hardness, by the fact that <the atoms> are large or small, and rare or dense, while heat and cold and the rest are explained by the figures <of the atoms>. In the second place, <it seems strange> to ascribe a resident and objective reality to the qualities heavy, light, hard, and soft (for the properties large and small, dense and rare are not relative to something other than <the substance itself>), and then to make heat, cold, and the rest entirely relative to sense, and this though he repeatedly says that the figure of heat is spherical.

(69) But the one glaring inconsistency running through the whole account is, that he no sooner declares <savors> to be subjective effects in sense than he distinguishes them by their figures; and he points out that the same substance appears bitter to some persons and sweet to others and has still a third quality for some other group. For the figure cannot possibly be a subjective effect, nor can one and the same figure be spherical for certain persons and of another shape for others (although such an assumption were perhaps inevitable if what is sweet for some is bitter for others), nor can the shapes <of atoms> change according to differences of state in us. And, in general, the <atomic> figure has been absolute existence, while sweetness and the sensuous object generally, as he says is relative and existent in something beyond itself.

It is strange, furthermore, to insist that to all those who perceive the same things there comes the same subjective appearance, and to examine the true character of these things, when he has already said that to persons in different conditions there come different subjective appearances, and again that no one attains the truth of things better than does another. (70) For it is probable that <in the attainment of truth> the better surpasses the worse, and the well the sick; since the <better and healthier> are more in accord with the reality of things.

But if there be no objective reality in sensory objects because they do not appear the same to all, there is manifestly none
in animals or other bodies; for men disagree about these things,
too. And yet even if the cause of sweet and bitter is not the same
for us all, at least the bitterness and sweetness appear the same
for all. Democritus himself seems a witness to this; for how
could that which is bitter for us be sweet or astringent for others,
unless these very qualities had a definite nature? (71) This he
makes even more explicit in those passages where he says that
the being of anything and the process by which it originated are
real; and particularly when he says of bitter, that "<here we>
have a portion of understanding." Upon such a showing, consequently, there would seem to be a general contradiction in his
refusal to ascribe any objective reality to sensory objects. But
there is, besides, the special contradiction indicated above, when
he assigns a figure to the bitter, as he does to the other <savors>,
and yet says that <the bitter> has no objective reality. For either
no <sensory object> has external reality, or else these tastes have
such reality, since a common cause underlies them.

Moreover both heat and cold, which are supposed to be the
primal source of things, probably have some objective reality;
but if these, then the others also. He does, however, ascribe a
certain substantive being to the qualities hard and soft, and heavy
and light;—although in spite of this they seem to be counted
<among the qualities> relative to us;—but he does not ascribe
such substantive being to heat, and cold, and the rest. And yet,
as he distinguishes the heavy and the light by the size <of their
atoms>, he ought to hold that all simple <bodies> have an impulse to move in the same direction; and consequently they would
be of one and the same "matter" and would have a common
nature. (72) Yet upon such questions he seems to have followed
those who make thought entirely a matter of change, a doctrine
from hoary antiquity; since all the ancients, whether poets or
sages, represented thought as dependent upon <bodily> disposition.

But in assigning an <atomic> figure to each of the savors,
Democritus has made this figure correspond to the effect which
the savor produces in our feelings. The <figure therefore should

be deduced>, not from the <external savors> merely, but from
our sense organs as well; above all, if these savors themselves are
but subjective effects in these sense-organs. A spherical figure
does not have the same "power" in every case, nor does any
other figure; <a savor> must consequently be characterized with
reference to the substrate affected, by stating whether it is composed of what is like or unlike <the substance of the sense or-
gan>, and how the change in the sensuous faculty comes to pass.
And furthermore there should be offered an explanation applicable alike to all the sensory qualities that arise by touch, and not
merely to those involved in taste. And yet these qualities <aris-
ing by touch> either show some difference when compared with
savors—a difference which he should make clear—or else he has
neglected to tell us what is the common explanation that here is
possible.

(73) The simple colors, he says, are four. What is smooth
is white; since what neither is rough nor casts shadows nor is
hard to penetrate,—all such substances are brilliant. But brilliant substances must also have open passages and be trans-
lucent. Now white substances that are hard have the structure
just described,—for instance, the inner surface of cockle shells;
for the substance here would be shadowless, "gleaming," and
with straight passages. But the white substances that are loose
and friable are composed of round particles, yet with these
placed oblique to one another and oblique in their conjunction
by pairs, while the arrangement as a whole is uniform in the
extreme. With such a structure these substances are loose because <their particles are> in contact only over a small <por-
tion of their surface>; friable, because their composition is so
uniform; shadowless, because they are smooth and flat. But
those substances are whiter, compared with one another, in
which the figures are more exactly as described above and are
freer from admixture with other figures and whose order and
position more nearly conform to the given description. From
such figures, then, is white derived.

(74) Black is composed of figures the very opposite <to
those of white>,—figures rough, irregular, and differing from
one another. For these cast shadows, and the passages amongst

them are not straight nor easy to thread. Their effluences, too, are sluggish and confused; for the character of the effluence also makes a difference in the inner presentation, as this emanation is changed by its retention of air.

(75) Red is composed of figures such as enter into heat, save that those of red are larger. For if the aggregations be larger although the figures are the same, they produce the quality of redness rather <than of heat>. Evidence that redness is derived from such <figures> is found in the fact that we redden as we become heated, as do other things placed in the fire until they have a fiery color. Those substances are redder that are composed of large figures—for example, the flame and coals of green wood <are redder> than those of dry. And iron, too, and other things placed in fire <become redder>. Those are most luminous, however, that contain the most fire and the subtilest, while those are redder that have coarser <fire> and less of it. Redder things, accordingly, are not so hot; for what is subtile is hot.

Green is composed of both the solid and the void,— the hue varying with the position and order of these constituents.

(76) Such are the figures which the simple colors possess; and each of these colors is the purer the less the admixture of other figures. The other colors are derived from these by mixture.

Golden and copper-color and all such tones, for instance, come from white and red, their brilliance being derived from the white, their ruddiness from the red component; for in combination the red sinks into the empty spaces of the white. Now if green be added to white and red, there results the most beautiful color; but the green component must be small, for any large admixture would not comport with the union of white with red. The tint will vary according to the amount <of green> that is introduced.

(77) Crimson comes from white, black, and red,—the largest "portion" being red, that of black small, and of white midway; for thus it makes an appearance delightful to the sense. That black and red are present in it is patent to the eye: its brilliance and lustre testify to the presence of white; for white produces such effects.

Woad hue is composed of deep black and golden green, but with the major "portion" black. Leek green is of crimson and woad, or of golden green and purplish. . . . For sulphur color is of this character, with a dash of brilliance. Indigo is a mixture of woad and fiery red, with round figures and figures needle-shaped to give a gleam to the color's darkness.

(78) Brown is derived from golden green and deep blue; but if more of the golden green be mixed, flame-color is the result; for the blackness is expelled because the <golden green> is shadowless. And red, too, when mixed with white, gives almost a "pure" golden green, and not a black; which accounts for the fact that plants at first are of such a green before there is a heating and dispersion.

This completes the tale of colors he recounts; although he holds that the colors, like the savors, are endless in number according to their combinations,—according as we remove some and add others and "combine" them in varying proportion. For no one of these colors would be the same as another.

(79) But first of all, his increase of the number of primaries presents a difficulty; for the other investigators propose white and black as the only simple colors. And in the second place, there is a difficulty when he fails to assign one and the same shape to all kinds of white, but attributes a different shape to the "hard" whites from that which he ascribes to the whites of "loose texture." For it is improbable that <the whiteness> would have a different cause in substances differing merely in their tactile character. And, too, the cause of the difference <between white and black> would not lie in the figure <of the constituent particles>, but in their position. For round figures, and indeed every kind of figure whatever, can cast shadows upon one another. And this is evident, for Democritus himself gives this reason for the smooth things that look black; for they appear thus, he holds, because they have the internal combination and arrangement characteristic of black. And again, <in giving his reason> for the white things that are rough; these are of large particles, he holds, and their junctions are not rounded off but are "battlemented," and the shapes of the figures are broken, like the earthworks in the approach to a city's wall. For such an ar-

rangement, he says, throws no shadow, and brilliance is not
hindered.

(80) Moreover, how can he say that the whiteness of certain creatures becomes black if they be so placed that shadows
are cast? He seems really to be talking about the nature of transparency and brilliance, rather than of whiteness. For to be easily
seen through and to have passages that do not run zig-zag are
features of transparency; but how many transparent substances
are white? And further, to assume straight passages in substances
that are white, and passages zig-zag in those that are black, implies that the very structure of the object enters <our sense
organ>. Vision, he says is due to an emanation and to the reflection in the organ of sight. But if this be so, what difference does
it make whether the passages <in the object> lie end to end or
zig-zag? Nor is it easy to believe that an emanation can by any
possibility arise from the void. The cause of this, therefore,
should be stated. For he seems to derive whiteness from light
or something else; and accordingly offers the grossness of the air
as also a reason why things seem dark.

(81) His explanation of black, farther, is not easy to comprehend; for a shadow is (in his theory) something black, and
at the same time it is an obscuration of what is white; white is
therefore essentially prior <to black>. Yet with this, he attributes
<black> not only to shading but to the grossness of the air and
of the entering emanation, as well as to disturbance of the eye.
But whether these arise from mere opacity, or from some other
source, and if so, what the character <of this farther source may
be>, he does not reveal.

(82) It is singular, also, to assign no shape to green but to
constitute it merely of the solid and the void. For these are present in all things, of whatsoever figures they are composed. He
should have given some distinctive <figure> to green, as he has
to the other colors. And if he holds <green> to be the opposite
of red, as black is of white, it ought to have an opposite shape;
but if in his view it is not the opposite, this itself would surprise
us that he does not regard his first principles as opposites, for
that is the universally accepted doctrine. Most of all, though, he
should have determined with accuracy which colors are simple,

and why some colors are compounded and others not; for there is the gravest difficulty with regard to the first principles. Yet this would doubtless prove a difficult task. For if one could say, of tastes for example, which of them are simple, there would be more in what one said <than is found in Democritus upon them>. As for smell, he says nothing definite except that something subtile emanating from heavy substances is the cause of odor. But what its character is, and by what this process is effected—which is perhaps the most important point of all,—on this we have never a word. There are some things of this kind, then, that Democritus has neglected.

137. Cic., *de Div.* II. 58, 120. Do we, therefore, believe that during sleep our minds move themselves, or as Democritus thought, that they are agitated by external and adventitious appearances?

138. ———— I. 3, 5. *Dox.* 224. Although . . . that weighty authority Democritus had in many passages approved of premonitions of future events, Dicaiarchus the Peripatetic held to premonitions in dreams and frenzies but rejected other types. 57, 131. [from Posidonius] Democritus, however, considered that the ancients wisely arranged for the inspection of sacrifices, whose condition and color give evidence of health or sickness and sometimes even of the future sterility or fertility of the fields.

139. Cens., *de Die.* 4, 9. Democritus the Abderite believed the first men were begotten of water and slime. Aet., *op. cit.* V. 19, 6. Democritus held that animals were first produced by the conjunction of jointless members, and moisture gave them life. Lact., *Inst. Div.* VII. 7, 9. The Stoics say that the world and all it contains were made for man's sake; and our Holy Scriptures teach the same thing. Democritus, therefore, erred when he thought that they emerged from the ground like worms, without a Maker, and without any reason.

140. Aet., *op. cit.* V. 4, 3. *Dox.* 417/8. Strato and Democritus say the power also [not merely the matter of the seed] is a body, for it is wind-like.

141. ——— 3, 6. *Dox.* 417. According to Democritus, [seed originates] from bodies as a whole and especially from the most important parts, such as the bones, the flesh, and the sinews.

143. Arist., *de Gen. Anima.* Δ 1. 764 a 6. Democritus of Abdera holds that the distinction between male and female takes place in the womb, not however as the result of heat and cold, but it depends on which parent furnishes the dominant seed, or more exactly that "chromosome" which originates in the organs which differentiate male from female. Cens., *op. cit.* 6, 5. Whichever parent's principle first occupies the spot, that one's nature, Democritus reports, is reproduced. Aet., *op. cit.* V. 7, 6. *Dox.* 420. The common parts arise from either one as it may happen, but the particularizing characteristics come from the dominant strain.

144. Arist., *de Gen. Anima.* B. 4. 740 a 33. The veins join on to the womb like roots through which the foetus receives nourishment. For this reason, the living thing remains in the womb, but not as Democritus says, so the parts may be molded to the parts of the womb. 7. 746 a 19. Those who say children are nourished in the womb by sucking bits of flesh are in error. Aet., *op. cit.* V. 16, 1. *Dox.* 426. Democritus and Epicurus say the foetus is nourished in the womb through its mouth. And so immediately when it is born, its mouth is put to the breast; for there are in the womb nipples and mouths by which it is nourished.

145. Arist., *de Gen. Anima.* B. 4. 740 a 13. All who like Democritus assert, the external parts of living beings are first developed, and the internal later, are in error. Cens., *op. cit.* 6, 1. Democritus says the belly and the head [come first], which have more of the void in them [than any other part].

146. Arist., *de Gen. Anima.* Δ 4. 769 b 30. Democritus said monstrosities occur because a prior fertilization mixes with a later. And when the later emission enters the womb the parts grow confusedly together. In the case of birds, since the fertilization occurs quickly, he says the eggs are always confused in their color, [text possibly corrupt].

147. ——— E. 8. 788 b 9. Democritus also has treated of these problems [teeth] . . . for he says the first set fall out because they grow too soon; for they grow according to nature when they are in their prime so to speak. And he explains their too early arrival as due to suckling.

148. ———, *de Part. Anim.* T. 4. 665 a 30. Bloodless animals have no viscera. And Democritus seems to have been mistaken in this respect, if indeed he thought they were indiscernible because the bloodless animals are so small.

149. ———, *de Gen. Anima.* B. 8. 747 a 29. For Democritus says the [genital] passages in mules are destroyed in the embryo because the process does not begin with animals of the same species.

150. [ARIST.] *Hist. Anim.* I. 39. 623 a 30. Spiders as soon as they are hatched can spin a web, not from within as if it were an excrement as Democritus says, but from the body like bark [of trees] or like animals which shed their hair or bristles, such as porcupines.

151. AEL., *A. N.* XII 16. Democritus says that pigs and dogs have large litters and gives the explanation that they have several wombs or receptacles for semen. The semen of one emission does not fill them all, but these animals repeat coitus two or three times so that the series fills the receptacles. The mule, he says, does not bear, for its womb, unlike that of other animals and so differently shaped, cannot receive seed; for the mule is not a product of nature, but rather the stratagem and contrivance of human forethought and adulterous daring, so to speak. "It seems to me—he said—an ass by chance forcibly impregnated a horse, and when men learned of it they made this form of fertilization customary." And those who know about these unions say that the very large Libyan asses cover the mare when shorn of her hair, for she who has the glory of her hair would not submit to such a mate.

152. ——— XII 17. Miscarriages, says Democritus, are more likely in southern climates than in the north. This is

plausible because the bodies of pregnant animals become flabby on account of the warmth and are distended. And when the body loosens up and does not fit well, the embryo also shifts its position, and as its temperature rises it slips from side to side and a miscarriage is easy. But if there are cold winds and icy weather, the embryo becomes solid, hard to move, and is not tossed about as by the waves of the sea. Such embryos, undisturbed as in a calm, become strong and healthy and await the natural time of birth. And so the Abderite concludes, "In cold weather it holds together but in hot there is often an abortion." And he says the veins and joints necessarily distend when there is too much heat.

160. Cic., *Tusc.* I. 34, 82. For assume that the soul is destroyed like the body. Is there, then, any pain or any sensation at all in the body after death? No one says there is, although Epicurus charges it against Democritus. Democritus' disciples, however, deny it. Tertul., *de An.* 51. Plato in the *Republic*, however, cites against this view the fact of the corpse of someone unburied for a long time, preserved without any deterioration in consequence of the inseparability of the soul. To this Democritus adds the growth of nails and hair a long time after burial. Cel., *de Med.* II. 6. Moreover the justly famed Democritus has maintained that even when life has ceased there are no certain symptoms of death in which physicians put their trust. Therefore he did not admit that there are any certain signs of future death.

162. Theoph., *de Caus. Plant.* II. 11, 7 *et sq.* When Democritus explains that straight plants bloom and die sooner than crooked ones because of the same necessary processes (for the nourishment on which the blossom and fruit depend is more quickly diffused through the straight plant, while in the other case more slowly because its [tracheal] tubes are constricted, and the roots themselves get the benefit, for the roots of these plants are both long and thick) he does not seem to be correct. (8) For he says that the roots of the straight plants are weak and for a double reason they break and the plant is destroyed; for both cold and heat descend quickly from the top to the roots because of the easy progress, and since the roots are weak they

cannot withstand the shock. In general many plants of this type begin to age from the bottom on account of the weakness of their roots. And further, the aerial parts because they are so slim are twisted by the winds and so disturb the roots. This results in harm and breakage and so decay attacks the whole tree. This, at any rate, is his account of the matter.

165. ALEX., *Quaest.* II. 23. (Why the lodestone attracts iron) [II 72, 82 Bruns] Democritus himself asserts that emanations arise and that like moves toward like, although everything moves toward the void also. On this basis he holds that the magnet and the iron are composed of similar atoms, the magnet however of finer atoms, more widely spaced, and inclosing more void than the iron. Therefore, since [its atoms] are more easily moved, they move faster to the iron (for motion proceeds toward the like), and entering the pores of the iron they set its component bodies in motion by slipping through them on account of their fineness. The bodies so set in motion leave the iron as an efflux and move toward the magnet, both because of the similarity in particles and because the magnet has more void. Then by reason of the wholesale egress of the bodies and their motion, the iron itself follows them and is also carried to the magnet. But the magnet does not move toward the iron because the iron does not have as many void spaces as the magnet. But granted that iron and lodestone are composed of like particles, how about amber and chaff? When anyone offers the same explanation for this case also, it must be recalled that amber attracts many things. Now if amber is composed of the same particles as all these, then the latter also are composed of similar particles and should attract each other.

169. [4N] CIC., *de Fin.* V. 8, 23. But the security of Democritus which is a sort of tranquillity of mind, which he has named Cheerfulness, should have been barred from this discussion because that very tranquillity of mind is itself the blessed life. 29, 87. Democritus—whether it is true or false we shall not inquire —is said to have put out his own eyes, presumably in order that his mind should be least distracted from contemplation. He neglected his inheritance, left his fields uncultivated, and

what else could he have been seeking than the blessed life? And even if he placed that life in knowing things, none the less from his investigations of nature he wished a good mind to result. For he called Cheerfulness, and often Confidence, that is a mind devoid of fear, the highest good. But though this is clear enough, it is not yet complete; for he said little about virtue, and that little was not so clear.

170. CLEM., *Strom.* II. 138 p. 503 P. [170 N.] Democritus begs to be excused from marriage and from the procreation of children because of their many annoyances and their distractions from more necessary matters. Epicurus also agrees with him.

a. The fragments.[23]

3. PLUT., *de Tranqu. An.* 2. STOB., *Flor.* IV. 103, 25. He that would be cheerful should not do too many things, either as a private individual or as a citizen, nor should the things which he chooses to do lie beyond his power and capacity, but he should take such care that even when luck goes his way and to all appearances is leading him on to more, he will disregard her and not attempt more than he is able. For sufficiency is safer than superfluity.

6. SEXT. EMP., *op. cit.* VII. 137. (In the book *On Ideas* he says:) Man must know by this rule, that he is far removed from truth.

7. (And again:) And this argument too makes it clear that we really know nothing about anything, but each one's opinion is the flow toward him [of sense images.]

8. (And again:) Although it will be clear that we are at a loss how to know what each thing really is.

9. ———, VII. 135. (But Democritus at times abolishes the things which appear to the senses and says that none of them appear really, but only seem to do so, and the only things which really exist are the atoms and the void. For he says,) By conven-

---

[23] Words enclosed in parentheses are context; words not so enclosed are quotation.

tion there is sweet; by convention, bitter; by convention, hot; by convention, cold; by convention, color; but in truth there exist atoms and void.

[Fr. 125 has the same quotation and adds] (He pictures the sensations speaking to reason as follows:) Miserable mind, will you reject us after receiving the grounds of belief from us? That rejection is ruin for you.

[Continuing Fr. 9.] (which means: Though Sense objects are thought to exist, they do not exist in truth, but only atoms and void. And in his *Verifications,* while professing to entrust the senses with the power of establishing belief, none the less we find that he condemns them. For he says:) We really perceive nothing strictly true, but only what changes with the condition of our body and the influences coming toward it or resisting it.

10. (And again he says:) It has now been truly shown in many ways that we do not perceive what each thing is or is not.

11. ——, VII. 138. [following B. 8.] (In *The Canons* he says there are two forms of knowledge, one through sensations, and one through reason. The one through reason he calls legitimate, testifying to its credibility in the discrimination of truth, but the one through sensations he names obscure, depriving it of inerrancy in the determination of truth. And he says verbatim:) There are two forms of knowledge, one legitimate, one obscure; the following all belong to the obscure form, sight, hearing, smell, taste, and touch. The other is legitimate, and is quite different from this. (Then, preferring the legitimate to the obscure he adds:) When the obscure can no longer see anything smaller, or hear or smell or taste or perceive by touch, and when into the more delicate [one is required to investigate, then there follows legitimate knowledge, which has a more delicate instrument for knowing.]

12.[24] CENS., *op. cit.* 18, 8. The [world] year of Philolaus . . . and Democritus comprises eighty-two years with twenty-eight intercalary [months].

[24] Nothing verbatim in 12, 14, 15, 26, 34.

14.1. Vɪᴛ., *de Arch.* IX. 6, 3. Concerning natural phenomena Thales of Miletus, Anaxagoras of Clazomenae, Pythagoras of Samos, Xenophon of Colophon, and Democritus of Abdera, left [carefully] thought-out explanations according to which these phenomena are governed by nature whatever effects they may have. Following their discoveries Eudoxus, Euctemon, Callippus, Meto, Philippus, Hipparchus, Aratus, and others, discovered through the technique of astronomical tables the rising and setting of the stars and the signs of the seasons and handed down the explanations to posterity. IX. 5, 4. I have explained in accordance with the views of the scientist Democritus the shapes and figures of the constellations designed by nature and the divine mind, or rather only those whose rising and setting we can observe and watch with our own eyes.

14.2. Eᴜᴅᴏx., *Ars. Astron.* col. 22, 21 [p. 25 Blass]. For Eudoxus and Democritus the winter solstice occurs sometimes on the twentieth, sometimes on the nineteenth of Athyr. 23, 3. From the autumnal equinox to the winter solstice is by Eudoxus' calculation 92 days; Democritus makes it 91. From the winter solstice to the spring equinox, both Eudoxus and Democritus count 91 days, Euctemon 92.

14.3. [Gᴇᴍɪɴ.] *Isag.* (Calendar perhaps from second century ʙ.ᴄ.) p. 218, 14 Mainit. (Scorpio) On the fourth day, says Democritus, the Pleiades set at daybreak; winter winds for the most part are wont to blow and cold and frost; and the trees begin to shed their leaves in abundance. p. 220, 5. On the thirteenth, says Democritus, Lyra rises with the sun; and the air is usually cold. p. 222, 9. (Sagittarius) On the sixteenth, says Democritus, Aquila rises with the sun, and is generally indicative of thunder and storms and water or winds or usually both. p. 226, 4. On the sixteenth, says Democritus, the northwest winds begin to blow and continue. On the forty-third day from the solstice. p. 226, 15. (Pisces) On the fourth, says Democritus, there commence the beautiful [unstable] days called halcyon. p. 226, 23. On the fourteenth, says Democritus, the cold winds blow, the so-called "bird-winds" for nine days at most. p. 228, 23.

(Aries) Democritus says the Pleiades disappear at sunrise, and remain invisible for forty nights.

15. AGATH., *Comp. Geo.* I. 1, 2. . . . The ancients believed the earth to be round and placed Greece as its center and Delphi at the center of Greece; for it was its navel. Democritus, a man of wide experience, first perceived that the earth is oblong in a ratio of three to two. With him Dicaiarchus the Peripatetic also agrees.

26. PROC., *in Crat.* 16 p. 6 Boiss. Pythagoras and Epicurus were of the opinion of Cratylus while Democritus and Aristotle held with Hermogenes.

. . . p. 7. In the expression "the Giver of names" [Pythagoras] hinted at the soul, which derives from mind. Things themselves are not primary realities as is the mind, and [the soul] has likenesses of them and essential, comprehensive notions like images of the realities, such as names which are imitations of the intellectual forms, the numbers. Accordingly, the being of everything derives from the self-conscious and wise mind, but names derive from soul, which imitates mind. Therefore, says Pythagoras, it is not any chance person who can give names to things, but only he who sees mind and the nature of things. Names, therefore, exist by nature. But Democritus by four lines of argument develops the conclusion that names are conventional. First, equivocation, where different things are called by the same name, hence the name is not by nature. Second synonymy. For if different names apply to one and the same thing, they would also apply to each other which is impossible. Third, the exchange of names; for if names were by nature, why did we call Aristocles Plato and Tyrtamus Theophrastus? Fourth, missing derivatives; for why is it that the verb "to think" comes from the noun "thought," while from the noun "justice" no verb is derived? Hence names exist by chance and not by nature. Democritus himself calls the first argument, ambiloquy; the second, equipollence; [the third, metonymy;] the fourth, nonymy.

31. CLEM., *Paed.* I. 6 p. 100 P. Medicine heals the diseases

of the body, according to Democritus, but wisdom frees the soul of passions.

34. DAVID, *Prol.* 38, 14 Busse. (As in the universe we see that one class, the deities, only rules, another class, mankind, both rules and is ruled—for men are ruled by the gods and rule the irrational animals—and another class, the irrational animals, is only ruled, so in the same manner these levels, according to Democritus, are found in) man who is a microcosm. (There is his reason which only rules, his passion which both rules and is ruled, and his appetites which are ruled only.) GAL., *de Usu. Partium* III. 241. (The ancients who were competent in science say that a living being is like a universe in miniature.)

THE GOLDEN MAXIMS.[25]

35. If anyone pay intelligent attention to these my maxims, many matters worthy of a good man shall he engage in, and many ignoble matters shall he escape.

37. He that chooses the goods of the soul chooses the more divine; he that chooses those of the body, chooses human goods.

38. It is good to prevent the wrongdoer, but at least not to join with him.

39. One ought to be good, or pretend to be.

40. Neither their bodies nor their wealth make men happy, but rectitude and much contemplation.

41. Not from fear, but from duty abstain from sins.

42. It is a great thing in misfortunes to think as one ought.

43. Repentance for shameful deeds is the salvation of life.

44. Speak true, not much.

45. He who wrongs is more wretched than he who is wronged.

46. Greatness of soul is to bear trouble patiently.

[25] The translation of these short fragments was taken from the handwritten notes of the late Professor William Romaine Newbold.

47. To yield to law, to the ruler, and to the wisest is becoming.

48. The good man does not value the fault-finding of the wicked.

49. It is hard to be governed by a worse man.

50. He that always yields to money could never be just.

51. Speech [or reason] often proves more persuasive than gold.

52. With one that fancies he has understanding, admonition is wasted toil.

53. Many that have learned no reason live reasonably; but many who act most disgracefully give the best of reasons.

54. Fools learn by misfortune.

65. One should cultivate much understanding, not much knowing.

66. To deliberate before one's acts, is better than to repent.

67. Do not trust all men, but those approved; the former is silly, the latter sensible.

69. For all men the good and the true are the same, but the pleasant varies.

70. Immoderate desire marks the child, not the man.

71. Untimely pleasures beget disgust.

72. Excessive desires for anything blind the soul to aught else.

73. Excessively to pursue the beautiful is righteous love.

74. Accept no pleasure that profits not.

75. It is better for the foolish to be ruled than to rule.

77. Glory and wealth without wisdom are not safe possessions.

78. To accumulate wealth is not useless, but nothing is worse than to do so by injustice.

83. The cause of sin is ignorance of the better.

84. Whoever commits disgraceful deeds should be ashamed first before himself.

85. He that contradicts and keeps on talking is unfitted to learn what he should.

86. To do all the talking and not to be willing to hear anything is greediness.

87. One should watch the bad man lest he seize his opportunity.

88. The envious man inflicts pain on himself as though he were an enemy.

89. The enemy is, not he that injures, but he that wants to.

90. The enmity of one's kinfolk is far worse than that of strangers.

91. Be not suspicious of everyone, but careful and wary.

92. One should accept favors with the expectation of returning them many fold.

93. When conferring a favor, keep your eye on the recipient lest he be a cheat who will requite good with evil.

96. Benevolent is, not he that looks to the return, but he that wills to do good.

102. In everything the fair is right; excess and deficiency please me not.

109. Censorious people are not adapted to friendship.

112. It is characteristic of a divine mind always to think on something beautiful.

118. DIONYS. quoted by EUS., *P.E.* XIV. 27, 4. (Democritus himself, so they tell us, said) I would rather discover one single

demonstration than rule over the Persians. (And that too though his demonstrations are vain and are no demonstrations at all because he starts from an empty principle and an erroneous hypothesis, and does not see the root of the matter and the common necessity of the nature of reality, but considers the observation of vain and random occurrences to be the highest wisdom; so he enthrones Luck as queen of divine things and of things in general, declaring that all things occur by her command; but he denies that she governs the lives of men, and charges those who worship her with ignorance.) [The fifth paragraph continues:]

119. ———— 5. (He commences his advice by saying) Men have devised the idol Luck as a cloak for their want of understanding. (For Luck naturally contends against counsel, and they say it rules over wisdom with great enmity, or rather they wholly suppress and annihilate wisdom and substitute luck, for wisdom, they say, is not lucky, but they celebrate luck as most wise.) STOB., op cit. II. 8, 16. Men have devised the idol Luck as a cloak for their lack of counsel. For luck opposes wisdom very little; most of life's tangles a keen and intelligent penetration straightens out.

125. Cf. IV. B. a. 9.

142. OLYMP., in Plat. Phil. 2, p. 242 Stallb. (Why does Socrates so greatly reverence the names of the gods? Is it because tradition has consecrated the proper names to the proper persons and it is unreasonable to change the unchangeable, or is it because the names belong to them by nature according to the argument in the Cratylus, or because they also are) vocal images of the gods (as Democritus says)? HIER., in Pyth. c. Aur. 25. (The name of Zeus is a symbol and image in sound of the creative reality. For those who first gave names to things did, in the excellence of their wisdom, like great sculptors in their statues, show forth in the names the powers of the things named.)

145. PLUT., de Puer. Ed. 14, p. 9. Language is the shadow of action.

146. ———, *de Prof. in Virt.* 10, p. 81. (Reason is rooted and nourished within oneself and according to Democritus) it habituates itself to derive its pleasures from itself.

149. ———, *Anim. an Corp.* 2, p. 500. (Let us say to ourselves that there are many diseases and passions, sir, which your body produces naturally of itself, and there are also many which attack it from without.) But if you will examine yourself from within you will discover a variegated and well stacked storehouse and treasury of evils, (as Democritus says, not flowing in from without, but having its own inherent, congenital sources produced by a total depravity abundant in passions.)

155. ———, *de Com. Not.* 39, p. 1079 e. (Again, therefore, see how he [Chrysippus] replied to Democritus who inquired naturally and wisely:) If a cone is cut by a plane parallel to its base, what must we think of the surfaces of the segments, are they equal or unequal? If they are unequal, the cone will be uneven since it will get step-like incisions or roughnesses. But if they are equal, the segments will be equal and the cone will seem to have the characteristics of a cylinder, for it will be composed of equal, not unequal, circles, which is most absurd.

156. ———, *Adv. Colot.* 4, p. 1108 f. ([Colotes] attacks [Democritus] because by saying each thing is no more this than that, he has confused life. But Democritus is so far removed from thinking that each thing is no more this than that, that he has attacked and written many persuasive arguments against the sophist Protagoras who did hold the principle under discussion. Colotes had never become acquainted with these things even in a dream and misunderstood the man's statement in which it is set forth that) Entity exists no more truly than non-entity. (By entity he means body and by non-entity the void, because the void too has a sort of nature and peculiar reality.)

159. ———, *Fragm. de Lib. et Aegr.* 2. (This seems to be an old law-suit between the body and the soul with respect to the passions. And Democritus putting the blame upon the soul for the misery of the body says:) If the body should bring the soul to trial for all the evils and miseries it has suffered throughout

life, and should itself be the judge of the indictment, it would gladly convict the soul because sometimes it destroyed the body through carelessness and broke it by drunkenness, and at other times it shattered and debauched it through lust, just as one might harshly accuse the user of an instrument or vessel which was left in poor condition.

160. PORPH., *de Abst.* IV. 21. (The evil, foolish, intemperate, and impious life, Democritus calls) not an evil life but a long extended death.

164. SEXT. EMP., *op. cit.* VII. 116. (The ancient . . . opinion that like can know like . . . (117) But Democritus states the argument with reference both to living and to inanimate objects:) Animals—he says—herd together with those of the same species, as pigeons with pigeons and cranes with cranes, and so on with the other irrational creatures also. It is the same with inanimate things as well, as can be seen in the case of seeds being sifted and of pebbles on the sea shore; for in the first case the whirling of the sieve separates out and heaps lentils with lentils and barley with barley and wheat with wheat, and in the second case the motion of the waves pushes the long stones into the same place with the long stones and the round with the round, as if the similarity of things in these cases possessed a sort of attractive power. (However, so Democritus says.)

165. ———— VII. 265. (Democritus whose voice has been compared to the voice of God says) the following things about everything [opening phrase of the *Lesser Cosmology?*] (and attempted to define the concept [of humanity] but could do no more than make the clumsy assertion:) Man is what we all know. CIC., *Ac. Pr.* II. 23, 73. (Why should I speak of Democritus? Whom can we compare with him not only for greatness of genius, but also of spirit? He who dared to begin) I speak these things about everything. (His statement confesses to no exception, for what can there be in addition to "everything." . . . Moreover, he does not agree with us who do not deny truth exists, although we deny it can be perceived. He flatly denies truth exists and holds that the senses are not dim but "blind," for that is what he calls

them.) ARIST., *de Part. Anim.* A. 1. 640 b. 29. (If each of the animals and their members exist by shape and color, Democritus was correct, for so he seems to have believed. At any rate he says it is clear to everyone what sort of shape man is, since he is known by his shape and color. And yet a corpse has the same shape, but it is not therefore a man.)

166. SEXT. EMP., *op. cit.* IX. 19. (Democritus asserts that) certain phantoms approach men, (some of which are productive of good, others of evil. Hence he prays) to meet propitious phantoms. (Although not indestructible these phantoms are hard to destroy and they are great and marvellous for they predict the future experience of men by being both seen and heard. For this reason the ancients seized upon the appearance of these things and considered it a god, as if God whose nature is indestructible were nothing else except these.)

172. STOB., *op. cit.*[26] From the very things from which our goods come we sometimes get evils, yet we can avoid these evils. For instance, deep water is useful for many things, and again it is evil, for there is danger of drowning. So a means was found— learning to swim.

173. Evils for man spring out of goods when one does not know how to guide and bear them easily. It is not right to reckon these among evils but among goods, and it is possible to use the goods if one will as a defense against the evils.

174. The cheerful man because he is always impelled to just and lawful deeds is happy, vigorous, and free from care, whether waking or dreaming. But whoever thinks naught of right and does not do what he ought, to him all such things are joyless and whatever he remembers brings him fear and self-reproach.

177. Fine talk never covers a mean deed, nor is a good deed marred by slander.

187. It is fitting that men have more regard for the soul than

[26] The remainder are all from Stobaeus.

the body, for the soul's perfection corrects the viciousness of the body, but the vigor of the body, without reason, does not make the soul a whit better.

189. It is best for man to pass his life with as much cheerfulness as possible and with as little distress. And this he would do, did he not find his pleasures in mortal affairs.

191. Men attain Cheerfulness through moderation in pleasure and equableness of life. Excess and want are ever alternating and causing great disturbances in the soul. Souls that are shifting from extreme to extreme are neither steadfast nor cheerful. You should, therefore, fix your mind upon what is possible and be content with what you have, giving little heed to those who are envied and admired, and not allowing your thoughts to dwell upon them. Rather, you should view the lives of the wretched and think of their suffering so that what you now have and possess may seem great and enviable to you, and that it be not your lot, while craving more, to suffer at heart. For he that envies those that have and that are thought happy by other men, and dwells on the thought all the time is compelled to be always trying new ways [of bettering his fortune] and is kept at it by his covetousness, until he does something fatal, forbidden by law. These things you should not seek, but should be content with your lot comparing your own condition with that of them who fare worse. You should take their sufferings to heart and congratulate yourself on faring so much better than they. For if you preserve this frame of mind, you will both live more cheerfully and brush aside not a few of the evils of life—envy, rivalry, and enmity.

194. The great pleasures arise from observing noble deeds.

221. The hope of evil gain is the beginning of ruin.

252. Of all other things, the needs of the city must be considered the most important so that it may be well governed. Unreasonable party strife and personal power must submit to the common good. For a well governed city is the surest regulator. The whole matter is contained in this: When the city is sound everything is sound, but when it is destroyed, everything is destroyed.

THE SOPHISTS

IN HIS CONCLUSION of the theory of "true-born" or objectively valid knowledge in the classical account of a universe explicable in terms of atoms and void, Democritus comes well within the tradition of the science which began in Miletus in "wonder." For if, as Aristotle wrote, (see above, Introductory, p. 27, 3) "in order to escape from ignorance," men "were pursuing science in order to know, and not for any utilitarian end," these systematic accounts had been enlarged to include man as well as speculation concerning the means by which he knows the cosmos and its processes. But when the great Atomist brings within the scope of the most scientifically formulated philosophy of ancient times an account of "obscure" or "bastard" knowledge, which may be summed up in the proposition, "sweet is by convention," his thought reflects the Sophists' great discovery of subjectivity.[1]

The significance of the emergence in the fifth century B.C. of the problem of subjective experience and its implications transcends the fact of the Sophistic influence upon Democritus and, indeed, goes beyond that of the discovery and its use by the Sophists themselves. The analysis of subjectivity and the consequent tendency of the Sophists to assert the ultimacy of subjective in contrast to objective judgment in fields as diverse as epistemology, morals, and politics marks a turning point in the history of philosophy. The reasons for the redirection of speculation are complex; the central fact, however, which indicates the

[1] See below, pp. 212 sq., for earlier suggestions of the problem.

turning away from the dominant interest in cosmological and physical subjects may be simply put: the most important consequence of Protagoras' theory that "Man is the measure. . . ." (see below, I. A. 14, 19, 21 a) is precisely the conviction that man, rather than physical or cosmological processes, rightly occupies the center of the speculative stage.

This consequence is evident in the views of the Sophists themselves. For reasons which will shortly be clear, the principal implications of Protagoras' theory, *homo mensura*, are individualism and relativism, and the Sophists, themselves, are understandably implicated both in their teaching and their thought. It is equally evident that to discover, among men who are individualists and who believe in the relativism of knowledge, morality, politics, and religion, a factor other than the individuality common to all presents a serious problem. The issue for the student is complicated by the diversity of the Sophists' interests and the pedagogical role they played in a Greece in which a tremendous increase of interest in all branches of knowledge is an important condition for the origin of Sophism itself (see below, p. 215). As we shall see, the Sophists are a diverse group. There are Sophists of Culture,[2] whose object was to stimulate the minds of the young and to examine a variety of fields of knowledge. To this group belong Protagoras and Gorgias, as well as Anonymus Iamblichi. Protagoras was the first man to organize speech and to lay the foundations of grammar, while Gorgias' principal interests lay in art and rhetoric. There are Encyclopaedists, the systematizers and classifiers of knowledge and information.[3] To this group belong the polymath, Hippias, the most learned and, by repute, the vainest of the Sophists; and Prodicus, who is said to have written a shallow ethics. There are Sophists of Eristic,[4] who specialized in debate and disputation and who tended to satisfy the contemporary demand for train-

[2] The selections relating to the Sophists of Culture begin below, p. 220.

[3] The "Encyclopaedists" are omitted from this book. The remaining fragments of their work, on the whole, are less important for our purposes than are such of Plato's *Dialogues* as the *Hippias Minor* and *Hippias Major,* which are readily available.

[4] The selections from the philosophy of the Sophists of Eristic begin below, p. 243.

ing in the arts of public life and the lawcourts. To this latter group
belonged Thrasymachus of Chalcedon, Polus, and Critias.

It is small wonder, in the face of such diversity of personality
and interests, that there has been serious doubt that the Sophists
comprise a "school" of philosophy. For while Plato, especially in
Apology and *Protagoras,* leaves the impression that the Sophists
were closely allied in their teachings and methods, that these
men were in close association, and that the adherents to their
beliefs esteemed them not only as individuals but as a close-knit
group,[5] so distinguished an historian as Grote [6] maintains, "It is
impossible . . . to predicate anything concerning doctrines,
methods, or tendencies, common and peculiar to all Sophists."
The situation is further complicated, first, by the fact that the
term *Sophist* was used widely and with little discrimination (see
below, Introductory, 1; I. A. 6), and secondly, by the diversity
of the applications of their central doctrines. It is doubtful,
indeed, that the Sophists were a "school" similar to the Milesian
or a "sect" like the Pythagorean. Still, there is no doubt that,
with such exceptions as Critias and Callicles who were influenced
by them, they were the first professional teachers of Greece (see
below, Introductory, 3; II. A. a. 14) and that, as such, they
travelled the length and breadth of Greece from 450 to 350 B.C.,
training the youth in rhetoric and in the art of disputation and
dialectic, instructing in subjects far wider in scope than the
traditional music and gymnastic, and subjecting knowledge to
new modes of classification and to new techniques for public
presentation.

To this somewhat external fact of a common profession, significant for other reasons which will shortly be evident, but a
fact which suggests that the Sophists had at least an aim in common, should be added their fundamental interest in man. Of the
Sophists of Culture, of the Eristics, or of the Encyclopaedists,
diverse as they are in personality and unequal as they are in
abilities, the Socrates of Plato's *Apology* could have remarked, as

<hr>

[5] Plato, *Protagoras,* pp. 314 sq.
[6] George Grote, *A History of Greece* (London, John Murray, 1869),
Vol. VIII, Part II, p. 175. Cf. H. Sidgwick, "The Sophists," *Journal of
Philology,* Vol. 4, No. 8, pp. 288-307, Vol. 5, No. 9, pp. 66-80.

he did of himself and with equal accuracy, that they had nothing to do with physical speculations, nor with the search "into things under the earth and in heaven" (see below, Ch. 7, p. 254; 15). Without too great arbitrariness, we may regard the Sophists as a group with a common profession of teaching; with a common interest in the meaning of human rather than physical nature; and with a tendency to interpret this object of common interest in terms of individualism and relativism.

The importance of their professional status is twofold. In the first place, the payment of large sums to the Sophists (see below, Introductory, 2, 3) was at least the ostensible reason for Plato's contemptuous attitude towards them and this, coupled with the reiterated charge that they taught without sound knowledge, whether of the specific subject or of the meaning of true philosophy (see below, Introductory, 4; II. A. a. 14), brought upon these assiduous gatherers and classifiers of information the suspicion of moral obliquity. Secondly, we discover precisely in the Sophists' fulfillment of their professional duties as pedagogues the most significant reason for the movement's spectacular rise and success. While it is no doubt true, as Plato urged, that certain individual Sophists either offered little or had little to offer of true wisdom in return for the fees collected; and while it is also probably true that the Eristic Sophists tended, as Aristotle intimates, to argue for the sake of argument without concern for the truth or falsity of their premises, it is essential to remember that large fees were forthcoming principally because the Sophistic method and the subjects taught satisfied a profound need. Accompanying the rise of democratic spirit in Greece (see below, p. 215), was a demand for instruction in arts more immediately applicable than music and gymnastic to the training of men for public life. The need was to teach "prudence," to enable a man "to speak and act for the best in the affairs of state" (see below, I. A. 5 [318D]).

It is a fair inference, moreover, that the Sophists prospered not only because there was need for instruction in the fields of knowledge in which they were interested, as well as training in the arts of rhetoric and disputation in which they were expert, but also because they fulfilled the task set for them. The "measure of the enemy" is not infrequently the defense raised against him. The "measure" of the Sophists as the "enemy" against whom Socrates and Plato waged philosophical combat is patent in the vigor of the arguments, in the basic character of the problems which Sophism forced its adversaries to examine, and in the philosophical techniques perfected for the solution to those problems. Thus, to speak only of Socrates, it is well to anticipate (see below, Ch. 7 on Socrates). In order to combat Sophistic arguments and rhetoric, the great Athenian perfected dialectic and irony; to oppose the theory of the ultimacy of "appearance" and of "sensation," Socrates brought forth the theory of concepts and of functional definition; to counteract "subjectivity," he laid the grounds for demonstrable and "objective" knowledge in the analysis of human nature, the precise field upon which Sophistic interest centered; and to defeat the claims of moral "relativism," he sought objective ethical principles through the examination of virtue and the virtues. It is profitable, also, to recall that in the reaction to Sophism, philosophy was led upon the path to the Platonic and Aristotelian systems of speculation, each sufficiently comprehensive to include the Sophistic interest in man and in subjectivity, as well as to revive Greek philosophy's original concentration upon ontology and cosmology.

The nerve of Sophistic doctrine itself is Protagoras' *homo mensura* (see below, I. A. 1, 14, 15; I. A. a. 1). While it is true, however, that, as Sextus Empiricus states Protagoras' theory, to make man the criterion of all objects is fundamental both to the theory of the greatest of Sophists and to the developments of Sophistic philosophy, it is nonetheless important to remember that the Sophists were not the first thinkers to investigate problems of perception or sensation (see above, Ch. 3, B. c; Ch. 5, I. B. d; Ch. 5, II. B. e. 1). Nor were the Sophists the first to suggest the relativism of knowledge made explicit by their interest in individualism (see above, Ch. 3, B. c, as well as B. a. 4, 37, 39, 52, 53-54, 57, 69, 78, 99; see also, above, Ch. 4, II B. a. 8 sq.; Ch. 4, II. B. b as well as the systematic distinction between *The Way of Truth* and *The Way of Opinion*). However, in spite of factors present in Sophism which are also discernible in previous and contemporary Greek political and moral relations and

in Greek speculation, it is nonetheless true that Protagoras' contribution is unique: He made the subjective experience not only
the ultimate and valid ground for experience and judgement; he
made the perceiver's experience the only experience, and the sole
possible ground for judgement (see below, I. A. 21 a). As Sextus
Empiricus correctly inferred, Protagoras "posits only what appears to each individual, and thus he introduces relativity" (see
below, I. A. 14).

The radical character of Protagoras' inference from the
Heraclitean doctrine that everything flows and is the combination of contraries is evident once we revert to the contrast between it and Democritus' theory of knowledge with which we
began. Sophism influenced the later Atomism [7] (see below, I. A.
15) and certainly such Democritean propositions as "sweet is by
convention" (see above, Ch. 5, IV. B. 49 and especially 135)
imply not only nominalism in judgements concerning sensation
but subjectivity and relativism of all knowledge got by the
senses as well. Still, as we have suggested, Democritus maintains also that there is objective knowledge got without the
intermediation of sensory organs and to this knowledge the tain
of neither nominalism nor relativism attaches (see above, Ch.
5, IV. B. 105; Ch. 5, IV. B. a. 11).

The importance of this contrast between Protagoras' and
Democritus' theory of knowledge may scarcely be overem-
phasized. The Sophist, in reducing all possible knowledge to
states of subjective experience, avoids the difficulty which confronts Democritus, who fails to explain how tastes can change if
atomic structures remain the same (see above, Ch. 5, IV. B. 132).
For this advantage, however, Protagoras pays a penalty: in his
reduction of what are ordinarily regarded as "judgements of fact"
to "judgements of individual taste," there is a consequent and
inevitable implication of individualism and relativism which de-
prives Sophistic philosophy of the strength inherent in the objectivity which is part of previous Greek speculative tradition.
To this tradition, especially in Eleatic rationalism (see above,

[7] The philosophical relations between Protagoras and Democritus have
frequently been misinterpreted in consequence of the tradition that the
Sophist was a pupil of the Atomist (I. A. 1 [50]).

Ch. 4, II. B. a. 8; Ch. 5, IV. B. a. 146; cf. Ch. 5, IV. B. 105),
Democritus returns in order to account for both subjective experience and objective knowledge. But Protagoras departs so
decisively from the tradition in which the Parmenidean *being*, the
Pythagorean *limited*, and the Anaxagorean *Nous* played indispensable roles, that his theory of experience denies the presuppositions of law and constancy implicit in the very nature of the
Heraclitean philosophy upon which his own epistemology rests
(see below, I. A. 1, I. A. a. 1; see above, Ch. 3, particularly
B. a. 10, 14, 16, 18, 37, 46, 81, 105, and B. c).

The importance of this radical departure from the rational
tradition in philosophy is evident in the historical evaluation of
the Sophists. It might justly be thought that the discovery of
"inner experience"; the investigations of the implications of subjectivity in morality, politics, law, religion, and theory of knowledge; and the direction of speculation into psychology would
be contributions of sufficient value to secure for the Sophists an
honored place in the history of speculation. Indeed, their studies
in grammar, rhetoric, and lexicography might in themselves have
warranted such a place and the germ of later theories in their
philosophy should have added lustre to their names. In their
speculation are anticipations of the Platonic theory of becoming [8] and of opinion, and the modern hypothesis of the social
contract, as well as theories of government in the interest of the
stronger and of the value of the individual. The magnitude of
their contribution has been diminished by history and it is of
value to suggest, if possible, some of the historical reasons for
this underestimation.

The basic reasons probably lie neither in the fact that the
Sophists were paid teachers nor in the discrete philosophical
problems they presented to Socrates and Plato. Behind these
somewhat superficial facts are discernible the two significant
reasons for the virulence of the opposition. The first is that their
professional pedagogy is but one aspect of the breaking down

---

[8] It may profitably be recalled that Plato was influenced by the
Heraclitean philosopher, Cratylus, who is treated as a Sophist in the dialogue, *Cratylus*. The Protagorean influence is evident in *Laws* 716 A,
where Plato writes that "God ought to be to us the measure of all things,
and not man, as men commonly say. . . ."

of the traditional and conservative Greek way of life during the period of the ascendancy, culmination, and decline of democracy. The second is that in Protagoras' proposition, "Man is the measure . . . ," Socrates and Plato are faced with a possible philosophical ground to fortify the individualism and relativism prevalent in nonphilosophical fields in consequence of the difficulties, governmental and commercial, which arose in the democracy. Indeed, in Gorgias' more complete skepticism (see below, II. A. a. 3) they face the prospect of the Sophistic use of the very dialectical method perfected by Zeno to establish the truth of Parmenides' *Being* (see above, Ch. 4, p. 98, and III), now employed to assert that nothing exists.

The issue is not, certainly, solely a speculative one, although the epistemological problem presented by Protagoras and the ontological, epistemological, and linguistic problems presented by Gorgias are sufficient to force Plato to the most strenuous efforts in order to invalidate the Sophists' arguments. Plato and Socrates were fundamentally concerned with the fact that Sophism employed philosophical techniques to supply instruments for the skepticism which means the destruction of philosophy itself. There were, however, moral issues in Sophism for Socrates (see below, Ch. 7, 22, 24, 30, 31), and moral and political issues for Plato— who, it will be recalled, believed that the ideal state would be one in which the philosopher is king and the king is philosopher —and these arose directly from the conditions of the times. Sophism reflected these conditions and presented philosophical grounds which tended to justify the breakdown of tradition and the breakdown of the distinction between law and custom. In consequence of the defeat of the Persians at Marathon in the times of Darius, and of the final driving out of the invaders a decade later, there came about in Greece an awakening of political sentiment. Greek youth, eager to participate in politics and in public affairs, sought training in arts best fitted to prepare them for their public tasks. The search brought forth the Sophists and, with the breakdown of the old aristocracy, it became clear that power and position—in a word, success—were within the grasp of any man, however humble his origin, provided that he could secure instruction. The Sophists did supply rhetoric and oratory, as well as subjects. They trained men for the law courts in debate all too often leading to Eristic (see below, *The Sophists of Eristic*).

Sophism, then, is a reflection of the times, and of the controversies and political stresses and strains of the times. In Plato's *Dialogues*, it is the Sophist and the political leaders like Thrasymachus and Callicles whom they produced, who expound theories of power, interest, and individualism in politics; it is Protagoras, the Sophist, who expounds his theory of perception, the virtues, and the gods; it is Gorgias, the Sophist, who displays his skepticism of knowledge; and it is Hippias, the Sophist, who in parading his extraordinary erudition, also demonstrates his incapacity to distinguish between denotation and connotation. But these figures who appear in Plato's writings and elsewhere are but distillations of the forces which Plato feared in the "beast," the people, who had, in his judgment, killed Socrates. Plato had characterized the men "whom the world calls Sophists" as "mercenary adventurers" who "do but teach the collective opinion of the many. . . ." This, he writes, is their wisdom and he compares them to a man "who should study the tempers and desires of a mighty strong beast who is fed by him." This man learns by "by what sounds . . . the beast is soothed or infuriated . . . and by constantly living with him . . . he makes a system or art, which he proceeds to teach, not that he has any real notion of what he is teaching, but he names this honorable and that dishonorable, or good or evil, or just or unjust, all in accordance with the tastes and tempers of the great brute, when he has learnt the meaning of his inarticulate grunts." [9]

Plato's inference is that the Sophist, like the man tending "the great brute," ends by pronouncing "what pleases him" to be good and what he dislikes to be evil. He concludes that the Sophist "can give no other account" of good and evil than that the just and noble are the necessary. The very controversies concerning the value of various forms of government implicit in Plato's remarks evidence themselves in Herodotus' writings.[10] The dangers inherent for law and politics and morality in

[9] Plato, *Republic* VI 494.
[10] *The History of Herodotus* III, 80-83.

Thrasymachus', Callicles', or Critias' contentions (see below, IV, V, VI) arise as well in the argument put with even greater brutality by the Athenians to the Melians: [11]

ATH. ". . . we Athenians will use no fine words; we will not go out of our way to prove at length that we have a right to rule, because we overthrew the Persians; or that we attack you now because we are suffering any injury at your hands. We should not convince you if we did; nor must you expect to convince us by arguing that, although a colony of the Lacedaemonians, you have taken no part in their expeditions, or that you have never done us any wrong. But you and we should say what we really think, and aim only at what is possible, for we both alike know that into the discussion of human affairs the question of justice only enters where there is equal power to enforce it, and that the powerful exact what they can, and the weak grant what they must. . . . You are weak and a single turn of the scale might be your ruin. Do not you be thus deluded; avoid the error of which so many are guilty, who . . . have recourse to the invisible, to prophecies and oracles and the like, which ruin men by the hopes which they inspire in them. . . . As for the Gods, we expect to have quite as much of their favor as you. . . . For of the Gods we believe, and of men we know, that by a law of their nature, wherever they can rule they will. This law was not made by us, and we are not the first who have acted upon it; we did but inherit it, and shall bequeath it to all time, and we know that you and all mankind, if you were as strong as we are, would do as we do. So much for the Gods; we have told you why we expect to stand as high in their good opinion as you. . . ."

The seeds of Sophistic philosophy fell on fertile soil. The issues at stake were too important for Plato to examine sophistry coolly. He saw in the teachings the reduction of law to custom and human agreement (see below, Introductory, 4). He saw this as anarchy, in contrast to law and objectivity, establishing claims by using philosophy's own weapons for the destruction of what he thought philosophy is. It is small wonder that with the strength of a powerful mind and with his superb control over philosophical instruments, Plato could bring it to pass that

[11] *Thucydides,* translated by Benjamin Jowett (Oxford, The Clarendon Press, 1900), Bk. V, 89 sq., pp. 168 et seq.

history underevaluates Sophism's principal contributions to the
knowledge of man and of his psychology.

INTRODUCTORY [12]

1. ARISTID., *Ars. Rhet.* 46. They seem to me not to know
either how the very name of philosophy stood with the Greeks
and what it signified, in fact absolutely nothing at all about this
matter. Didn't Herodotus call Solon a Sophist, and Pythagoras
too? And hasn't Androtion named the Seven,—I mean of course
the Seven Wise Men,—Sophists; and again called the celebrated
Socrates himself a Sophist? And then those who concerned themselves with controversy and those self-styled dialecticians, did
not Isocrates call them Sophists but call himself a philosopher,
along with the orators and those who are occupied with political
management? And don't some of his pupils apply these designa-
tions in the same way? Doesn't Lysias call Plato a Sophist, and
also Aeschines? One might take the view that he is making an
allegation. However, the others, while accusing those others, did
not attach the same name to them. Moreover, if it were possible
for someone who was making an allegation against Plato to do so
by calling him a Sophist, what would anyone call those others?
But the name Sophist was, I believe, a fairly general designation,
and philosophy could thus be a love of the beautiful and a preoccupation with inquiry. And this is not the present way, but
education generally. . . . Plato appears somehow always to
vilify the Sophist regularly, and Plato, I really believe, was the
one who revolted against the designation. And the reason for
this is that he despised the majority. But clearly he also applied
this appellation with utmost reverence. The god, at any rate,
whom he claims is the wisest and with whom the whole of truth
resides, he has called somewhere "a perfect Sophist."

[12] The new translations of the philosophy of the Sophists printed in this
edition are the work of Professor Alister Cameron. All passages from Plato
are in Benjamin Jowett's translation, from *The Dialogues of Plato* (Oxford,
Oxford University Press, 1871). The sources of other translations are given
in footnotes. The enumeration of the fragments follows that in H. Diels'
Die Fragmente der Vorsokratiker, 3rd ed. (Berlin, Wiedmannsche Buchhandlung, 1906).

2. PLATO, *Soph.* 231 D. In the first place, he [the Sophist] was discovered to be a paid hunter after wealth and youth. . . . In the second place, he was a merchant in the goods of the soul. . . . In the third place, he has turned out to be a retailer of the same sort of wares. . . . In the fourth place, he himself manufactured the learned wares which he sold. . . . Fifth . . . he belonged to the fighting class, and was further distinguished as a hero of debate, who professed the Eristic art. . . . The sixth point was doubtful, and yet we at last agreed that he was a purger of souls, who cleared away notions obstructive to knowledge.

3. ———, *Apology* 19-20. *Socrates:* As little foundation is there for the report that I am a teacher, and take money; this accusation has no more truth in it than the other. Although, if a man were really able to instruct mankind, to receive money for giving instruction would, in my opinion, be an honor to him. There is Gorgias of Leontium, and Prodicus of Ceos, and Hippias of Elis, who go the round of the cities, and are able to persuade the young men to leave their own citizens by whom they might be taught for nothing, and come to them whom they not only pay, but are thankful if they may be allowed to pay them.

4. ———, *Laws* 889 E. And they say that politics cooperate with nature, but in a less degree, and have more of art; also that legislation is entirely a work of art, and is based on assumptions which are not true. . . . These people would say that the gods exist not by nature, but by art, and by the laws of states, which are different in different places, according to the agreement of those who make them; and that the honorable is one thing by nature and another thing by law, and that the principles of justice have no existence at all in nature, but that mankind are always disputing about them and altering them; and that the alterations which are made by art and by law have no basis in nature, but are of authority for the moment and at the time at which they are made. . . . These, my friends, are the sayings of wise men, poets and prose writers, which find a way into the minds of youth. They are told by them that the highest right is

might, and in this way the young fall into impieties, under the idea that the gods are not such as the law bids them imagine; and hence arise factions, these philosophers inviting them to lead a true life according to nature, that is, to live in real dominion over others, and not in legal subjection to them.

THE SOPHISTS OF CULTURE

To that group of professional teachers whose primary interest lay in a variety of fields of human knowledge, including poetry, rhetoric, politics, speech, and morality, and in the stimulation of the minds of the young in preparation for public life, belong the two most significant philosophical figures among the Sophists, Protagoras and Gorgias. To it, also, belong the writings of an unknown Sophist, referred to as Anonymus Iamblichi, whose work is of especial interest because of the moral theories put forward and of the light it throws upon speculation which affected Plato.

I. PROTAGORAS

Protagoras' *homo mensura* (see below, I. A. 14, 15, 21a; I. A. a. 1) is, as was pointed out above, central to the meaning and historical development of Sophism. Protagoras was a native of Abdera. Burnet fixes the date of his birth not later than 432 B.C., and of his death early in the Peloponnesian War.[13] Protagoras, who wrote a book called *The Truth* (probably identical with *The Throwers*) and one entitled *On the Gods*, was the most successful Sophist. His fees for teaching are described as large; "all men praise him. . . . He is reputed to be the most accomplished of speakers." He is described in Plato's *Protagoras* as having been followed to Athens by a "train of listeners," who assembled to hear "the wisest of all living men."

In Plato's *Protagoras* this philosopher from Abdera tells Hippocrates (see below, I. A. 5, 318 D) that one who comes to

[13] See below, p. 222, for Protagoras' life.

him "will learn that which he comes to learn. And this is prudence in affairs private as well as public; he will learn to order his own house in the best manner, and he will be able to speak and act for the best in the affairs of state." Protagoras' interests, however, lay not alone in this field of "prudence." He is said to have laid the foundations of grammar and to have studied the parts of speech. Significantly, he carried philosophical inference into the realm of religion (see below, I. A. 1 [51]). Tradition, in fact, has it that Protagoras was persecuted as an atheist, that his treatise was burned, and that, driven from Athens, the great Sophist died on his voyage to Sicily.

Some modern scholars have interpreted Protagoras' central theory that man is the measure of all things to mean that "man" is "generic man" or "humanity." Similarly, some interpretations of Protagoras' remark concerning the existence or nonexistence of the gods imply that the Sophist intended to rule this type of speculation, necessarily incomplete in the scope of a lifetime, from the province of philosophy. It is doubtful that either the interpretation of man or of the problem of the existence of the gods would accord with what Protagoras meant and what was the usual interpretation in ancient times (see below, I. A. 21a; I. A. a. 1, 4). Protagoras, in accepting the Heraclitean theory of the flux of all things, is led by his own interest in epistemology to interpret perception in terms of motions. Since both the perceiver and the object of perception are in constant motion, perception itself will be a form of motion or perceiving which gives "birth to" qualities and sensation. Moreover, since Protagoras reduces all knowing to perceiving, the consequence is that knowledge is not only relative but is relative to each perceiver at the moment of the conjunction of the motions involved (see below, I. A. 14; I. A. a. 1).

It would appear probable that Protagoras applied to the problem of the existence or nonexistence of the gods the same theory of relativism. The consequent individualism in the epistemological theory would suggest that Plato's presentation of Protagoras' political and moral theory is authentic (Plato, *Protagoras*). Plato's account implies that the Sophist held neither that there is a virtue common to all virtues nor that man is by nature or essentially virtuous. Rather, the implication in Protagoras' theory would appear to be that man is virtuous by necessity, with the implication that if external sanctions were removed, he would revert to the state of pre-compact or natural egoism.

A. LIFE AND TEACHING

1. D.L., *Lives* IX. (50 sq.) Protagoras,[14] son of Artemon or, according to Apollodorus and Dinon in the fifth book of his *History of Persia,* of Maeandrius, was born at Abdera (so says Heraclides of Pontus in his treatise *On Laws,* and also that he made laws for Thurii) or, according to Eupolis in his *Flatterers,* at Teos; for the latter says:

Inside we've got Protagoras of Teos

He and Prodicus of Ceos gave public readings for which fees were charged, and Plato in the *Protagoras* calls Prodicus deep-voiced. Protagoras studied under Democritus. The latter was nicknamed "Wisdom," according to Favorinus in his *Miscellaneous History.*

(51) Protagoras was the first to maintain that there are two sides to every question, opposed to each other, and he even argued in this fashion, being the first to do so. Furthermore he began a work thus: "Man . . . are not." He used to say that soul was nothing apart from the senses, as we learn from Plato in the *Theaetetus,* and that everything is true. In another work he began thus: "As to the gods, I have no means of knowing either that they exist . . . human life." (52) For this introduction to his book the Athenians expelled him; and they burnt his works in the market-place, after sending round a herald to collect them from all who had copies in their possession.

He was the first to exact a fee of a hundred minae and the first to distinguish the tenses of verbs, to emphasize the importance of seizing the right moment, to institute contests in

---

[14] Reprinted by permission of the publishers and The Loeb Classical Library from Diogenes Laertius, *Lives of Eminent Philosophers,* translated by R. D. Hicks (Cambridge, Harvard University Press, 1925).

debating, and to teach rival pleaders the tricks of their trade. Furthermore, in his dialectic he neglected the meaning in favor of verbal quibbling, and he was the father of the whole tribe of eristical disputants now so much in evidence; insomuch that Timon too speaks of him as

> Protagoras, all mankind's epitome,
> Cunning, I trow, to war with words.

(53) He too first introduced the method of discussion which is called Socratic. Again, as we learn from Plato in the *Euthydemus,* he was the first to use in discussion the argument of Antisthenes which strives to prove that contradiction is impossible, and the first to point out how to attack and refute any proposition laid down: so Artemidorus the dialectician in his treatise *In Reply to Chrysippus.* He too invented the shoulder-pad on which porters carry their burdens, so we are told by Aristotle in his treatise *On Education;* for he himself had been a porter, says Epicurus somewhere. This was how he was taken up by Democritus, who saw how skilfully his bundles of wood were tied. (54) He was the first to mark off the parts of discourse into four, namely, wish, question, answer, command; others divide into seven parts, narration, question, answer, command, rehearsal, wish, summoning; these he called the basic forms of speech. . . .

The first of his books he read in public was that *On the Gods,* the introduction to which we quoted above; he read it at Athens in Euripides' house, or, as some say, in Megaclides'; others again make the place the Lyceum and the reader his disciple Archagoras, Theodotus' son, who gave him the son of Polyzelus, one of the four hundred; Aristotle, however, says it was Euathlus.

(55) . . . Philochorus says that, when he was on a voyage to Sicily, his ship went down, and that Euripides hints at this in his *Ixion.* (56) According to some his death occurred, when he was on a journey, at nearly ninety years of age, though Apollodorus makes his age seventy, assigns forty years for his career as a Sophist, and puts his *floruit* in the 84th Olympiad [444-441 B.C.]. . . .

5. PLATO, *Protag.* 317 B. . . . I take an entirely opposite course, and acknowledge myself to be a Sophist and instructor of mankind; . . . 317 C. And I have been now many years in the profession—for all my years when added up are many: there is no one here present of whom I might not be the father. . . . 318 A. Young man, if you associate with me, on the very first day you will return home a better man than you came, and better on the second day than on the first, and better every day than you were on the day before. . . . 318 D. If Hippocrates comes to me he will not experience the sort of drudgery with which other Sophists are in the habit of insulting their pupils; who, when they have just escaped from the arts, are taken and driven back into them by these teachers, and made to learn calculation, and astronomy, and geometry, and music (he gave a look at Hippias as he said this); but if he comes to me, he will learn that which he comes to learn. And this is prudence in affairs private as well as public; he will learn to order his own house in the best manner, and he will be able to speak and act for the best in the affairs of the state. . . . 319 A. Do I understand you, I said; and is your meaning that you teach the art of politics, and that you promise to make men good citizens? That, Socrates, is exactly the profession which I make. . . . 349 A. Moreover such confidence have you in yourself, that although other Sophists conceal their profession, you proclaim in the face of Hellas that you are a Sophist or teacher of virtue and education, and are the first who demanded pay in return.

6. —— 328 B. And therefore I have introduced the following mode of payment:—When a man has been my pupil, if he likes he pays my price, but there is no compulsion; and if he does not like, he has only to go into a temple and take an oath of the value of the instructions, and he pays no more than he declares to be their value.

14. SEXT. EMP., *Pyrrh. H.* I. 216 sq. Protagoras [15] also holds that "Man is the measure of all things, of existing things that they

[15] *Outlines of Pyrrhonism,* translated by R. G. Bury, in *Sextus Empiricus,* I. 216 sq. (London, W. Heinemann, 1933). From The Loeb Classical Library. Reprinted by permission of the President and Fellows of Harvard College.

exist, and of non-existing things that they exist not"; and by "measure" he means the criterion, and by "things" the objects, so that he is virtually asserting that "Man is the criterion of all objects, of those which exist that they exist, and of those which exist not that they exist not." And consequently he posits only what appears to each individual, and thus he introduces relativity.

(217) What he states then is this—that matter is in flux, and as it flows additions are made continuously in the place of the effluxions, and the senses are transformed and altered according to the times of life and to all the other conditions of the bodies. (218) He says also that the "reasons" of all the appearances subsist in matter, so that matter, so far as depends on itself, is capable of being all those things which appear to all. And men, he says, apprehend different things at different times owing to their differing dispositions; for he who is in a natural state apprehends those things subsisting in matter which are able to appear to those in a natural state, and those who are in a non-natural state the things which can appear to those in a non-natural state. (219) Moreover, precisely the same account applies to the variations due to age, and to the sleeping or waking state, and to each several kind of condition. Thus, according to him, Man becomes the criterion of real existences; for all things that appear to men also exist, and things that appear to no man have no existence either.

We see, then, that he dogmatizes about the fluidity of matter and also about the subsistence therein of the "reasons" of all appearances, these being non-evident matters about which we suspend judgment.

15. ———, *Adv. Math.* VII. 389. One [16] cannot say that every presentation is true, because this refutes itself, as Democritus and Plato taught in opposing Protagoras; for if every presentation is true, the judgment that not every presentation is true, being based on a presentation, will also be true, and thus the judgment that every presentation is true will become false.

[16] *Ibid.* Reprinted by permission of the President and Fellows of Harvard College.

16. HERM., *I. G. P.* 9. But Protagoras draws me to the other side, where he takes his stand, when he maintains: that man is the criterion and decision of things; that those which come under the observation of the senses *are* things, but those which do not do not exist in the forms of being.

19. . . . ARIST., MET. 4. 1007 b 18. Again,[17] if all contradictory statements are true of the same subject at the same time, evidently all things will be one. For the same thing will be a trireme, a wall, and a man, if of everything it is possible either to affirm or to deny anything (and this premiss must be accepted by those who share the views of Protagoras). For if any one thinks that the man is not a trireme, evidently he is not a trireme; so that he also *is* a trireme, if, as they say, contradictory statements are both true. ———— 6. 1062 b 13. He [Protagoras] said that man is the measure of all things, meaning simply that that which seems to each man also assuredly is. If this is so, it follows that the same thing both is and is not, and is bad and good, and that the contents of all other opposite statements are true, because often a particular thing appears beautiful to some and the contrary of beautiful to others, and that which appears to each man is the measure.

21. ————, *Rhet.* B. 24. 1402 a 23. This [18] sort of argument illustrates what is meant by making the worse argument seem the better. Hence people were right in objecting to the training Protagoras undertook to give them. It was a fraud; the probability it handled was not genuine but spurious, and has a place in no art except Rhetoric and Eristic. Steph. Byz. Eudoxus relates that Protagoras made the worse also the better reason and taught his pupils to blame and praise the same man.

21a. PLATO, *Theaet.* 166 D seq. [Apology of Protagoras] For I declare that the truth is as I have written, and that each of us is a measure of existence and of non-existence. Yet one man may be a thousand times better than another in proportion as different things are and appear to him. And I am far from

---

[17] Translated by W. D. Ross, *The Works of Aristotle Translated into English,* ed. by W. D. Ross (Oxford, The Clarendon Press, 1928).
[18] *Ibid.* (Translated by W. Rhys Roberts.)

saying that wisdom and the wise man have no existence; but I say that the wise man is he who makes the evils which appear and are to a man, into goods which are and appear to him. 167 B. But as the inferior habit of mind has thoughts of kindred nature, so I conceive that a good mind causes men to have good thoughts; and these which the inexperienced call true, I maintain to be only better, and not truer than others. And, O my dear Socrates, I do not call wise men tadpoles: far from it; I say that they are physicians of the human body, and the husbandmen of plants—for the husbandmen also take away the evil and disordered sensations of plants, and infuse into them good and healthy sensations—aye and true ones; and the wise and good rhetoricians make the good instead of the evil to seem just to states; for whatever appears to a state to be just and fair, so long as it is regarded as such, is just and fair to it; but the teacher of wisdom causes the good to take the place of the evil, both in appearance and in reality. And in like manner the Sophist who is able to train his pupils in this spirit is a wise man, and deserves to be well paid by them. And so one man is wiser than another; and no one thinks falsely, and you, whether you will or not, must endure to be a measure. On these foundations the argument stands firm.

23. ——— 162 D. [Protagoras speaks] Good people, young and old, you meet and harangue, and bring in the gods, whose existence or non-existence I banish from writing and speech.

a. The fragments.

1. SEXT., *Adv. Math.* VII. 60. Some,[19] too, have counted Protagoras of Abdera among the company of those philosophers who abolish the criterion, since he asserts that all sense impressions and opinions are true and that truth is a relative thing inasmuch as everything that has appeared to someone or been opined by someone is at once real in relation to him. Certainly, at the opening of his book *The Down-Throwers* he has pro-

---

[19] Translated as *Against the Logicians* by R. G. Bury in *Sextus Empiricus*, Vol. II, Book 1, 60 sq. (London, W. Heinemann, 1925). From The Loeb Classical Library. Reprinted by permission of the President and Fellows of Harvard College.

claimed that "Of all things the measure is man, of existing things that they exist and of non-existing things that they exist not."

2. PLATO, *Theaet.* 151 E-152 A. [Socrates and Theaetetus] [Socrates] Well, you have delivered yourself of a very important doctrine about knowledge; it is indeed the opinion of Protagoras, who has another way of expressing it. Man, he says, is the measure of all things, of the existence of things that are, and of the non-existence of things that are not:—You have read him? —— O yes, again and again. —— Does he not say that things are to you such as they appear to you, and to me such as they appear to me, and that you and I are men? . . . the same wind is blowing, and yet one of us may be cold and the other not, or one may be slightly and the other very cold? —— Quite true. —— Now is the wind, regarded not in relation to us but absolutely, cold or not; or are we to say, with Protagoras, that the wind is cold to him who is cold, and not to him who is not? —— I suppose the last. —— Then it must appear so to each of them? —— Yes. —— And "appears to him" means the same as "he perceives." —— True. —— Then appearing and perceiving coincide in the case of hot and cold, and in similar instances; for things appear, or may be supposed to be, to each one such as he perceives them? (161 C) [Socrates] I am charmed with his doctrine, that what appears is to each one, but I wonder that he did not begin his book on Truth with a declaration that a pig or a dog-faced baboon, or some other yet stranger monster which has sensation, is the measure of all things; then he might have shown a magnificent contempt for our opinion of him by informing us at the outset that while we were reverencing him like a God for his wisdom he was no better than a tadpole, not to speak of his fellow-men.

4. EUS., *P. E.* XIV. 3, 7. Protagoras got a reputation for being an unbeliever from having been an associate of Democritus. He is said at least to have used this sort of beginning in his work *Concerning the Gods:* "I do not know about the gods. . . ."

5. D.L., *op. cit.* IX. 51. "As to the gods, I have no means of

knowing either that they exist or that they do not exist. For many are the obstacles that impede knowledge, both the obscurity of the question and the shortness of human life."

II. GORGIAS

In Gorgias' philosophy, the epistemological interest of Sophism which had been expressed in Protagoras' theory that man is the measure of all things is shown as it is extended to include ontology and communication (see below, II. A. a. 3). The skepticism which touches upon the existence or nonexistence of *Being* is explicable on fairly simple grounds: both Protagoras and Gorgias had been influenced by the Eleatic philosophy and Gorgias applied the dialectic of Zeno to the *Being*, for the defense of which Zeno had perfected the instrument (see above, Ch. 4, III). Gorgias expresses his skepticism, however, not only in the proposition, "Nothing exists," but also adds that if anything exists, it is unknowable by man. In this, he follows Protagoras' lead. He goes beyond his predecessor, however, in the final proposition, which asserts that if anything does exist and may be known, it is inexpressible and incommunicable to one's neighbor.

This extension of the central doctrine of subjectivity to the problems of *Being* is suggested by the title of Gorgias' book, *Concerning Nature* or *Concerning the Non-Existent*. Its extension to language is probably a natural consequence of Gorgias' principal interest in rhetoric and of the requirements of his diplomatic career. A native of Leontium in Sicily, the dates of his birth and death have been suggested as 483-375 B.C. Gorgias first arrived in Athens in 427 B.C., as head of an embassy, to secure aid against Syracuse. Tradition has it that he starved himself to death in Larisa. Something both of Gorgias' temperament and of his profession as a rhetorician are suggested by his willingness to speak on any subject (see below, II. A. 1a) and by the "grand and bold style" with which he equipped his pupils and with which he answered all comers (see below, II, A. 19). Gorgias' description of what Socrates calls the "artificer of persuasion" suggests something of the power which the Sophist judged would be within the grasp of one trained in rhetoric.

Gorgias is principally interesting historically because he showed that the dialectical weapons forged for the defense of the theory of *Being* could be used to support an argument which denies the possibility of predicating anything of anything. It is this view that Plato examines with great care in his later dialogues.

A. LIFE AND TEACHING

1. PHILOS., *V. S.* 19, (1) Sicily,[20] produced Gorgias of Leontini, and we must consider that the art of the Sophists carries back to him as though he were its father. For if we reflect how many additions Aeschylus made to tragedy when he furnished her with her proper costume and the buskin that gave the actor's height, with the types of heroes, with messengers who tell what has happened at home and abroad, and with the conventions as to what must be done both before and behind the scenes, then we find that this is what Gorgias in his turn did for his fellow-craftsmen. (2) For he set an example to the Sophists with his virile and energetic style, his daring and unusual expressions, his inspired impressiveness, and his use of the grand style for great themes; and also with his habit of breaking off his clauses and making sudden transitions, by which devices a speech gains in sweetness and sublimity; and he also clothed his style with poetic words for the sake of ornament and dignity. (3) That he also improvised with the greatest facility I have stated at the beginning of my narrative; and when, already advanced in years, he delivered discourses at Athens, there is nothing surprising in the fact that he won applause from the crowd; but he also, as is well known, enthralled the most illustrious men, not only Critias and Alcibiades, who were both young men, but also Thucydides and Pericles who

[20] Philostratus, *Lives of the Sophists*, 9, translated by Wilmer Cave Wright, *Philostratus and Eunapius* (London, W. Heinemann, 1927). From The Loeb Classical Library. Reprinted by permission of the President and Fellows of Harvard College.

were by that time well on in years. Agathon also, the tragic poet,
whom Comedy calls a clever poet and "lovely in his speech,"
often imitates Gorgias in his iambics.

(4) Moreover, he played a distinguished part at the religious festivals of the Greeks, and declaimed his *Pythian Oration* from the altar; and for this his statue was dedicated in
gold and was set up in the temple of the Pythian god. His
Olympian Oration dealt with a theme of the highest importance
to the state. For, seeing that Greece was divided against itself,
he came forward as the advocate of reconciliation, and tried to
turn their energies against the barbarians and to persuade them
not to regard one another's cities as the prize to be won by
their arms, but rather the land of the barbarians. . . .

(6) It is said that though Gorgias attained to the age of
108, his body was not weakened by old age, but to the end of
his life he was in sound condition, and his senses were the senses
of a young man.

1a. ———— (1). Gorgias of Leontini founded the older type
of Sophistic in Thessaly. . . . It was Gorgias who founded the
art of extempore oratory. For when he appeared in the theatre
at Athens he had the courage to say, "Do you propose a theme";
and he was the first to risk this bold announcement, whereby he
as good as advertised that he was omniscient and would speak
on any subject whatever, trusting to the inspiration of the
moment.

4. D.L., *op. cit.* XII. 53. (1) At this time the Leontini in
Sicily, a colony of Chalcis, but also kin of the Athenians, happened to be under attack from the Syracusans. Harassed by the
war and in danger of being overwhelmed by the superiority of
the Syracusans, they sent an embassy to the Athenians calling
upon the people to come to their aid as quickly as possible and
rescue their city from danger. (2) The ranking ambassador was
Gorgias the orator, distinguished far beyond his fellows by his
skill in speech. He was the first inventor of rhetorical arts and
so excelled others in the profession of Sophistry that he received
a hundred minae from his pupils. (3) He, then, having reached
Athens, was presented to the assembly and talked to the

Athenians about the alliance, and astonished the Athenians with the strangeness of his diction, for they were naturally clever and had a taste for eloquence. (4) He was, in fact, first to use figures of speech that were unusual and marked by artistry, antitheses, balanced periods, equal measure, uniform endings and such like, which then, because of the strangeness of the effect, won acceptance but now seem to be mannered and appear to be composed with a repetition and extravagance that is ridiculous. (5) In the end he did persuade the Athenians to enter an alliance with the Leontini and, much admired for his rhetorical art, he returned to Leontini.

19. PLATO, *Meno* 70 A-B. O Meno, there was a time when the Thessalians were famous among the other Hellenes only for their riches and their riding; but now, if I am not mistaken, they are equally famous for their wisdom, especially at Larisa, which is the native city of your friend Aristippus. And this is Gorgias' doing; for when he came there, the flower of the Aleuadae, among them your admirer Aristippus, and the other chiefs of the Thessalians, fell in love with his wisdom. And he has taught you the habit of answering questions in a grand and bold style, which becomes those who know, and is the style in which he himself answers all comers; and any Hellene who likes may ask him anything.

a. The fragments

1. ISOCR., *Orat.* 10, 3. For how could one surpass Gorgias, who dared to assert that nothing exists of the things that are, or Zeno, who ventured to prove the same things as possible and again as impossible. 15, 268. The speculations of the ancient Sophists, who maintain, some of them, that the sum of things is made up of infinite elements . . . Parmenides and Melissus, of one; and Gorgias, of none at all.

3. SEXT., *Adv. Math.* VII. (65). Gorgias [21] of Leontini be-

---

[21] Translated as *Against the Logicians* by R. G. Bury in *Sextus Empiricus*, Vol. II, 65 sq. (London, W. Heinemann, 1935). From The Loeb Classical Library. Reprinted by permission of the President and Fellows of Harvard College.

longed to the same party as those who abolish the criterion, although he did not adopt the same line of attack as Protagoras. For in his book entitled *Concerning the Non-existent* or *Concerning Nature* he tries to establish successively three main points—firstly, that nothing exists; secondly, that even if anything exists it is inapprehensible by man; thirdly, that even if anything is apprehensible, yet of a surety it is inexpressible and incommunicable to one's neighbor. (66) Now that nothing exists, he argues in the following fashion: If anything exists, either it is the existent that exists or the non-existent, or both the existent and the non-existent exist. But neither does the existent exist, as he will establish, nor the non-existent, as he will demonstrate, nor both the existent and the non-existent, as he will also make plain. Nothing, therefore, exists. (67) Now the non-existent does not exist. For if the non-existent exists, it will at one and the same time exist and not exist; for in so far as it is conceived as non-existent it will not exist, but in so far as it is non-existent it will again exist. But it is wholly absurd that a thing should both exist and exist not at one and the same time. Therefore the non-existent does not exist. Moreover, if the non-existent exists, the existent will not exist; for these are contrary the one to the other, and if existence is a property of the non-existent, non-existence will be a property of the existent. But it is not the fact that the existent does not exist; neither, then, will the non-existent exist.

(68) Furthermore, the existent does not exist either. For if the existent exists, it is either eternal or created or at once both eternal and created; but, as we shall prove, it is neither eternal nor created nor both; therefore the existent does not exist. For if the existent is eternal (the hypothesis we must take first), it has no beginning; (69) for everything created has some beginning, but the eternal being uncreated had no beginning. And having no beginning it is infinite. And if it is infinite, it is nowhere. For if it is anywhere, that wherein it is is different from it, and thus the existent, being encompassed by something, will no longer be infinite; for that which encompasses is larger than that which is encompassed, whereas nothing is larger than the infinite; so that the infinite is not anywhere.

(70) Nor, again, is it encompassed by itself. For, if so, that wherein it is will be identical with that which is therein, and the existent will become two things, place and body (for that wherein it is is place, and that which is therein is body). But this is absurd; so that the existent is not in itself either. Consequently, if the existent is eternal it is infinite, and if it is infinite it is nowhere, and if it is nowhere it does not exist. So then, if the existent is eternal, it is not even existent at all.

(71) Nor, again, can the existent be created. For if it has been created, it has been created either out of the existent or out of the non-existent. But it has not been created out of the existent; for if it is existent it has not been created but exists already; nor out of the non-existent; for the non-existent cannot create anything because what is creative of anything must of necessity partake of real existence. Neither, then, is the existent created.

(72) In the same way, it is not both together—at once eternal and created; for these are destructive the one of the other, and if the existent is eternal it has not been created, while if it has been created it is not eternal. So then, if the existent is neither eternal nor created nor both at once, the existent will not exist.

(73) Moreover, if it exists, it is either one or many; but, as we shall show, it is neither one nor many; therefore the existent does not exist. For if it is one, it is either a discrete quantity or a continuum or a magnitude or a body. But whichever of these it be, it is not one; but if it be a discrete quantity it will be divided, and if it be a continuum it will be cut in sections; and similarly, if it be conceived as a magnitude it will not be indivisible, while if it is a body it will be threefold, for it will possess length and breadth and depth. But it is absurd to say that the existent is none of these; therefore the existent is not one. Yet neither is it many. (74) For if it is not one, neither is it many; for the many is a sum of the ones, and hence if the one is destroyed the many also are destroyed with it.

Well, then, it is plain from this that neither does the existent exist nor the non-existent exist; (75) and that they do not both exist—both the existent and the non-existent—is easy to prove.

For if the non-existent exists and the existent exists, the non-existent will be identical with the existent so far as regards existing; and for this reason neither of them exists. For it is admitted that the non-existent does not exist; and it has been proved that the existent is identical therewith; therefore it too will not exist. (76) And what is more, if the existent is identical with the non-existent, both of them cannot exist; for if the pair of them both exist, there is identity, and if there is identity, there is no longer a pair. From which it follows that nothing exists; for if neither the existent exists nor the non-existent nor both, and besides these no other alternative is conceived, nothing exists.

(77) In the next place it must be shown that even if anything exists it is unknowable and inconceivable by man. If, says Gorgias, the things thought are not existent, the existent is not thought. And this is logical; for just as, if it is a property of the things thought to be white it would be a property of white things to be thought—so, if it is a property of things thought not to be existent, it will necessarily be a property of things existent not to be thought. (78) Consequently, this is a sound and consistent syllogism—"If the things thought are not existent, the existent is not thought." But the things thought (for we must take them first) are not existent, as we shall establish; therefore, the existent is not thought. And, in fact, that the things thought are not existent is plain; (79) for if the things thought are existent, all the things thought exist, and in the way, too, in which one has thought them. But this is contrary to sense. For if someone thinks of a man flying or of a chariot running over the sea, it does not follow at once that a man is flying or a chariot running over the sea. So that the things thought are not existent. (80) Furthermore, if the things thought are existent, the non-existent things will not be thought. For opposites are properties of opposites, and the non-existent is the opposite of the existent; and because of this, if "to be thought" is a property of the existent, "not to be thought" will most certainly be a property of the non-existent. But this is absurd; for Scylla and Chimaera and many non-existent things are thought. Therefore the existent is not thought. (81) And just as the things seen are called visible because of the fact that they are seen, and the

audible termed audible because of the fact that they are heard,
and we do not reject the visible things because they are not
heard, nor dismiss the audible things because they are not seen
(for each object ought to be judged by its own special sense and
not by another),—so also the things thought will exist, even if
they should not be viewed by the sight nor heard by the hearing, because they are perceived by their own proper criterion.
(82) If, then, a man thinks that a chariot is running over the sea,
even if he does not behold it he ought to believe that there
exists a chariot running over the sea. But this is absurd; therefore the existent is not thought and apprehended.

(83) And even if it should be apprehended, it is incommunicable to another person. For if the existent things are objects, externally existing, of vision and of hearing and of the
senses in general, and of these the visible things are apprehensible by sight and the audible by hearing, and not conversely,—
how, in this case, can these things be indicated to another person? (84) For the means by which we indicate is speech, and
speech is not the real and existent things; therefore we do not
indicate to our neighbors the existent things but speech, which
is other than the existing realities. Thus, just as the visible thing
will not become audible, and *vice versa,* so too, since the existent
subsists externally, it will not become our speech; and not being
speech it will not be made clear to another person.

(85) Speech, moreover, as he asserts, is formed from the
impressions caused by external objects, that is to say the sensibles; for from the occurrence of flavor there is produced in
us the speech uttered respecting this quality, and by the inci-
dence of color speech respecting color. And if this be so, it
is not speech that serves to reveal the external object, but the
external object that proves to be explanatory of speech. (86)
Moreover, it is not possible to assert that speech subsists in the
same fashion as the visible and audible things, so that the subsisting and existent things can be indicated by it as by a thing
subsisting and existent. For, says he, even if speech subsists, yet
it differs from the rest of subsisting things, and the visible bodies
differ very greatly from spoken words; for the visible object is
perceptible by one sense-organ and speech by another. There-

fore speech does not manifest most of the subsisting things, just
as they themselves do not make plain one another's nature.

(87) Such, then, being the difficulties raised by Gorgias, if
we go by them the criterion of truth is swept away; for there
can be no criterion for that which neither exists nor can be
known nor is naturally capable of being explained to another
person.

4. PLATO, *Meno* 76 A sq. [Meno and Socrates] And now,
Socrates, what is color? —— You are outrageous, Meno, in
thus plaguing a poor old man to give you an answer, when
you will not take the trouble of remembering what is Gorgias'
definition of virtue. —— 76 C. Would you like me to answer
you after the manner of Gorgias, which is familiar to you?
—— I should like nothing better. —— Do not he and you
and Empedocles say that there are certain effluences of existence? —— Certainly. —— And passages into which and
through which the effluences pass? —— Exactly. —— And
some of the effluences fit into the passages, and some of them
are too small or too large? —— True. —— And there is such
a thing as sight? —— Yes. —— And now, as Pindar says,
'read my meaning':—color is an effluence of form, commensurate with sight, and palpable to sense. —— That, Socrates,
appears to me to be an admirable answer. —— Why, yes, because it happens to be one which you have been in the habit of
hearing: and your wit will have discovered, I suspect, that you
may explain in the same way the nature of sound and smell, and
of many other similar phenomena. —— Quite true. —— The
answer, Meno, was in the orthodox solemn vein.

6. PLAN., *ad Hermog.* V. 548. . . . (He [Gorgias] is prais-
ing those Athenians who had been distinguished for bravery in
battle.)

What did these men not have that men should? And what
had they that men should not? May I be empowered to say what
I will and will what I should, thus hiding from heaven's retribu-
tion and escaping man's ill-will? For these men were possessed
of divine virtue but human mortality; in much they preferred
gentle fairness to arrogant righteousness, and in much, to the

letter of the law, propriety in what is said, believing this to be the most divine and universal law, to speak, to be silent, to do and <to desist> in the right matter at the right moment, and theirs was a twofold training in the necessary things, in mind <and in body> counselling the one, perfecting the other, guardians of those unjustly unfortunate but scourges of those unjustly fortunate, bold towards the common good, agreeable towards the seemly, putting a stop to the unreason <of the body> by the reason of the mind, violent to the violent, restrained to the restrained, without fear to those who have no fear, fearful among the fearful. In witness of this they set up symbols of victory over their enemies, ornaments of Zeus, offerings from themselves, not untried in ingrowing war or lawful loves or armed conflict or gracious peace, reverent towards the gods with justice, pious towards their parents with tendance, just towards their fellow-citizens with equality, righteous towards their friends with fidelity. Thus it is that the longing for them did not die with their death but lives deathless for those not living in bodies which are not deathless.

14. Arist., *Soph. El.* 34. 183 b 36. For the [22] training given by the paid professors of contentious arguments was like the treatment of the matter by Gorgias. For they used to hand out speeches to be learned by heart, some rhetorical, others in the form of question and answer, each side supposing that their arguments on either side generally fall among them. And therefore the teaching they gave their pupils was ready but rough. For they used to suppose that they trained people by imparting to them not the art but its products, as though any one professing that he would impart a form of knowledge to obviate any pain in the feet, were then not to teach a man the art of shoemaking or the sources whence he can acquire anything of the kind, but were to present him with several kinds of shoes of all sorts. . . .

21. Plut., *de Adul. et Am.* 23, p. 64 C. For the friend will not, as Gorgias declared, claim service for himself from a friend

[22] Translated by W. D. Ross, *op. cit.*

in just matters but himself serve him in many unjust matters as well.

26. PROC., *in Crat.* 758. It is not a simple truth which Gorgias said. And he said that being is unknowable if it does not achieve appearance, and appearance is of no consequence if it does not achieve being.

III. ANONYMUS IAMBLICHI

In Chapter 20 of Iamblichus' *Protrepticus* appear the writings of an unknown Sophist whose speculations upon the relation of natural virtue to training in virtuous action present clearly the controversy between nature and convention which Eristic Sophistry argued at such length. The theories are referred to "Anonymus Iamblichi" and are generally agreed to date from the end of the fifth century B.C. Not only do they reflect Eristic views, however, but suggest in the author's comments upon the growth of justice, law, and society, and upon the relation of specific virtues to good ends, matters which preoccupy Plato and closely parallel the philosophical views enunciated by the great Sophist whose name provides the title to Plato's *Protagoras*.

While the general argument of Anonymus Iamblichi concerns the need for consistent application to and training in virtuous acts to fortify natural capacity, an important section (see below, III. 3 [1]) raises the fundamental issue of justifying specific virtues only by their relation to "good and useful ends." The writer concludes that the misuse of virtue results in the agent being "utterly bad." The student of moral and political philosophy discovers in these writings equally valuable analyses of the grounds for law and justice. The author denies that obedience to laws is cowardice (see below, III. 6 [1]) and considers the hypothetical case of a man "tougher than steel in body and soul" who might try to "overreach" all others. He concludes that such a man would not go unscathed (see below, III. 6 [2]), on the ground that power is consequent to law and justice. Anonymus Iamblichi anticipates Thomas Hobbes' picture

of the horrors of "warre," with its lawlessness and fear, and traces
to the evils of the lawless state and to "overreaching" the origin
of tyranny.

1. (1) Whatever anyone wishes to bring to the highest perfection, whether it be wisdom, courage, eloquence, the whole
of virtue or some part of it, can be accomplished from these
following: (2) In the first place, there must be the natural
capacity, which is a gift of fortune, but in addition a man must
become a lover of the things that are beautiful and good, in-
dustrious and a precocious learner, passing much time with
them. (3) And if even one of these is absent, it is not possible
to bring anything to the highest pitch; but when a man has all
these, whatever he may cultivate, in this he becomes unsur-
passable.

2. (1) In whatever a man wishes to win reputation among
men, and to be known for what he is, he must begin this straight-
away when young and apply himself consistently throughout,
not in different ways at different times. (2) For each of these
that has been cultivated for a long time, having been begun
early and having grown to completion, wins a secure reputation
and renown, because it is then accepted without hesitation and
does not incur the ill will of men. . . . (6) Further, if the time
given to each action and matter is long, the thing which is being
trained also becomes strong in time; but a brief time cannot accomplish this result. (7) And one could learn the art of discourse
and having learned it could become no worse than his teacher in
a short time; but virtue of any sort is the product of many actions
and this it is impossible for any one who has begun late to accomplish in a short time; but one must be brought up with it and
grow up with it, shielded from bad things, both words and habits,
but practising and perfecting the other things assiduously and
for a long time. . . .

3. (1) Whenever anyone has striven for one of these things
and has succeeded in accomplishing and acquiring it, whether
it be eloquence, wisdom or strength, he must use it for good
and lawful ends. And if anyone shall use the good in his pos-

session for unjust and unlawful ends, this is the worst sort of thing, and it is better for it not to be present at all. (2) And just as he who has any of these things becomes perfectly good by using them for good ends, so he becomes correspondingly utterly bad by using them for wicked ends. (3) Again, he who is reaching for the whole of virtue, must consider from what word or deed he would become best. And the one useful to most would be such. (4) If someone will benefit his neighbors by giving money, he will be compelled to be bad in turn in collecting money. . . . (5) How could anyone, then, not with the distribution of money but indeed in some other way, be a benefactor of men, and this not with evil but with virtue? And still further, how could the recipient retain the gift permanently? (6) This will happen if he defend the laws and justice, for it is this which brings men and cities together and binds them.

4. (1) Moreover, every man must be preeminently master of himself. Such he would certainly be if he should be superior to money—which is the cause of corruption for all—unsparing of his life and soul, being both zealous for just things and pursuing virtue. For in these two things most men are weak. . . .

6. (1) Still further, one must not aim at overreaching others, nor believe that the strength which lies in overreaching is virtue, and obedience to the laws, cowardice. For this is the vilest state of mind and from it arises everything which is opposed to the good things, evil and hurt. . . . (2) If indeed there could be anyone having from the beginning such a nature as this, invulnerable in body, without sickness or suffering, a tremendous man tougher than steel in body and soul, perhaps one would have believed that the strength which lies in overreaching others would suffice for such a person (on the theory that such a man without knuckling under to the law could remain unscathed). He is, of course, not right in his supposition. (3) For even if there should be such a person (as there could not), if he were an ally of the laws and justices, strengthening them and using his strength for them and the things serviceable to them, in this way such a man would survive, otherwise he could not keep his ground. (4) For, evidently, all men become hostile to a

person of this nature because of their own law-abiding, and the
mass either by skill or power would be too much for and prevail
over such a man. (5) Thus it appears that even power itself,
that is to say real power, survives through the law and because
of justice.

7. . . . (12) And tyranny, too, so great an evil as it is,
comes from nothing but lawlessness. And some men believe—
that is, those who reason falsely—that a tyrant is produced by
some other cause and that men are deprived of their freedom
without their being responsible, but because they have been
forced by the tyrant in power. And their reckoning is wrong in
this. (13) For whoever thinks a king or a tyrant arises from
anything but lawlessness and overreaching, is a fool. For whenever everybody has recourse to evil, then this comes about. For
it is impossible for men to live without laws and justice. (14) For
whenever these two things pass out from the mass, law and
justice, then their guardianship and protection retreats into one.
For how otherwise could single rule come round to one unless
the law which is of service to the many had been thrust out?
(15) For it is necessary for this man, who will put down justice
and will appropriate law that is common and serviceable to all,
to be tougher than steel, if he, being one among many, means
to strip these from the mass of men.

THE SOPHISTS OF ERISTIC

Plato's condemnation of the Sophists in the *Laws* (see
above, Introductory, p. 219, 4) is principally directed against the
masters of dialectical disputation who practised Eristic Sophistry.
In the course of satisfying the contemporary demand for training in disputation as a means to success in public life and in the
law courts, the efforts of these professional teachers not un-
naturally came to appeal primarily to men ambitious for material
success. The consequence would appear to have been an increased preference for teaching verbal tricks rather than in-
sistence upon soundly argued philosophical discourse. The
resulting emphasis led to an interest in contest or strife for its

own sake rather than in the determination of the truth or falsity of the propositions under examination.

Once having derived from Protagoras' proposition, *homo mensura*, the distinction between art or convention and nature, the Eristics proceeded to make explicit its implications in the fields of religion, law, and morality. Plato implies that Sophism tended to reduce the grounds for religious belief, moral practice, and legal observance to mere convention.

The specific arguments of Eristic Sophistry are adequately displayed in the political and religious theories attributed to Thrasymachus, Callicles, and Critias.

IV. THRASYMACHUS

Thrasymachus of Chalcedon was a teacher of rhetoric whose very name is used by Aristotle to illustrate the argument that a line of meanings is derived from names: "And Herodicus said of Thrasymachus, 'You are always *bold in battle*.'" The author of a treatise called μεγάλη τέχνη, Thrasymachus appears in Plato's *Republic* as a boisterous and irrepressible but thoroughly honest advocate of the theory that "justice is in the interest of the stronger" (see below, IV. a. 6a).[23] It is noteworthy that, while Thrasymachus in his scorn of Socrates' irony and subtlety impetuously puts forward an argument which he is shown to be unable to defend. Socrates' superior dialectical skill is directed in *Republic* to the refutation of that very argument, reformulated by Glaucon and Adeimantus.

a. The fragments.

6a. PLATO, *Rep.* 338 C. I [Thrasymachus] proclaim that justice is nothing else than the interest of the stronger.

8. HERM., *d. Plat. Phaedr.* 239. Thrasymachus, in his own speech, said something of this sort, that the gods do not see human matters, for they would not overlook the greatest of all man's goods, justice. For we see that men do not make use of it.

[23] See also Plato, *Republic*, 336 C.

b. Imitation.

PLATO, *Rep.* 1. 336 B sq. And now I will not have you say that justice is duty or advantage or profit or gain or interest, for this sort of nonsense will not do for me; I must have clearness and accuracy. . . . I proclaim that justice is nothing else than the interest of the stronger. . . . Forms of government differ; there are tyrannies, and there are democracies, and there are aristocracies. . . . And the government is the ruling power in each state. . . . And the different forms of government make laws democratical, aristocratical, tyrannical, with a view to their several interests; and these laws, which are made by them for their own interests, are the justice which they deliver to their subjects, and him who transgresses them they punish as a breaker of the law, and unjust. And that is what I mean when I say that in all states there is the same principle of justice, which is the interest of the government; and as the government must be supposed to have power, the only reasonable conclusion is, that everywhere there is one principle of justice, which is the interest of the stronger.

V. CALLICLES

Callicles of Acharnae presents a subtler form of the Eristic argument concerning law and justice than that attributed to Thrasymachus and, in doing so, emphasizes the distinction drawn by Sophists between convention and nature. Nothing more than may be inferred from Plato's *Gorgias* is known of Callicles and even his argument concerning the methods by which the many weak control the strong individual is better known in its Nietzchean than in its original formulation. Callicles maintains that were the strong individual, shackled by the weak, sufficiently powerful to throw off the conventions of society, his actions would then be "just" according to nature. It is notable that Callicles' argument contradicts that put forward by Anonymus Iamblichi (see above, III).

PLATO, *Gorgias* 482 E seq. *Callicles:* For the suffering of injustice is not the part of a man, but a slave, who indeed had better die than live; since when he is wronged and trampled upon, he is unable to help himself, or any other about whom he cares. The reason, as I conceive, is that the makers of laws are the majority who are weak; and they make laws and distribute praises and censures with a view to themselves and to their own interests; and they terrify the stronger sort of men, and those who are able to get the better of them, in order that they may not get the better of them; and they say, that dishonesty is shameful and unjust; meaning, by the word injustice, the desire of a man to have more than his neighbors; for knowing their own inferiority, I suspect that they are too glad of equality. And therefore the endeavor to have more than the many, is conventionally said to be shameful and unjust, and is called injustice, whereas nature herself intimates that it is just for the better to have more than the worse, the more powerful than the weaker; and in many ways she shows, among men as well as among animals, and indeed among whole cities and races, that justice consists in the superior ruling over and having more than the inferior. For on what principle of justice did Xerxes invade Hellas, or his father the Scythians? (not to speak of numberless other examples). Nay, but these are the men who act according to nature; yes, by Heaven, and according to the law of nature: not, perhaps, according to that artificial law, which we invent and impose upon our fellows, of whom we take the best and strongest from their youth upwards, and tame them like young lions,—charming them with the sound of the voice, and saying to them, that with equality they must be content, and that the equal is the honorable and the just. But if there were a man who had sufficient force, he would shake off and break through, and escape from all this; he would trample under foot all our formulas and spells and charms, and all our laws which are against nature: the slave would rise in rebellion and be lord over us, and the light of natural justice would shine forth. And this I take to be the sentiment of Pindar, when he says in his poem, that

Law is the king of all, of mortals as well as of immortals;

this, as he says,

Makes might to be right, doing violence with the highest hand;
and as I infer from the deeds of Heracles, for without buying
them. . . .

. . . I do not remember the exact words, but the meaning
is, that without buying them, and without their being given to
him, he carried off the oxen of Geryon, according to the law of
natural right, and that the oxen and other possessions of the
weaker and inferior properly belong to the stronger and superior.

VI. CRITIAS

The subtlety of Callicles' theory of law and justice is par-
alleled by Critias' attempt to apply the distinction between convention and nature to the field of religion. Protagoras (see above,
I. A. a. 4) had expressed doubt concerning both the existence
of the gods and the possibility of securing sound knowledge
concerning the problem. Critias' assumptions concerning the
origin and nature of religious belief begins with an hypothetical
state of war, in which men live without the control of either law
or order. The argument proceeds to show that, inasmuch as
penal laws for the punishment of discoverable crimes are in-
adequate to prevent hidden derelictions, a clever man sought
to overcome this obstacle by inculcating fear of invisible gods
who see all things and who apply divine sanctions. It should
be noted that Critias regards this invention as "the truth concealing under words untrue."

Critias' life and career are as interesting to the philosopher
as is his theory of religion. He was one of the "Thirty Tyrants"
of Athens (and known as the cruelest of the lot), appointed to
his office by the Lacedaemonians in 404 B.C., and killed in battle
by the returning Democrats. An orator and poet, Critias in his
youth had been a pupil of Socrates, and Xenophon, in the
Memorabilia of Socrates, writes that Socrates' accusers made
much of this fact. They asserted that Socrates, in teaching Critias
and Alcibiades, had instructed two men unequalled in the evils

they had done to the state. It may well be recalled, in estimating Plato's strictures upon the Eristics, that Xenophon remarks of both Critias and Alcibiades that ambition was their very life-blood and that they associated with Socrates not so much to model their lives on his but to perfect themselves in speech and action. Xenophon asserts that Critias and Alcibiades left Socrates when they thought themselves superior to their fellow pupils and concludes that it was solely for political ends that they had associated themselves with him.

The fragments.

9. STOB., *Flor.* III. 29, 11. More men are good by training than by nature.

22. ———, III. 37, 15. A worthy character is steadier than the law. For never could an orator pervert it but often he confuses the law this way, that way, and so often brings it to ruin.

25. SEXT. EMP., *Adv. Math.* IX. 54 sq. And [24] Critias, one of the Tyrants at Athens, seems to belong to the company of the atheists when he says that the ancient lawgivers invented God as a kind of overseer of the right and wrong actions of men, in order to make sure that nobody injured his neighbors privily through fear of vengeance at the hands of the Gods; and his statement runs thus:—

> A time there was when anarchy did rule
> The lives of men, which then were like the beasts',
> Enslaved to force; nor was there then reward
> For good men, nor for wicked punishment.
> Next, as I deem, did men establish laws
> For punishment, that Justice might be lord
> Of all mankind, and Insolence enchain'd;
> And whosoe'er did sin was penalized.
> Next, as the laws did hold men back from deeds
> Of open violence, but still such deeds
> Were done in secret,—then, as I maintain,

[24] Translated as *Against the Physicists* I. 54, by R. G. Bury in *Sextus Empiricus*, Vol. III, 31 sq. (London, W. Heinemann, 1936). From The Loeb Classical Library. Reprinted by permission of the President and Fellows of Harvard College.

Some shrewd man first, a man in counsel wise,
Discovered unto men the fear of Gods,
Thereby to frighten sinners should they sin
E'en secretly in deed, or word, or thought.
Hence was it that he brought in Deity,
Telling how God enjoys an endless life,
Hears with his mind and sees, and taketh thought
And heeds things, and his nature is divine,
So that he hearkens to men's every word
And has the power to see men's every act.
E'en if you plan in silence some ill deed,
The Gods will surely mark it; for in them
Wisdom resides. So, speaking words like these,
Most cunning doctrine did he introduce,
The truth concealing under speech untrue.
The place he spoke of as God's abode
Was that whereby he could affright men most,—
The place from which, he knew, both terrors came
And easements unto men of toilsome life—
To wit the vault above, wherein do dwell
The lightnings, he beheld, and awesome claps
Of thunder, and the starry face of heaven,
Fair-spangled by that cunning craftsman Time,—
Whence, too, the meteor's glowing mass doth speed
And liquid rain descends upon the earth.
Such were the fears wherewith he hedged men round,
And so to God he gave a fitting home,
By this his speech, and in a fitting place,
And thus extinguished lawlessness by laws.

And, after proceeding a little farther, he adds:

Thus first did some man, as I deem, persuade
Men to suppose a race of Gods exists.

49. PSEUDODION., *Ars. Rhet.* 6. II. 277, 10. For a man, once
he is born, nothing but death is sure; while he lives it is certain
that he cannot move out of the way of ruin. . . .

PART II

🔲🔲🔲🔲🔲 7

SOCRATES

PHILOSOPHY, born in Miletus early in the sixth century B.C. (see above, Introduction and Ch. 1) is reborn in Athens in the latter part of the fifth century. The genius of Socrates endows philosophy with its "second nature" and in doing so this extraordinary citizen of Athens performs a task no less original than that accomplished by the Milesian, Thales. Early Greek philosophy begins with the speculation of one of the Seven Wise Men and is brought to a term by an original genius.

As Gomperz has argued (see above, pp. 7 sq.) the earliest philosophy, both in its initial stages and in its development, was conditioned by religious beliefs and practices, as well as by materials and techniques which had their origin in mathematics, geography, cosmology, astronomy, and a variety of other scientific disciplines. Similarly, Socrates' original contribution to philosophy emerges from among clearly definable conditions. His philosophy is conditioned by earlier speculation which had established a tradition of rationalist philosophizing within which diverse thinkers had sought to make intelligible the relation between processes of change and what remains permanent throughout change. There was also, as we have observed, the powerful influence of the Sophists upon Socrates' entire philosophical enterprise (see above, Ch. 6).

Yet, in neither the earliest Greek philosophy nor in Socrates' later contribution did the conditions wholly determine the mature speculation which emerged. The issues in which the

251

natural philosophers and the Sophists were interested are evident in Socratic speculation, but Socrates uses what he inherits and experiences in ways at once unique and original. He turns his attention from the problem of change and permanence in the macrocosm to the problems of change in the perceptual situation and to permanence in the self and in concepts. He submits percepts, which were the sole epistemological concern of the Sophists, to investigation; but he does so in order to relate them to concepts. He "searches into himself and into other men" for objective knowledge as distinct from subjective states. He converts the function of dialectic from that of defending an argument—as it had been employed by Zeno and Melissus (see above, Ch. 4)—or of combatting an opponent on eristic grounds alone—as it had been used by Thrasymachus and other of the Sophists (see above, Ch. 6)—to that of "beating out" the truth. And the truth which percepts suggest and which dialectic "beats out" is discovered in proper classification, gotten by induction rather than as the product of arbitrary defining (see above, Ch. 2, pp. 51-52, on Pythagoreans).

Thus in these and in many other instances which might be mentioned, we may trace the antecedents of Socratic philosophy in the thought both of Socrates' predecessors and contemporaries. What we shall not come upon, however, in the philosophies which provided the conditions with which his own philosophy began is Socrates' discovery that philosophy is an art, that it has its own subject matter, and that it employs a unique method (see below, 3).[1]

The root of Socrates' originality is twofold. His person and his character are at once so complex and diverse that for many the man himself appears to embody an unending set of paradoxes. In addition to the puzzles of who and what he is and of what he accomplished, one encounters as well the evidences of a brilliance in conversation seldom if ever equalled; events in an extraordinary civil and military life; a trial and death described with consummate literary skill by a devoted disciple, Plato, who is himself one of the greatest philosophers who ever

---

[1] The references are to selections from writings concerning Socrates' life and thought, which begin below, p. 273.

lived. The result is that the word, *Socrates,* has tended to set alight men's imaginations. There can be little doubt that some portion of the originality ascribed to Socrates has its source in the image men have constructed of this man of genius. Like all such constructions, it is an image to which other images have been attracted and which, in its turn, has acquired creative functions. The result is, for example, that we associate the dictum, "Know thyself," almost wholly with Socrates, rather than with the oracle at Delphi (see below, 3, 29, 31). It may well be that the same aspects of creative powers which adhere to the image of Socrates have rendered Socratic at least some of the sayings and actions which have become integral to the cultural history of the West. Among these, in all likelihood, are the assumptions that virtue is knowledge (see below, 31); that the wisest man is he who knows that he knows nothing (see below, 3), that the unexamined life is not worth living, and that man's most important task is the tendance of the soul.

So difficult, indeed, has the problem become of differentiating the historical Socrates from the image of the man that scholarship has swung like a pendulum between the thesis that there is an historic Socrates and the alternative that the Socrates we know is largely a construct of Platonic, Xenophonic, Aristotelian, and Aristophanic skills.

It is a basic assumption of this book of selections, however, that there is a second root for Socratic originality in addition ,o that nourished in men's imaginations. There are, as we shall see, sound grounds for this assumption, more particularly in Socrates' renunciation of natural philosophy and his criticism of Sophist speculation. If we approach the problem on this assumption, we are provided with two valuable perspectives. The first gives us an independent and intelligible view of early Greek philosophy; the second a better understanding of one of history's great men. As we turn to Socrates, we are at once aware that he knows and expresses clearly the radical differences between other men's interpretations of what philosophy is and his own conviction of what philosophy must be.

"The simple truth is, O Athenians, that I have nothing to do with these studies," says Socrates, after remarking that his slanderers have described him as "a curious person, who searches into things under the earth and in heaven." (Plato, *Apology* 19 C, sq.) He is defending himself before the Athenian court in 400-399 B.C. A capital charge has been brought against him. The judges have been told that Socrates had made the worse appear the better reason, that he had corrupted the youth, and that he had introduced new gods into the city (see below, 32).[2] The charges had been brought by Anytus, a politician, Lycon, an artisan, and Meletus, a poet or son of a poet of that name. It is Meletus who brings the accusation of impiety against Socrates and to this Socrates makes a significant reply. His accusers, he says, have brought against him the "ready-made charges which are used against all philosophers about teaching things up in the clouds and under the earth, and having no gods, and making the worse appear the better cause. . . ."[3]

As the trial proceeds, Meletus' accusations become more specific. He asserts that Socrates is an atheist and then, even more specifically, that Socrates "says that the sun is stone and the moon earth."[4] Meletus, Socrates replies, has mistaken him for Anaxagoras[5] (see also above, Ch. 5, II. B. d. 3 and below, 16).

Socrates' defense at this point is at its most sophistic level and is as little likely to convince the present-day reader as it did the Athenian judges. What is significant is the evidence that the accusers are convinced that Socrates is both a natural philosopher and a Sophist. They believe the latter because of his "eloquence," despite his disclaimer to the contrary. Socrates urges, moreover, that there is as little foundation for the assumption that he is a teacher, who, like the Sophists, takes money, as there is in the assumption that he is interested in cosmology (see below, 17; and above, Ch. 6, Introductory, 3). It is with reference to the latter assumption that Socrates explains the origin of the "ready-made" charges against "all philosophers"[6] and offers an explanation of the force this charge carries. The accusation is familiar,

[2] See also Plato, *Apology* 18 B, sq.
[3] *Ibid.*, 19 B.
[4] *Ibid.*, 26 D.
[5] *Ibid.*
[6] *Ibid.*, 23 D.

not only because it had been brought against Anaxagoras, a protege of Pericles, (see above, p. 134) but also because it is a repetition of calumnies made by Aristophanes, the comic poet, a quarter of a century before Socrates' trial. Socrates tells the Athenians that the notion of Socrates as a "curious person, who searches into things under the earth and in heaven" and as one who "makes the worse appear the better causes" is one "you have seen for yourselves in the comedy of Aristophanes." [7] What they had seen was *The Clouds*, written in 423 B.C. Here Socrates is shown suspended in a basket and caricatured as a man treading air and contemplating the sun.

At his trial, Socrates maintains that Aristophanes had introduced "a man he calls Socrates," who speaks "a deal of nonsense concerning matters of which I do not pretend to know either much or little. . . ." It is evident, however, that Socrates had in fact "paid some attention" to the "cause of all things." [8] He tells Cebes (see below, 14) that when he was young he had a "prodigious desire" to know "natural science," having been led to the subject by its "lofty aims, as being the science which has to do with the causes of things, and which teaches why a thing is, and is created and destroyed. . . ." Socrates adds that he had gone on to consider "the things of heaven and earth," only to conclude that he was "wholly incapable of these inquiries."

We shall return to this passage in Plato's *Phaedo* (see below, 14). At the moment, it is of value to have before us other evidences of Socrates' earlier interest in the "causes of all things." It is significant, for example, that both Theophrastus and Diogenes Laertius mention that Socrates had been a student of Anaxagoras and later of Archelaus (see below, 1). Socrates had talked to Parmenides (see above, Ch. 4, II. B. b. 2). And, of greater weight is the evidence afforded by Xenophon in the *Memorabilia of Socrates* and in various of Aristotle's writings.

---

[7] *Ibid.*, 18, 19 B-C.

[8] See A. E. Taylor, "The Phrontisterion," *Varia Socratica* (Oxford, James Parker & Co., 1911), pp. 129 sq. Taylor believes that what is said in *The Clouds* shows that Socrates "stood from the first in very close relation" with Anaxagoras and Archelaus. Taylor also links Socrates to Pythagorean science through his possession of "mathematical attainments of an advanced kind" (see below, 10).

Xenophon, after Plato the principal source for our information concerning Socrates, was the Athenian who served as commander under Cyrus the Younger. The attack on the army of Artaxerxes II failed and Xenophon commanded the Ten Thousand in the famous retreat described in the *Anabasis*. A cavalryman, the son of a landowner, a member of the class of knights, Xenophon portrayed Socrates from the point of view of an informed and able Athenian who in 399 B.C. had been exiled from Athens. In the first book of the *Memorabilia*, Xenophon tells us that, in Socrates' opinion, it was "sheer folly" to speculate on the cosmos, its operation, and the laws which govern it (see below, 15). Socrates marvels that men should believe that they can resolve such riddles; disagreement among the cosmologists leads him to compare them to madmen. "Madmen" they may have been in Socrates' judgment and men engaged in "folly" but he does, nevertheless, characterize them and summarize their views as one fully informed in the subject. Thus, Xenophon's Socrates disposes in turn, succinctly, specifically, and accurately, of the philosophies of Heraclitus, the Eleatics, Xenophanes, Parmenides, Leucippus, and Democritus (see below, 15).

Aristotle, the third of the important sources of our information concerning Socrates' philosophy, informs us that Socrates was "busying himself about ethical matters and neglecting the world of nature as a whole" (see below, 23). It is notable, however, that Aristotle writes that "in Socrates' time an advance was made so far as the method was concerned," i.e., a method for defining "being," but that "at that time philosophers gave up the study of Nature and turned to the practical subject of goodness, and to political science." [9] Aristotle's remark indicates that Socrates was himself as well versed in the natural philosophy he differentiated from the philosophy of the Sophists as Aristotle is in the basis for the distinction between the study of nature and that of ethics. That Socrates knows "natural philosophy" as well as Sophism is clear, also, from other words he speaks at the trial. He tells the court that he does not mean to disparage any student of natural philosophy; but he waxes ironical in his denial that

[9] Aristotle, *de Partibus Animalium*, I. 1. 642 a 26.

he is a Sophist: "If a man is able to teach," he says, "I honor him for being paid." [10] Socrates believes that the natural philosophers are deluded in their efforts to explain the cosmos and its causes; but he sharply differentiates them from the professional teachers, men who, in his opinion, are dangerous both to the state and to the individual. He dissociates himself from the Sophists' belief that percepts are ultimate, from their conviction that judgments are valid only for the subject who makes them, and from their inferences that morality and religion are relative. He distinguishes himself from those who provide "set speeches," ornamented "with words and phrases." Nevertheless, having come, as Aristotle saw, to the problem of "essence" and "being" in the area of "goodness" in individual and political conduct, Socrates attacks in the main those who believe that "the principles of justice have no existence at all in nature" [11] (see also above, Ch. 6, Introductory, 4). This tells us, however, that his attack upon Sophism is likewise an oblique one directed against the natural philosophy which served as a basis for Sophistic speculation concerning subjective experience and morals.[12]

Still, the Socrates who defends himself before the Athenian court does not do so as an historian of ideas but as an Athenian and a man facing a death sentence. What was he and what are the principal facts of his life?

Socrates was born in Athens in 470-69 B.C. His father, Sophroniscus, was a stonemason; his mother, Phaenarete, a midwife (see below, 1). Socrates followed his father's trade literally. Diogenes Laertius tells us that the draped figures of the Graces on the Parthenon had been attributed to him. He followed his mother's craft figuratively. He tells us that he brings ideas to birth (see below, 12). He married Xantippe, whose name has become a symbol for shrew. Antisthenes remarks of her that she was the "most insupportable woman that is, has been, or ever

[10] Plato, *op. cit.*, 19 E, sq.

[11] Aristotle, *loc. cit.*

[12] See above, pp. 221 sq., for the relation of Protagoras' philosophy to Heraclitean speculation, and pp. 229 sq. for Gorgias' indebtedness to Parmenides and Zeno. See also Plato's *Theaetetus,* quoted above, Ch. 6, I. A. 21 a.

will be," and Socrates explains his marriage to her on the ground that if he can endure her he will have no difficulty in coping with the rest of the world (see below, 10).

Socrates belonged to the tribe of Antiochis. He held but one state office, that of senator. At his trial, he tells the court that he was the only one of the Prytanes who opposed an illegal attempt to try the generals after the battle with the Spartans at Arginusae (see below, 4). It had been proposed that the generals be tried collectively for their failure to take up the bodies of the dead. In consequence of his refusal to join in this attempt by the authorities at judicial murder, an effort was made to arrest and impeach him.

Again, in the course of Plato's account of the trial in the *Apology*, Socrates informs his judges that the oligarchy of the Thirty had sent him and four others to bring in Leon of Salamis, a wealthy banker whose property was to be seized. Socrates, convinced that this is an effort to implicate him in a political murder, tells his judges that he "went quietly home." Leon of Salamis was killed but Socrates took no part in the murder: "The strong arm of that oppressive power did not frighten me into doing wrong. I cared not a straw for death and . . . my only fear was the fear of doing an unrighteous or unholy thing (see below, 4). He distinguished himself in battle, serving at Potidaea (432 B.C.), at Delium (424 B.C.), and at Amphipolis (422 B.C.). Alcibiades describes Socrates as a formidable figure on the field of battle and one unexcelled in his capacity to endure hardship in camp (see below, 6).

Socrates was brought to trial and convicted in 399 B.C., by a vote of 280 to 220. He refused to specify a fine sufficient to warrant the court in substituting a money payment for penalty of death.[13] Indeed, he suggested that the Athenians might properly place and maintain his statue in the Prytaneum, honoring him in this way for his services to the state. Before his trial, Socrates had been advised to prepare his defense. Juries, he was told, often acquit the guilty and condemn the innocent. To this he replied that he had been preparing for his trial throughout his entire life (see below, 33). After his condemnation, Socrates

---

[13] Xenophon, *Memorabilia of Socrates*, IV. 4.

refused to become party to a plan which might have enabled him to escape from prison and flee Athens (see below, 33). He believed that his duty as a citizen required obedience to the laws of the state, however injustly these might be administered. Socrates' trial took place the day before the sacred ship which the Athenians sent each year to Delos was crowned. During the period of the ship's voyage, the city was not permitted to be polluted by public executions. A month after his condemnation, Socrates drank the hemlock and died in his prison cell, surrounded by friends and disciples (see below, 36).

If we accept this account of Socrates' life, trial, and death— bearing in mind that no single detail of it has not been subject to controversy—we may proceed to some of the interpretations of this man's thought and actions and, at the outset, to those which have contributed to the image of Socrates which has served to light men's imaginations for over two millennia.

Plato in the dialogues, *Apology, Euthyphro, Crito,* and *Phaedo* and Xenophon in his *Memorabilia of Socrates* do not radically disagree concerning Socrates' life and death. There are, however, radical differences in the Platonic and Xenophonic interpretations of Socrates as a philosopher.

Plato's Socrates in *Phaedo* speaks to his friends of "proofs" for the immortality of the soul and he does so in terms of a theory of Ideas, concepts, or universals in which these objects of the philosopher's search for knowledge transcend the world of change, becoming, and percepts. Xenophon's account of Socrates is in large part one which concerns a man intent upon helping men to "become good men and true, capable of doing their duty by house and household, by relatives and friends, by city and fellow-citizens." As Alcibiades describes Socrates in Plato's *Symposium,* the philosopher is an earthy enough character. But, for the most part, Plato's Socrates is, in a metaphorical sense, otherworldly. His Socrates voices the conviction [14] that "the true philosophers are ever studying death," are eager for the release of the soul from the body, and know that true knowledge of the absolutes, the Ideas, can be gotten only by thought, not through feelings.

[14] Plato, *Phaedo,* 67 D-E.

Xenophon's Socrates is otherworldly in a literal sense: He is contemptuous of material goods and luxuries. Antiphon, who tells Socrates that he had supposed that philosophy must add to happiness, remarks that the fruits Socrates has reaped are apparently very different: ". . . You are living a life that would drive even a slave to desert his master. Your meat and drink are of the poorest: the cloak you wear is not only a poor thing, but is never changed, summer or winter; and you never wear shoes or tunic. . . ." Socrates, remarking that he feels certain Antiphon "would choose death in preference to a life" like his own, concludes only that "to have no wants is divine." [15]

The significant point of the different interpretations is not so much that Plato is both a poet and a dramatist in writing the *Dialogues* and that Xenophon contents himself with straightforward prose. It is, rather that Plato's Socrates is the discoverer of concepts; that, as Aristotle tells us, Socrates "did not make the universals or definitions exist apart. . . ." whereas "Plato . . . held that the problem applied not to sensible things but to entities of another kind. . . ." (see below, 23). Moreover, Plato portrays Socrates as the embodiment of philosophy and examines the philosophical life as a search for reality separate and apart from the world of phenomena. In consequence of Plato's separation of universals from this world, Socrates is depicted as a man who progressively comes to deny value to the world of perception. Philosophy becomes the process of ascending to the suprasensible world of Ideas and Socrates becomes an integral part of an ideal philosophy, the goal of which is to show how this world may be transcended. The prisoners make their ascent, in the *Republic,* from the Cave to the Idea of the Good. The man in search of beauty must move, in the *Symposium,* from the world of fair forms to that of absolute and transcendent beauty. The gods, in *Phaedrus,* journey by chariot to a "heaven beyond heaven."

Xenophon's Socrates is earthbound. He is the Socrates of whom Cicero writes in the *Tusculan Disputations* that he was ". . . the first to call philosophy down from the heavens and set her in the cities of men and bring her also into their homes

[15] Xenophon, *op. cit.,* I. 6. 2.

and compel her to ask questions about life and morality and things good and evil. . . ." Plato's Socrates continues the search for absolute justice, even after the searchers come upon justice "tumbling at our feet." Xenophon's Socrates is portrayed in endless discussions with the greatest variety of Athenians (see below, 2), searching into himself and into other men; offering counsel on practical matters and helping them to solve their moral problems (see below, 31); discussing the duties owed by son to father; expatiating upon the proper care of a household and the proper rule of a kingdom [16] and visiting the painter and the sculptor, inquiring into the nature of their arts (see below, 13). Xenophon's is the portrait of a shrewd man, capable of coping and eager to cope with the ambitious, the untrained, and the arrogant. His mission is to teach men to recognize their own powers and limitations.

Each portrait of Socrates expresses its maker's conviction that this is the true Socrates. Each mirrors the person and character of a great and complex man. Even Aristotle, whose method of writing philosophy largely precludes the use of portrait or characterization, and who gives us in the first history of philosophy a sober account of his "lisping" predecessors, does not wholly escape the impact of the man and of his death. It is true that, for Aristotle, Socrates is primarily the thinker who sought to "syllogize" and define (see below, 23). And it is no doubt true, as Jaeger writes,[17] that Aristotle learned of Socrates by reading and not through "any living presence of the Socratic spirit in the Academy of the sixties." Still, it is a no less sound tradition that at the death of Alexander the Great, when Aristotle fell under suspicion as the world conqueror's master spy in Athens, Aristotle is said to have left Athens for Euboea, "Lest the Athenians sin twice against philosophy." [18]

But if Plato, Xenophon and even Aristotle felt the force of what Cicero was to call "the greatness" of Socrates' "genius," they are not alone in this, nor are they alone in offering conflicting accounts of the man and of this thought. In Cicero's opinion,

[16] *Ibid.*

[17] Werner Jaeger, *Aristotle* (Oxford, Clarendon Press, 1934), p. 13.

[18] "Non concedam Atheniensibus bis peccare in Philosophiam." Ammonius Hermeiou, *Vita Aristoteles* (Leiden, 1621), p. 68.

Socrates' many-sided methods of discussion and the varied nature of its subjects led not only the men of the so-called Socratic schools but others as well to produce "many warring sects." Antistenes, the Cynic, is said by Diogenes Laertius to have walked each day from the Peiraeus to the city of Athens in order to hear Socrates. The author of the *Lives of Eminent Philosophers* tells us also that Aristippus was drawn from Cyrene to Athens by Socrates' renown. Antisthenes learned from Socrates "his hardihood, emulating his disregard of feeling, and thus inaugurated the Cynic way of life." But, whereas Antisthenes formulated his Socratic philosophy in the conviction that he would "rather be mad than feel pleasure," Aristippus, the Cyrenaic, formulated *his* Socratic philosophy in accord with the assertion that "bodily pleasures are far better than mental pleasures, and bodily pains far worse than mental pains." There came to Socrates, as well, Euclides of Megara, a student of Parmenidean philosophy, who seized on Socrates' search for knowledge in conceptual terms as the most significant aspect of the great Athenian's teaching. Euclides used dialectic and asserted that the contradictory of the good does not exist.

The spectacle of the men of the "Socratic schools" discovering what for each is the ground for Socratic philosophy and each interpreting the philosopher and his philosophy in a different way repeats itself long after the Cyrenaics and the Cynics and the Megareans have given way to the Epicureans and the Stoics and the latter have given way to the philosophers of the Renaissance and of modern times. For Erasmus, Socrates was "St. Socrates." For some, in a more recent era, he was as much of a quibbler and master of irony as Thrasymachus believes him to be in the discussion which enlivens the first book of Plato's *Republic* (see below, 22). Socrates has been taken by some who emphasize the dictum, "Know thyself," to be one of history's most ardent individualists, the arch rebel against tyranny, whether of rulers or of dogmatists controlling men's minds. For others, on the contrary, he is a mere instrument, used by such reactionary aristocrats as Crito and Critias and later as a literary figure by Plato, to halt in its stride any philosophical, literary, or artistic movement towards novelty. For Nietzsche,

Socrates is the great "nay-sayer" to feeling and instinct, the great "yea-sayer" to reason. For Hegel, Socrates is a tragic character who suffered death because in his relation to the state subjectivity and objectivity come into collision. The result of this conflict of rights is that one set of values is destroyed. "His own world could not understand Socrates," writes Hegel and one need not accept Hegel's dialectic of history to be convinced that Socrates' fellow-Athenians had no conception of the meaning of this gadfly's mission (see below, 4). Socrates understood his mission to be one "given to the state by God," so that the state may be stirred to life. His task is to fasten upon the citizens, "arousing and persuading and representing" them "all day long and in all places." [19] The Athenians failed to understand Socrates' task, which he took to be the improvement of men's souls. Evidently, they were no less blind to his use of art, which developed from the conviction that neither he nor any other man would knowingly practise a technique intended to corrupt rather than benefit the men with whom a man must live (see below, 24). They killed him because they mistook him for one who sought to introduce a new religion into Athens. They seem never to have realized that he brought, rather, a new philosophy.

These diverse interpretations lead again to the first root of Socrates' originality. The image of this philosopher plays no small role in the rebirth of philosophy at his hands. A phrase in Cicero's *Tusculan Disputations* provides a sound starting point for further speculation concerning Socratic creativity. Cicero remarks on "the greatness of Socrates' genius," and the word *genius,* in some of the senses in which men of the eighteenth century used it,[20] helps us better to understand the role Socrates has played in the speculative tradition of the West. It is clear, in the first place, that Socrates' image has been that of the "tutelary genius," which Shaftesbury well describes as "the imagination or supposition of a . . . presence," needed to inspire a mind "with more than what I feel at ordinary hours." In the instance of Socrates, one part of this "supposition," this ideal model, is com-

---

[19] Plato, *Apology,* 30E-31A.
[20] See my *The Artist as Creator* (Baltimore, The Johns Hopkins Press, 1956), Chs. 4-6.

prised of the rationalist philosopher, who transfers the object of his rationalism from cosmic "substances" to the self and to concepts. For what Socrates sought was "knowledge" and, if we are to believe Aristotle, he erred in identifying prudence with scientific knowledge rather than with virtue (see below, 28). Socrates perfected a rationalist dialectic for "beating out" the truth which, in his opinion, must be sought beyond appearances. He established the conception of an art as a rational technique (see below, 19, 20) by means of which men could demonstrate and make intelligible what is done, made, or thought. He undertook to define and classify the arts, including philosophy, in terms of the autonomy and uniqueness of their subject-matter (see below, 25). He directed his dialectical search "into himself and other men" in order to establish the soul and concepts as objects of knowledge (see below, 13).

Simultaneously—and here appears the other side of the coin of "genius,"—one notes the demonic in contrast to the rationalist in Socrates' nature. He listened to his own *daimon* and communed with his "inner self" (see below, 4, 34). Precisely as he adopted for his own uses the rationalism of the natural philosophers, so he adapts to his own uses the subjectivity which is the core of Sophist theory of knowledge and in so doing provides the *fons et origo* for the mysticism of Plato, Plotinus, and St. Augustine. These aspects of Socratic genius are manifestations of diverse and ostensibly incompatible characteristics: of a man great by nature and as a result of discipline; of one whose art is intelligible but whose person and wisdom are not comprehensible in rational terms alone; of a man who practises an art and observes a mystery, who traditionally stirs other men to originality, and yet one who in moments of stress and danger provides steadfastness for those who require a symbol of courage.

Yet, both the rational and the demonic aspects of his life and thought may be made compatible in terms of Socrates' appetite for knowledge of what men think and what they do. He pursued his search for knowledge in the town: "I am a lover of knowledge," he says, "and the men who dwell in the city are my teachers, and not the trees, or the country." [21]

[21] Plato, *Phaedrus* 230 D.

In Athens, he set about his task, that of achieving sound knowledge in his "search into himself and into other men." Xenophon tells us (see below, 2) that "Socrates went in the morning to the places for walking and the gymnasia. . . . He was generally engaged in discourse and all who pleased were at liberty to hear him." Those who listened in the public places heard a Socrates who discussed, argued, questioned, and waxed ironical. He spoke to the great,—to Alcibiades, Critias, Parmenides,—and to the slave; to devoted disciples; to imitators of his dialectical method; to enthusiasts; to the overly ambitious; to the well- and the ill-informed. We see him at the house of Callias, arguing with the great Sophist, Protagoras, and at the shop of Cleiton, the sculptor, and Parrhasius, the painter (see below, 27).

Thus, as Xenophon tells us, Socrates was "continually in men's sight." With equal accuracy, it may be said that men, including himself, were always in his sight and that precisely as Socrates was physically within the Athenian's sight in the fifth century B.C., so he has never since been out of men's mind's eye.

This constant encounter and endless dialogue account for the incredible variety men have discovered in Socrates and the seemingly irreconcilable evaluations they have made of him. The "images" they got of the man are, in fact, the precise and specific details of a Socrates we have interpreted as a man urged on both rationally and demonically, as a man searching for complete intelligibility and yet dependent upon the most subjective of states in his communions with himself.

As we see Socrates through the eyes of the men who gathered about him in the *Agora,* we are made aware of striking contrasts. These begin with Socrates' physical appearance. Alcibiades compares him to the carved head of a Silenus (see below, 8). Socrates describes himself in terms ordinarily reserved for caricature (see below, 9). Yet, as Alcibiades carries to its conclusion the comparison of the man to the head of a Silenus, he tells us that he looked within and saw in Socrates "divine and golden images of . . . fascinating beauty."

The contrast between the inner and outward self is but the beginning of the paradox. Alcibiades describes Socrates, the formidable soldier on the battlefield (see below, 5). Plato presents him as a no less formidable disputant, employing dialectic to rout the rude and combative Eristic, Thrasymachus (see below, 22; above, Ch. 6, IV). Nor is Socrates gentler in dealing with the renowned Protagoras, who becomes ruffled and excited as the conversation proceeds.[22] Yet this expert hoplite and flinty disputant offers the most self-effacing of prayers for himself and for *Phaedrus* (see below, 7).

The contrast pervades more than physical appearance and conversational techniques. Socrates never evades the most difficult problems, nor did he need or use set speeches to counter an opponent. "Discussion," he believes, "is one thing, making an oration is quite another." Alcibiades [23] remarks that he would be greatly surprised if Socrates "yielded to any living man in the power of holding and apprehending an argument." Yet, as Alcibiades also observes, Socrates expresses his philosophy in the language of pack-asses and smiths and cobblers and curriers (see below, 11). He was, says Alcibiades, "always repeating the same things in the same words" and an ignorant man might be disposed to laugh at Socrates. But the words, in fact, are "the only words which have a meaning in them. . . ."

The same sense of paradox is evoked by Socrates in less obvious respects than those to which we have just made men-tion. In a notable example, Socrates asserts in Plato's *Crito*, "I am not the kind of man to obey anything else but the dictate of reason, and not only on this occasion, but at all times I follow the one that seems to be best" (see below, 35). Yet, this master of dialectic and definition, who searches for concepts by use of reason (see below, 13, 30, 31) stands silent in the armed camp. The unforgettable scene is recalled by Alcibiades. Socrates remained fixed in thought until out of curiosity some Ionians brought their mats and slept in the open air to watch him, "while he stood all night and all day and the following morning; and with the return of light he offered up a prayer to the sun, and went his way" (see below, 6).

[22] Plato, *Protagoras,* 333 D-E.
[23] Plato, *Symposium* 221. Contrast with Gorgias' method (see above, Ch. 6, II. a. 14).

This is not the only occasion on which this rationalist philosopher communed with himself in silence. In moments of greatest stress (see below, 33), he takes counsel of his *daimon*. These moments would appear to have been occasions for dialogues with himself. It may be that they suggest for Socrates the basic significance of the dictum, "Know thyself," the belief that the ultimate truths of philosophy may not be expressed in words or designated in symbols.

The facts are that Socrates is both rationalist and mystic and that these terms suggest properly the extremes of experience to which Socrates submitted himself. As we have observed, he meets and discusses the most diverse subjects with the greatest variety of men. He brought within the compass of his experience the self, which for him is one of the objects of his search. It may be surmised, in fact, that in attempting to know himself he encountered, in the laboratory of his own mind, material as varied as that he came upon in examining the slave boy and in instructing Alcibiades in virtue.

Socrates pursued this course because the search into himself and into other men is integral to his method of induction. In submitting himself to the widest and most varied experiences of himself and other men in the only external world in which he was interested—that of men and of the town—Socrates sought the unities which would explain the diversity. Once this point is understood, the degree of paradox in Socrates' character is notably diminished and with it the no less paradoxical appearance of his actions.

Socrates' philosophical method begins in induction (see below, 23). It is evident, however, that while he regards these direct experiences of the self and of other men as necessary for a philosophy, they are not sufficient. The percepts gotten in such experiences must be submitted to dialectic, by means of which their truth is "beaten out." What are "beaten out" are objects of knowledge,—the self and concepts which are not perceived (see below, 11, 23, 31). Socrates' concepts are the "essences" of the percepts, the single and ultimate meanings of the multiple and diverse objects and events of perceptual experience. The percepts are what the Heraclitean world of flux and change is for the perceiver (see below, 23). They are the world in which processes move from contrary to contrary (see above, Ch. 5, IV. B. 135 [50] sq.), a world of becoming to which the Sophists limit knowing (see above, Ch. 6). For Socrates, experience of percepts is necessary for the knowing process but a knowledge of concepts is essential if we are to classify correctly and order our experience of the self and of the external world (see below, 23). "Two things may be fairly ascribed to Socrates," writes Aristotle, "inductive arguments and universal definitions" (see below, 23). Aristotle also tells us, that Socrates searched for the "essence" and adds that speculation about contraries is science. It is this "science" with which Socrates deals directly.

It is within this framework of reference that Socrates distinguishes philosophy from other disciplines, and marks off his own speculations from those of his predecessors. Plato tells us in the *Apology* how Socrates went about the first task, that of differentiating philosophy from other arts (see below, 3). Appropriately enough, Plato describes Socrates' search for what philosophy is in terms of the most obvious of all Socratic paradoxes. In order to determine the truth or falsity of the Delphic oracle's pronouncement that Socrates was the wisest man in Greece, (see below, 32) [24] Socrates inquires of other men. He concludes, after his questionings, that the oracle is correct. He, Socrates, knows that he knows nothing and his own wisdom is established in comprehending what this lack of knowledge means. He arrives at this paradoxical position by questioning the poets, the artisans, and the politicians (see below, 3).

The portion of Plato's *Apology* which concerns these questionings merits especial attention. It is important not alone because it shows Socrates in search of a wise man or because it argues the ignorance of the poets, the politicians, and the artisans. It is also important because it shows the way Socrates sets philosophy apart from other arts, precisely as he had differentiated it from natural philosophy and Sophism. It tells us what Socrates believed the art of philosophy must be.

The poets, we learn, "say many fine things, but do not understand the meaning of them" (cf. 25, below). Poets write poetry

[24] See also Plato, *Apology*, 21 E sq.

by "a sort of genius and inspiration." There is, in poetry, no unique subject matter. The poet is a mime and does not practice a unique art. The poetic and the tragic arts are not autonomous. In contrast to the poets, the artisans do use and know the art they practise. Theirs is an intelligible technique, but it is one successful only in relation to a precisely limited subject matter. Socrates admits that the artisans know many things of which he is ignorant. But, because they were good workmen, "they thought they also knew all sorts of high matters." They evidently believe that because their art is intelligible, they can transfer its techniques at will to any and all subject matters. The politicians err because they are convinced that they *know* but in fact know nothing. "I," says Socrates, "neither know nor think that I know."

The conclusion to Socrates' search is not merely, as this final sentence would suggest, a negative one. Socrates has grasped the essential point in distinguishing the philosopher's art from that of the poet, the artisan, the politician, and the physicist. Socrates is in search of proper classification for the sake of knowledge. He has achieved the conception of specific arts which are "masters of their own subject matter" (see below, 25).

Socrates submits Sophism to the same test. For the Sophists, the subject matter of philosophy is "percepts." The Sophist method is that of definition, but their defining is conventional, nominal, and arbitrary (see above, Ch. 6). They err not only because for them "percepts" constitute the whole of the subject matter of philosophy, but also because they misuse Parmenides' and Zeno's dialectic: they use it to show that knowing, being, and communicating are not possible (see, for example, Ch. 6, above, II. A. a. 14).

As we have observed, Socrates' attack upon the Sophists is by implication a denial of the validity of natural philosophy. His denial, however, is implicit not only in his attacks on the Sophists; he makes it explicit in his own philosophy as well. His definitions are brought to the test of experience, as those of the Pythagoreans and the geometers were not (see above, Ch. 2, pp. 51-52).[25]

[25] See, also, above, Aristotle's comment, Ch. 2, C. b. 3; and below, 17, where Socrates' comments on astronomers and geometers are given.

There are, however, sharper and more explicit differences between the earlier Greek and Socratic philosophy. In the *Phaedo*, in a passage to which we have already referred (see above, p. 254), Socrates remarks (see below, 16) that he had been interested in a book by Anaxagoras. He expresses dissatisfaction with Anaxagoras' failure to develop correctly the conception of *Nous* and with the pluralist's failure to describe mind in any other than material terms (see above, Ch. 5, II. B. b. 12, II. B. c). Socrates here criticizes not only a physical and materialist conception of soul or mind, but also attacks the underlying theory of the natural philosophers that mechanism and necessity are the necessary and sufficient principles of explanation. "There is," he says, "a strange confusion of cause and conditions in all this" (see below, 16).

To natural philosophy and its emphasis upon necessity and mechanism as the presuppositions of philosophical speculation, Socrates opposes the twofold theory of choice and teleology (see below, 16, 21). The "best" serves Socrates as the principle he judges to be strongest. In relation to it, he describes his inductive procedure: "I first assumed some principle which I judged to be the strongest, and then I affirmed as true whatever seemed to agree with this, whether relating to the causes or to something else; and that which disagreed, I regarded as untrue . . ." (see below, 20).

Socrates' teleology is, in fact, a reinterpretation of Anaxagoras' conception of Mind ordering the cosmos, despite its contrast to Anaxagoras' interpretation of the ordering principle, Mind, as material and mechanist in character (see above, Ch. 5, p. 137, and II. B. c. 1). On the other hand, Socratic teleology is in sharp contrast to the basic beliefs of the Atomists. For Leucippus, necessity is the governing principle in the universe. For Democritus, mechanism and necessity are the necessary and sufficient frameworks of reference for the explanation of all events in the world of becoming (see above, p. 24, and Ch. 5, The Atomists). The Atomists explicitly exclude purpose as an explanatory principle in the cosmic process (see above, Ch. 5, IV. B. 66). Socrates introduces teleological principles (see below, 30) and with them, functional definition (see below, 13, 31).

The methodology is intended to permit his arguments to proceed from percepts to concepts. Percepts which appear to differ may be identical in relation to "the best"; percepts which appear to be identical may differ because they do not function in terms of an identical end. The classification of percepts requires concepts, i.e., essences for their comprehension (see below, 31).

The teleological mode of classification clearly holds for Socrates' conception of philosophy in general. His outstanding and abiding interest, however, is in such moral concepts as "courage," "wisdom," and "justice." The Socratic dictum, "virtue is knowledge" (see below, 27-30), leads Socrates to an examination of man's virtue or excellence. This virtue is not only the concept by means of which we correctly classify the specific virtues and specific acts; it is also the self into which Socrates searches. It is the object, as well, both of knowledge and of the perfection of the self. Whereas the earlier natural philosophers had speculated upon "air," "fire," "water," and "seeds" persisting throughout change, Socrates searches for the self which retains its identity throughout a man's specific actions and individual decisions.

Xenophon portrays a Socrates for whom the practical, rather than the theoretical, problems of philosophy are of primary interest. His is the Socrates who believes that a man who knows what is good will do no evil (see below, 26, 28, 29). There are in the *Memorabilia* many accounts of Socratic examinations of moral issues. Not the least interesting of these is that with Euthydemus (see below, 31) in which the close relation between knowledge of what to do and of sound classification is a major issue. These investigations underline the differences between Socrates' interests and those of the natural philosophers. They serve, as well, to draw attention to Socrates' beliefs in the objective nature of virtue and of the self, beliefs which are in striking contrast to those of the Sophists.

Socrates was heir to much in philosophy but this does nothing to diminish the fact of his originality, any more than does the additional fact that men imitated the dialectic he used.[26] For Socrates and in him, philosophy becomes the separate art

[26] Plato, *Apology*, 23 C.

which is at once master of its unique subject matter and one
practised by use of its own unique technique (see below, 27).

❁   ❁   ❁   ❁

Our principal interest in this conclusion to a study of early
Greek philosophy has been to examine Socrates in relation to
his predecessors and to indicate how, from his renunciation of
both natural philosophy and Sophism, he proceeded to his own
contribution to speculation. It is difficult, however, to conclude
any study of Socrates without a mention of Socrates' relation to
Plato, his great disciple, a subject which leads far beyond the
confines of a book on early Greek philosophy. Still, it is not
irrelevant to note that what Plato, Xenophon, and Aristotle
report concerning Socrates' evaluation of natural philosophy
reduces the likelihood that he is the source for those arguments
in Plato's *Dialogues* which more particularly concern the metaphysical and ontological status of the Ideas. It is a fair inference
from Socrates' views on the physicists, that Aristotle is correct
in his assertion that it was Plato, not Socrates, who gave the
universals or definitions an existence apart from sensible objects (see below, 23, 24).

The same conclusion is implicit in our interpretation of
Socrates as a rare instance of original genius. Even during his
lifetime, some of Socrates' disciples followed him and his method
in a wholly mimetic fashion and this is, indeed, an integral part
of the chronicle of genius. It is also true, however, that some
disciples of a genius have been original and creative and surely
among these we may count Plato. Perhaps it is Kant who offers
the soundest explanation of the relationship between such creative minds as Socrates' and Plato's: The skill each original genius
displays is imparted to him by nature and cannot be com-
municated, "and so it dies with him, until nature endows another in the same way, so that he only needs an example in
order to put in operation in a similar fashion the talent of which
he is conscious." It is reflections such as this which lead one to
accept Geoffrey Mure's wise inference: [27] "To suggest that from

[27] Geoffrey Mure, *Aristotle* (New York, Oxford University Press,
1932) p. 26n.

the ages of thirty to sixty . . . Plato should have thought nothing worth publication save mere reproductions of his master's
philosophy is to deny all power of vital development to the
Socratic inspiration."

In any case, whatever conclusions one may reach concerning the Socratic problem, a book of selections from early Greek
philosophy reaches its proper conclusion in an account of the
life, death, and speculation of a great man. It does so more particularly in a philosophy which is better understood because
Socrates adopted not only an epimethean attitude towards the
traditions of natural philosophy and Sophism but also a prome-
thean one from which emerged one classical answer to the question, What is philosophy?

LIFE AND TEACHING [28]

1. D.L., *Lives* II. 18. Socrates was the son of Sophroniscus,
a sculptor, and of Phaenarete, a midwife, as we read in the
Theaetetus of Plato; he was a citizen of Athens and belonged to
the deme of Alopece. . . . 19. According to some authors, he
was a pupil of Anaxagoras. . . . When Anaxagoras was condemned, he became a pupil of Archelaus, the physicist. . . .
Duris makes him out to have been a slave and to have been employed on stonework, and the draped figures of the Graces on
the Acropolis have by some been attributed to him. . . . 44.
He was born, according to Apollodorus in his *Chronology*, in the
archonship of Apsephion, in the fourth year of the 77th Olympiad,

[28] The translations used here are from Benjamin Jowett's *The Dialogues
of Plato* (Oxford, Oxford University Press, 1871), and *The Works of
Aristotle Translated into English*, edited by W. D. Ross (Oxford, Oxford
University Press, 1928); Xenophon's *Memorabilia of Socrates*, translated by
E. C. Marchant, Xenophon's *Anabasis, Symposium, and Apology*, translated
by Charleton L. Brownson and O. J. Todd, and Diogenes Laertius' *Lives of
Eminent Philosophers*, translated by R. D. Hicks, all from (Cambridge,
Harvard University Press, 1923, 1918-1922, and 1925, respectively), reprinted by permission of the publishers and The Loeb Classical Library. The
selection and order of the excerpts which follow are my own and are intended both to provide basic information concerning Socrates and provide
the reader with the grounds for the principal arguments in the Introduction
to this part of the *Selections*. I have found H. Ritter and L. Preller's *Historia Philosophiae Graecae* (Hamburg, F. Perth, 1838) most useful.

on the 6th day of the month of Thargelion, when the Athenians purify their city, which according to the Delians is the birthday of Artemis. He died in the first year of the 95th Olympiad at the age of seventy (400-399 B.C.).

Socrates' daily life.

2. XEN., *Mem.* I. 1. 10. He was constantly in public, for he went in the morning to the places for walking and the gymnasia; at the time when the market was full he was to be seen there; and the rest of the day he was where he was likely to meet the greatest number of people; he was generally engaged in discourse, and all who pleased were at liberty to hear him; 11. Yet no one ever either saw Socrates doing, or heard him saying, anything impious or profane. . . .[29]

Socrates' search for a man wiser than himself.

3. PLATO, *Apology* 21 A. sq. You must have known Chaerephon; he was early a friend of mine, and also a friend of yours, for he shared in the exile of the people, and returned with you. Well, Chaerephon . . . went to Delphi and boldly asked the oracle to tell him whether—as I was saying, I must beg you not to interrupt—he asked the oracle to tell him whether there was any one wiser than I was, and the Pythian prophetess answered, that there was no one wiser. . . .

Why do I mention this? Because I am going to explain to you why I have such an evil name. When I heard the answer, I said to myself, What can the god mean? and what is the interpretation of this riddle? For I know that I have no wisdom, small or great. What then can he mean when he says that I am the wisest of men? And yet he is a god, and cannot lie; that would be against his nature. After long consideration, I at least thought of a method of trying the question. I reflected that if I could only find a man wiser than myself, then I might go to the god with a refutation in my hand. I should say to him, "Here is a man who is wiser than I am; and you said that I was the wisest." Accordingly I went to one who had the reputation of wisdom, and

---

[29] *Xenophon's Memorabilia of Socrates*, translated by J. S. Watson (New York, Harper & Row, Publishers, Inc., 1855), p. 352.

observed him—his name I need not mention; he was a politician whom I selected for examination—and the result was as follows: When I began to talk with him, I could not help thinking that he was not really wise, although he was thought wise by many, and wiser still by himself; and I went and tried to explain to him that he thought himself wise, but was not really wise; and the consequence was that he hated me, and his enmity was shared by several who were present and heard me. So I left him, saying to myself, as I went away . . . I am better off than he is,—for he knows nothing, and thinks that he knows. I neither know nor think that I know. . . . After this I went to one man after another. . . . 22 A. I will tell you the tale of my wanderings and of the 'Herculean' labors, as I may call them, which I endured only to find at last the oracle irrefutable. When I left the politicians, I went to the poets; tragic, dithyrambic, and all sorts. And there, I said to myself, you will be detected; now you will find out that you are more ignorant than they are. Accordingly, I took them some of the most elaborate passages in their own writings, and asked what was the meaning of them— thinking that they would teach me something. Will you believe me? I am almost ashamed to speak of this, but still I must say that there is hardly a person present who would not have talked better about their poetry than they did themselves. That showed me in an instant that not by wisdom do poets write poetry, but by a sort of genius and inspiration; they are like diviners or soothsayers who also say many fine things, but do not understand the meaning of them. And the poets appeared to me to be much in the same case; and I further observed that upon the strength of their poetry they believed themselves to be the wisest of men in other things in which they were not wise. . . .

At last I went to the artisans, for I was conscious that I knew nothing at all, as I may say, and I was sure that they knew many fine things; and in this I was not mistaken, for they did know many things of which I was ignorant, and in this they certainly were wiser than I was. But I observed that even the good artisans fell into the same error as the poets;—because they were good workmen they thought that they also knew all sorts of high matters, and this defect in them overshadowed their

wisdom. . . . 23. This investigation has led to my having many
enemies of the worst and most dangerous kind, and has given
occasion also to many calumnies. . . .

Socrates describes himself and his mission.

4. ———— 28 D. Strange, indeed, would be my conduct, O
men of Athens, if I who, when I was ordered by the generals
whom you chose to command me at Potidaea and Amphipolis
and Delium, remained where they placed me, like any other
man, facing death; if, I say, now, when, as I conceive and imagine,
God orders me to fullfil the philosopher's mission of searching
into myself and other men, I were to desert my post through
fear of death, or any other fear. . . . 30 C. If you kill me you
will not easily find another like me, who, if I may use such a
ludicrous figure of speech, am a sort of gadfly, given to the state
by the God; and the state is like a great and noble steed who is
tardy in his motions owing to his very size and requires to be
stirred into life. . . . 31 C. Some one may wonder why I go
about in private giving advice and busying myself with the
concerns of others, but do not venture to come forward in
public and advise the state. I will tell you the reason of this.
You have often heard me speak of an oracle or sign which comes
to me, and is the divinity which Meletus ridicules in the indictment. This sign I have had ever since I was a child. The sign is
a voice which comes to me and always forbids me to do something which I am going to do, but never commands me to do
anything, and this is what stands in the way of my being a
politician. And rightly, as I think. For I am certain, O men of
Athens, that if I had engaged in politics, I should have perished
long ago, and done no good either to you or to myself. . . .
32 A. I can give you proofs of this, not words only, but deeds,
which you value more than words. Let me tell you a passage
of my own life which will prove to you that I should never
have yielded to injustice from any fear of death, and that if I
had not yielded I should have died at once. I will tell you a
story—tasteless perhaps and commonplace, but nevertheless
true. The only office of state which I ever held, O men of Athens,
was that of senator; the tribe Antiochis, which is my tribe, had

the presidency at the trial of the generals who had not taken up the bodies of the slain after the battle of Arginusae; and you proposed to try them all together, which was illegal, as you all thought afterwards; but at the time I was the only one of the Prytanes who was opposed to the illegality, and I gave my vote against you; and when the orators threatened to impeach and arrest me, and have me taken away, and you called and shouted, I made up my mind that I would run the risk, having law and justice with me, rather than take part in your injustice because I feared imprisonment or death. This happened in the days of the democracy. But when the oligarchy of the Thirty was in power, they sent for me and four others into the rotunda, and bade us bring Leon the Salaminian from Salamis, as they wanted to execute him. This was a specimen of the sort of commands which they were always giving with the view of implicating as many as possible in their crimes; and then I showed, not in word only but in deed, that, if I may be allowed to use such an expression, I cared not a straw for death, and that my only fear was the fear of doing an unrighteous or unholy thing. For the strong arm of the oppressive power did not frighten me into doing wrong; and when we came out of the rotunda the other four went to Salamis and fetched Leon, but I went quietly home. For which I might have lost my life, had not the power of the Thirty shortly afterwards come to an end. And to this many will witness.

Alcibiades describes Socrates in battle.

5. ———, *Symp.* 220 D. ALCIBIADES: I will also tell . . . . of his courage in battle; for who but he saved my life? Now this was the engagement in which I received the prize of valor: for I was wounded and he would not leave me, but rescued me and my arms. . . . There was another occasion on which he was very noticeable, this was in the flight of the army after the battle of Delium. . . . 221 A. He and Laches were retreating as the troops were in flight, and I met them and told them not to be discouraged, and promised to remain with them; and there you might see him, Aristophanes, as you describe, just as he is in the streets of Athens, stalking like a pelican, and rolling his

eyes, calmly contemplating enemies as well as friends, and making very intelligible to anybody, even from a distance, that whoever attacks him will be likely to meet with a stout resistance. . . .

Alcibiades describes Socrates' endurance.

6. ———— 219 E. sq. ALCIBIADES: In the faculty of endurance he was superior not only to me but to everybody; there was no one to be compared to him. Yet at a festival he was the only person who had any real powers of enjoyment, and though not willing to drink, he could if compelled beat us all at that, and the most wonderful thing of all was that no human being had ever seen Socrates drunk; and that, if I am not mistaken, will soon be tested. His endurance of cold was also surprising. There was a severe frost, for the winter in that region is really tremendous, and everybody else either remained indoors, or if they went out had on no end of clothing, and were well shod, and had their feet swathed in felt and fleeces: in the midst of this, Socrates, with his bare feet on the ice, and in his ordinary dress, marched better than any of the other soldiers who had their shoes on, and they looked daggers at him because he seemed to despise them. . . . One morning he was thinking about something which he could not resolve; and he would not give up, but continued thinking from early dawn until noon—there he stood fixed in thought; and at noon attention was drawn to him, and the rumor ran through the wondering crowd that Socrates had been standing and thinking about something ever since the break of day. At last, in the evening after supper, some Ionians out of curiosity (I should explain that this was not in winter but in summer), brought out their mats and slept in the open air that they might watch him and see whether he would stand all night. There he stood all night as well as all day and the following morning; and with the return of light he offered up a prayer to the sun, and went his way. . . .

Socrates' prayer.

7. ————, *Phaedrus* 279 B. SOCRATES: Beloved Pan, and all ye other gods who haunt this place, give me beauty in the inward

soul; and may the outward and inward man be at one. May I
reckon the wise to be the wealthy, and may I have such a quantity of gold as none but a temperate man and none but he can
carry. Anything more? That prayer, I think, is enough for me.

Alcibiades describes Socrates:
his appearance and the inner man.

8. ———, *Symp.* 216 D. sq. ALCIBIADES: Is he not like a
Silenus in this? Yes, surely: that is, his outer mask, which is the
carved head of the Silenus; but when he is opened, what tem-
perance there is . . . residing therein. . . . When I opened
him, and looked within at his serious purpose, I saw in him
divine and golden images of such fascinating beauty that I was
ready to do in a moment whatever Socrates commanded. . . .

Socrates describes himself.

9. XEN., *Ban.* V. 6-7. SOCRATES: . . . My eyes are finer ones
than yours. . . . Because, while yours see only straight ahead,
mine, by bulging out as they do, see also to the sides. . . . Your
nostrils look down toward the ground, but mine are wide open
and turned outward so that I can catch scents from all about. . . .
It does not put a barricade between the eyes but allows them
unobstructed vision of whatever they desire to see; whereas a
high nose, as if in despite, has walled the eyes off one from the
other. CRITOBOLUS: As for the mouth, I concede that point. For
if it is created for the purpose of biting off food, you could bite
off a far bigger mouthful than I could. . . .

Xantippe.

10. . . . II. 9-10. ANTISTHENES: If that is your view, Socrates, how does it come that you don't practise what you preach
by yourself educating Xantippe, but live with a wife who is the
hardest to get along with of all the women there are—yes, or
all that ever were, I suspect, or ever will be? SOCRATES: Because
I observe that men who wish to become expert horsemen do not
get the most docile horses but rather those that are high-mettled,
believing that if they can manage this kind, they will easily
handle any other. My course is similar. Mankind at large is what

I wish to deal with; and so I have got her, well assured that if I can endure her, I shall have no difficulty in my relations with all the rest of human kind.

Socrates' language.

11. PLATO, *Symp.* 221 E. ALCIBIADES: . . . His words are ridiculous when you first hear them; he clothes himself in language that is as the skin of the wanton satyr—for his talk is of pack-asses and smiths and cobblers and curriers, and he is always repeating the same things in the same words, so that an ignorant man who did not know him might feel disposed to laugh at him; (222 A) but he who pierces the mask and sees what is within will find that they are the only words which have a meaning in them. . . .

Socrates, the midwife of ideas.

12. ——, *Theaet.* 149 A. sq. SOCRATES: I am the son of a midwife, brave and burly, whose name was Phaenarete. . . . And I myself practise midwifery. . . . I attend men and not women, and I practise on their souls when they are in labor, and not on their bodies; and the triumph of my art is in examining whether the thought which the mind of the young man is bringing to birth is a false idol or a noble and true creation. And like the midwives, I am barren, and the reproach often made against me, that I ask questions of others and have not the wit to answer them myself, is very just; the reason is, that the god compels me to be a midwife, but forbids me to bring forth. And therefore I am not wise, nor have I anything which is the invention or offspring of my own soul. . . .

Percepts, concepts, and teleology.

13. XEN., *Mem.* III. 8. 4. Again, Aristippus asked him whether he knew of anything beautiful: "Yes, many things," he replied. "All like one another?" "On the contrary, some are as unlike as they can be." "How then can that which is unlike the beautiful be beautiful?" "The reason, of course, is that a beautiful wrestler is unlike a beautiful runner, a shield beautiful for defence is utterly unlike a javelin beautiful for swift

and powerful hurling." 5. ". . . Men . . . are called 'beautiful and good' in the same respect and in relation to the same things: it is in relation to the same things that men's bodies look beautiful and good and that all other things men use are thought beautiful and good, in relation to those things for which they are useful." 6. "Is a dung basket beautiful then?" "Of course, and a golden shield is ugly, if the one is well made for its special work and the other badly." "Do you mean that the same things are both beautiful and ugly?" 7. "Of course—and both good and bad. For what is good for hunger is often bad for fever, and what is good for fever bad for hunger. . . . For all things are good and beautiful in relation to those purposes for which they are well adapted, bad and ugly in relation to those for which they are ill adapted. . . ."

Socrates' early interest in natural science.

14. PLATO, *Phaedo* 96 A-100 A. SOCRATES: When I was young, Cebes, I had a prodigious desire to know that department of philosophy which is called Natural Science; this appeared to me to have lofty aims, as being the science which has to do with the causes of things, and which teaches why a thing is, and is created and destroyed; . . . At last I concluded that I was wholly incapable of these inquiries, as I will satisfactorily prove to you. . . . Nor am I any longer satisfied that I understand the reason why one or anything else either is generated or destroyed or is at all, but I have in my mind some confused notion of another method, and can never admit this. . . .

On natural philosophy and causal explanation.

15. XEN., *Mem.* I. i. 11-17. He did not even discuss that topic so favored by other talkers, "the Nature of the Universe"; and avoided speculation on the so-called "Cosmos" of the Professors, how it works, and on the laws that govern the phenomena of the heavens; indeed he would argue that to trouble one's mind with such problems is sheer folly. In the first place, he would inquire, did these thinkers suppose that their knowledge of human affairs was so complete that they must seek these

new fields for the exercise of their brains; or that it was their duty to neglect human affairs and consider only things divine? Moreover, he marvelled at their blindness in not seeing that man cannot solve these riddles; since even the most conceited talkers on these problems did not agree in their theories, but behaved to one another like madmen. . . . So is it, he held, with those who worry with "Universal Nature." Some hold that *What is* is one, others that it is infinite in number; some that all things are in perpetual motion, others that nothing can ever be moved at any time; some that all life is birth and decay, others that nothing can ever be born or ever die. . . .

His own conversation was ever of human things. The problems he discussed were, What is godly, what is ungodly; what is beautiful, what is ugly; what is just, what is unjust; what is prudence, what is madness; what is courage, what is cowardice; what is a state, what is a statesman; what is government, what is a governor. . . .

On Anaxagoras: "mind," the "best," and teleology.

16. PLATO, *Phaedo* 97 B sq. Then I heard someone who had a book of Anaxagoras, as he said, out of which he read that mind was the disposer and cause of all, and I was quite delighted at the notion of this, which appeared admirable, and I said to myself: If mind is the disposer, mind will dispose all for the best, and put each particular in the best place; and I argued that if any one desired to find out the cause of the generation or destruction or existence of anything, he must find out what state of being or suffering or doing was best for that thing, and therefore a man had only to consider the best for himself and others, and then he would also know the worse, for the same science comprised both. And I rejoiced to think that I had found in Anaxagoras a teacher of the causes of existence such as I desired, and I imagined that he would tell me first whether the earth is flat or round; and then he would further explain the cause and the necessity of this, and would teach me the nature of the best and show that this was best; and if he said that the earth was in the center, he would explain that this position was the best, and I should be satisfied if this were shown to me,

and not want any other sort of cause. And I thought that I would then go on and ask him about the sun and moon and stars, and that he would explain to me their comparative swiftness, and their returnings and various states, and how their several affections, active and passive, were all for the best. For I could not imagine that when he spoke of mind as the disposer of them, he would give any other account of their being as they are, except that this was best, and I thought that when he had explained to me in detail the cause of each and the cause of all, he would go on to explain to me what was best for each and what was good for all. . . .

What hopes I had formed, and how grievously was I disappointed! As I proceeded, I found my philosopher altogether forsaking mind or any other principle of order, but having recourse to air, and ether, and water, and other eccentricities. I might compare him to a person who began by maintaining generally that mind is the cause of the actions of Socrates, but who, when he endeavoured to explain the causes of my several actions in detail, went on to show that I sit here because my body is made up of bones and muscles; . . . and he would assign ten thousand other causes of the same sort, forgetting to mention the true cause, which is, that the Athenians have thought fit to condemn me, and accordingly I have thought it better and more right to remain here and undergo my sentence. . . . (99 A.) There is surely a strange confusion of causes and conditions in all this. It may be said, indeed, that without bones and muscles and the other parts of the body I cannot execute my purposes. But to say that I do as I do because of them, and that this is the way in which mind acts, and not from the choice of the best is a very careless and idle way of speaking. . . .

On geometry.

17. XEN., *Mem.* IV. 7. 2. ". . . He said that the study of geometry should be pursued until the student was competent to measure a parcel of land accurately in case he wanted to take over, convey or divide it, or to compute the yield. . . . Similarly he recommended them to make themselves familiar with as-

tronomy, but only so far as to be able to find the time of night, month and year . . . their periods of revolution and the causes of these. Of such researches, again he said that he could not see what useful purpose they served. He had indeed attended lectures on these subjects too; but these again, he said, were enough to occupy a lifetime to the complete exclusion of many useful studies.

On the gods.

18. ———, IV. 7. 6. In general, with regard to the phenomena of the heavens, he deprecated curiosity to learn how the deity contrives them: he held that their secrets could not be discovered by man, and believed that any attempt to search out what the gods had not chosen to reveal must be displeasing to them.

Socrates on Sophists.

18a. PLATO, *Apology* 19-20. See above, Ch. 6, Introductory, 3.

Socrates on Protagoras' theory of perceiving.

19. ———, *Theaet.* 166 D. See above, Ch. 6, I. A. 21a.

Socrates on method.

20. ———, *Phaedo* 100 A. SOCRATES: However, this was the method which I adopted: I first assumed some principle which I judged to be the strongest, and then I affirmed as true whatever seemed to agree with this, whether relating to the cause or to anything else; and that which disagreed I regarded as untrue. . . .

Induction.

21. XEN., *Mem.* IV. 6. 13. Whenever anyone argued with him on any point without being able to make himself clear, asserting but not proving, that so and so was wiser or an able politician or braver or what not, he would lead the whole discussion back to the definition required. . . . 15. By this process of leading back the argument even his adversary came to see

the truth clearly. Whenever he himself argued out a question, he advanced by steps that gained general assent, holding this to be the only sure method. . . .

Socratic irony.

22. PLATO, *Rep.* I. 336 E. SOCRATES: Thrasymachus, I said, with a quiver, have mercy on us. Our error, if we were guilty of any error, was certainly unintentional; and therefore you, in your wisdom, should have pity on us, and not be angry with us. . . . Do not imagine, then, that we are pretending to seek for justice, which is a treasure far more precious than gold. . . . THRAS.: How characteristic of Socrates! he replied, with a bitter laugh;—that's your ironical way! Did I not foresee—did I not tell you all, that he would refuse to answer, and try irony or any other shift in order that he might avoid answering?

Aristotle on Socrates and definition.

23. ARIST., *Met.* I. 6. 987 b 1. Socrates [30] . . . was busying himself about ethical matters and neglecting the world of nature as a whole but seeking the universal in these ethical matters, and fixed thought for the first time on definitions; Plato accepted his teaching, but held that the problem applied not to sensible things but to entities of another kind. . . . —— XIII. 4. 1078 b 18. . . . "Socrates [31] was occupying himself with the excellences of character, and in connection with them became the first to raise the problem of universal definition (. . . but it was natural that Socrates should be seeking the essence, for he was seeking to syllogize, and "what a thing is" is the starting-point of syllogisms; . . . For two things may be fairly ascribed to Socrates—inductive arguments and universal definition, both of which are concerned with the starting point of science):—but Socrates did not make the universals or definitions exist apart. . . .

On art.

24. PLATO, *Apology* 25 A sq. SOCRATES: Then every Athenian

[30] Translated by W. D. Ross, *op. cit.*
[31] *Ibid.*

improves and elevates them [the youth]; all with the exception
of myself; and I alone am their corruptor? . . . I am very unfortunate if that is true. But suppose I ask you a question:
Would you say that this also holds true in the case of horses?
Does one man do them harm and all the world good? Is not the
exact opposite of this true? One man is able to do them good,
or at least not many;—the trainer of horses, that is to say, does
them good, and others who have to do with them rather injure
them. . . . Happy indeed would be the condition of youth
if they had one corruptor only, and all the rest of the world
were their improvers. . . . And now, Meletus, I must ask you
another question: Which is better, to live among bad citizens,
or among good ones? . . . Do not the good do their neighbors
good, and the bad do them evil? . . . And is there any one who
would rather be injured than benefited by those who live with
him? . . . And am I, at my age, in such darkness and ignorance
as not to know that if a man with whom I have to live is corrupted by me, I am very likely to be harmed by him, and yet
I corrupt him, and intentionally, too;—that is what you are
saying, and of that you will never persuade me or any other
human being. . . .

On the autonomy of the single arts.

25. ———, *Ion* 532 D. SOCRATES: . . . When a man has
acquired a knowledge of a whole art, the inquiry into good and
bad is one and the same. . . . 537 C. And every art is appointed
by God to have knowledge of a certain work; for that which we
know by the art of the pilot we do not know by the art of medicine. . . . Nor do we know by the art of the carpenter that
which we know by the art of medicine. . . . When the subject
of knowledge is different, the art is different. . . . For surely,
if the subject of knowledge were the same, there would be no
meaning in saying that the arts were different. . . . 538 A. Tell
me . . . whether this holds universally? Must the same art have
the same subject of knowledge, and any other have other subjects of knowledge? . . . Then he who has no knowledge of a
particular art will have no right judgment of the sayings and
doings of that art. . . . By the help of which art, Ion, do you

know whether horses are well managed, by your skill as a horse-
man or as a performer on the lyre?

On inspiration and poetic invention.

26. ———, 534 B. SOCRATES: For the poet is a light and
winged and holy thing, and there is no invention in him until
he has been inspired and is out of his senses, and the mind is
no longer in him. . . . For not by art does the poet sing, but
by power divine. . . .

Conversations on painting and sculpture.

27. XEN., *Mem.* III. 10. 1. . . . On entering the house of
Parrhasius the painter one day, he asked in the course of a
conversation with him: "Is painting a representation of things
seen, Parrhasius? Anyhow, you painters with your colors represent and reproduce figures high and low, in light and in shadow,
hard and soft, rough and smooth, young and old. . . . 2. And
further, when you copy types of beauty, it is so difficult to find
a perfect model that you combine the most beautiful details of
several, and thus contrive to make the whole figure look beautiful. . . . 3. . . . Do you also reproduce the character of the
soul, the character that is in the highest degree captivating, delightful, friendly, fascinating, lovable? Or is it impossible to
imitate that?" . . . 4. "Do human beings commonly express
the feelings of sympathy and aversion by their looks?" . . .
"Then cannot thus much be imitated in the eyes?" . . . 6. On
another occasion he visited Cleiton the sculptor, and while con-
versing with him said: "Cleiton, that your statues of runners,
wrestlers, boxers, and fighters are beautiful I see and know. But
how do you produce in them that illusion of life which is their
most alluring charm to the beholder?" . . . 7. "Is it," he added,
"by faithfully representing the form of living beings that you
make your statues look as if they lived?" . . . "Then is it not
by accurately representing the different parts of the body as they
are affected by the pose—the flesh wrinkled or tense, the limbs
compressed or outstretched, the muscles taut or loose—that you
make them look more like real members and more convincing?" . . . 8. "Does not the exact imitation of the feelings that

affect bodies in action also produce a sense of satisfaction in the spectator?" . . . "Then must not the threatening look in the eyes of fighters be accurately represented, and the triumphant expression on the face of conquerors be imitated?" . . . "It follows, then, that the sculptor must represent in his figures the activities of the soul."

Phronesis.

28. Arist., *Eth. Eud.* VII. 13. 1245 b 32. . . . The Socratic saying that nothing is stronger than prudence is right. But when Socrates said this of knowledge, he was wrong. For prudence is virtue and not scientific knowledge, but another kind of cognition.[32]

On virtue and knowledge.

29. Xen., *Mem.* III. ix. 4. Between Wisdom and Prudence he drew no distinction; but if a man knows and practises what is beautiful and good, knows and avoids what is base, that man he judged to be both wise and prudent. When asked further whether he thought that those who know what they ought to do and yet do the opposite are at once wise and vicious, he answered: "No; not so much that, as both unwise and vicious. For I think that all men have a choice between various courses, and choose and follow the one which they think conduces most to their advantage. Therefore I hold that those who follow the wrong course are neither wise nor prudent. 5. He said that Justice and every other form of Virtue is Wisdom.[33] . . . For Socrates was entirely opposed to the view in question, holding that there is no such thing as incontinence; no one, he said, when he judges acts against what he judges best—people act so only by reason of ignorance. . . .

Virtue as knowledge and as end.

30. Arist., *Eth. Eud.* I. 5. 1216 b 3. Socrates, then, the elder, thought the knowledge of virtue to be the end, and used to inquire what is justice, what bravery, and each of the parts of

---

[32] Cf. Aristotle, *Magna Moralia* I. 1. 1183 b 9.
[33] Cf. Aristotle, *Nicomachean Ethics*, VII. 1145 b 21.

virtue; and his conduct was reasonable, for he thought all the virtues to be kinds of knowledge, so that to know justice and to be just came simultaneously; for the moment we have learned geometry or architecture we are architects and geometers. Therefore he inquired what virtue is, not how or from what it arises. . . .

Conversation with Euthydemus on justice and self-knowledge.

31. XEN., *Mem.* IV. 2. 11. Then Socrates exclaimed: "Surely, Euthydemus, you don't covet the kind of excellence that makes good statesmen and managers, competent rulers and benefactors of themselves and mankind in general?" . . . "Why," cried Socrates, "it is the noblest kind of excellence, the greatest of the arts that you covet, for it belongs to kings and is dubbed 'kingly.' However," he added, "have you reflected whether it be possible to excel in these matters without being a just man?" . . . "Then tell me, have you got that?" . . . "And have just men, like carpenters, their works?" . . . "And as carpenters can point out their works, should just men be able to rehearse theirs?" "Do you suppose," retorted Euthydemus, "that I am unable to rehearse the works of justice? Of course I can,—and the works of injustice too, since there are many opportunities of seeing and hearing of them every day." "I propose, then, that we write *J* in this column and *I* in that, and then proceed to place under these letters, *J* and *I*, what we take to be the works of justice and injustice respectively." . . . Having written down the letters as he proposed, Socrates went on: "Lying occurs among men, does it not?" "Yes, it does." "Under which heading, then, are we to put that?" "Under the heading of injustice, clearly." "Deceit, too, is found, is it not." "Certainly." "Under which heading will that go?" "Under injustice again, of course." "What about doing mischief?" "That too." "Then we shall assign none of these things to justice, Euthydemus?" "No, it would be monstrous to do so." "Now suppose a man who has been elected general enslaves an unjust and hostile city, shall we say that he acts unjustly?" "Oh no!" "We shall say that his actions are just, shall we not?" "Certainly." . . . 16. "Then I propose to revise our classification, and to say: It is just to do such things to

enemies, but it is unjust to do them to friends, towards whom
one's conduct should be scrupulously honest." . . . "Now suppose that a general, seeing that his army is downhearted, tells a
lie and says that reinforcements are approaching, and by means
of this lie checks discouragement among the men, under which
heading shall we put this deception?" "Under justice, I think."
. . . "You mean, do you, that even with friends straightforward
dealing is not invariably right?" "It isn't, indeed! I retract what
I said before, if you will let me." . . . 24. Hereupon Socrates
exclaimed: "Tell me, Euthydemus, have you ever been to
Delphi?" "Yes, certainly, twice." "Then did you notice somewhere on the temple the inscription, 'Know thyself'?" "I did."
"And did you pay no heed to the inscription, or did you attend
to it and try to consider who you were?" . . . 25. "And what
do you suppose a man must know to know himself, his name
merely? Or must he consider what sort of a creature he is for
human use and get to know his own powers;" . . . 26. "Is it not
clear too that through self-knowledge men come to much good,
and through self-deception to much harm? For those who know
themselves, know what things are expedient for themselves and
discern their own powers and limitations. And by doing what
they understand, they get what they want and prosper: by re-
fraining from attempting what they do not understand, they
make no mistakes and avoid failure." . . . "Socrates," answered
Euthydemus, "you may rest assured that I fully appreciate the
importance of knowing oneself. But where does the process of
self-examination begin? I look to you for a statement, please."
"Well," said Socrates, "I may assume, I take it, that you know
what things are good and what are evil?" "Of course. . . ."
"Come then, state them for my benefit." "Well, that's a simple
matter. First health in itself is, I suppose a good, sickness an
evil. Next the various causes of these two conditions—meat,
drink, habits—are good or evil according as they promote health
or sickness." "Then health and sickness too must be good when
their effect is good, and evil when it is evil." "But when can
health possibly be the cause of evil, or sickness of good?" "Why,
in many cases; for instance, a disastrous campaign or a fatal

voyage: the able-bodied who go are lost, the weaklings who stay behind are saved."

The indictment, the daimon, and the gods.

32. ———— I. 1. i. I have often wondered by what arguments those who drew up the indictment against Socrates could persuade the Athenians that his life was forfeit to the state. The indictment against him was to this effect: *Socrates is guilty of rejecting the gods acknowledged by the state and of bringing in strange deities: he is also guilty of corrupting the youth.* 2. . . . Indeed it had become notorious that Socrates claimed to be guided by "the deity": it was out of this claim, I think, that the charge of bringing in strange deities arose. . . . 4. . . . Whereas most men say that the birds or the folk they meet dissuade or encourage them, Socrates said what he meant: for he said that the deity gave him a sign. . . . 8. You may plant a field well; but you know not who shall gather the fruits . . . ; versed in statecraft, you know not whether it is profitable to guide the state; . . . 9. If any man thinks that these matters are wholly within the grasp of the human mind and nothing in them is beyond our reason, that man, he said, is irrational. But it is no less irrational to seek the guidance of heaven in matters which men are permitted by the gods to decide for themselves by study: to ask, for instance, Is it better to get an experienced coachman to drive my carriage or a man without experience? . . . To put such questions to the gods seemed to his mind profane. In short, what the gods have granted us to do by help of learning, we must learn; what is hidden from mortals we should try to find out from the gods by divination; for to him that is in their grace the gods grant a sign.

Socrates: his life as preparation for his trial.

33. ———— IV. 8. 3 sq. I will repeat what Hermogenes, son of Hipponicus, told me about him. "When Meletus had actually formulated his indictment," he said, "Socrates talked freely in my presence, but made no reference to the case. I told him that he ought to be thinking about his defence. His first remark was,

'Don't you think that I have been preparing for it all my life?'
And when I asked him how, he said that he had been constantly
occupied in the consideration of right and wrong, and in doing
what was right and avoiding what was wrong, which he regarded as the best preparation for a defence. Then I said, 'Don't
you see, Socrates, that the juries in our courts are apt to be
misled by argument, so that they often put the innocent to death,
and acquit the guilty?' 'Ah, yes, Hermogenes,' he answered, 'but
when I did try to think out my defence to the jury, the deity at
once resisted.' 'Strange words,' said I; and he, 'Do you think
it strange, if it seems better to God that I should die now? Don't
you see that to this day I never would acknowledge that any
man had lived a better or a pleasanter life than I? For they live
best, I think, who strive best to become as good as possible: and
the pleasant life is theirs who are conscious that they are growing
in goodness. . . . But now, if I am to die unjustly, they who
unjustly kill me will bear the shame of it. For if to do injustice
is shameful, whatever is unjustly done must surely bring
shame. . . .

Socrates on the afterlife.

34. PLATO, *Apology* 40 A sq. Now as you see there has come
upon me that which may be thought, and is generally believed
to be, the last and worst evil. But the oracle made no sign of
opposition. . . . I regard this as a proof that what has happened
to me is a good, and that those of us who think that death is an
evil are in error. . . . Let us reflect in another way, and we shall
see that there is great reason to hope that death is a good, for
one of two things:—either death is a state of nothingness and
utter unconsciousness, or, as men say, there is a change and mi-
gration of the soul from this world to another. Now if you suppose that there is no consciousness, but a sleep like the sleep
of him who is undisturbed even by the sight of dreams, death
will be an unspeakable gain. . . . Now if death is like this, I
say that to die is gain; for eternity is then only a single night.
But if death is the journey to another place, and there, as men
say, all the dead are, what good, O my friends and judges, can

be greater than this? . . . What would not a man give if he might converse with Orpheus, and Musaeus and Hesiod and Homer? Nay, if this be true, let me die again and again. . . . Above all, I shall be able to continue my search into true and false knowledge; as in this world, so also in that; I shall find out who is wise, and who pretends to be wise, and is not. . . . The hour of departure has arrived, and we go our ways—I to die, and you to live. Which is better God only knows.

Reason and man-made laws.

35. ———, *Crito* 46 B. SOCRATES: For I am and always have been one of those natures who must be guided by reason, whatever the reason may be which upon reflection appears to me to be the best. . . . 45. A. CRITO: . . . There are persons who at no great cost are willing to save you and bring you out of prison. . . . 48 B. Soc.: And I should like to know whether I may say . . . not life, but a good life, is to be chiefly valued? . . . 50 A. Soc.: Imagine that I am about to play truant (you may call the proceeding by any name you like), and the laws and the government come and interrogate me: "Tell us, Socrates," they say; "what are you about? Are you going by an act of yours to overturn us—the laws and the whole state, as far as in you lies? Do you imagine that a state can subsist and not be overthrown, in which the decisions of law have no power, but are set aside and overthrown by individuals?" . . . And we might reply, "Yes, but the state has injured us and given an unjust sentence." . . . 51 E. But he who has experience of the manner in which we order justice and administer the state, and still remains, has entered into an implied contract that he will do as we command him. . . . He has made an agreement with us that he will duly obey our commands . . . and we do not rudely impose them, but give him the alternative of obeying or convincing us. . . . 54 B. Soc.: The law would say. . . . Think not of life and children first, and of justice afterwards, but of justice first. . . . Now you depart in innocence, a sufferer and not a doer of evil; a victim, not of the laws, but of men. . . .

The death of Socrates.

36. ———, *Phaedo* 116 B sq. SOCRATES: . . . . let the cup be brought, if the poison is prepared: if not let the attendant prepare some.

Yet, said Crito, the sun is still upon the hilltops, and many a one has taken the draught late. . . . Do not hasten, then, there is still time.

Socrates said: Yes, Crito, and they of whom you speak are right in doing thus, for they think that they will gain by the delay; but I am right in not doing thus, for I do not think that I should gain anything by drinking the poison a little later; I should be sparing and saving a life which is already gone; I could only laugh at myself for this. Please then to do as I say, and not to refuse me. . . . (117 A.)

Crito, when he heard this, made a sign to the servant. . . . Then holding the cup to his lips, quite readily and cheerfully he drank off the poison. And hitherto most of us had been able to control our sorrow; but now when we saw him drinking, and saw too that he had finished the draught, we could no longer forbear, and in spite of myself my own tears were flowing fast. . . . Socrates alone retained his calmness: What is this strange outcry? he said. I sent away the women mainly in order that they might not offend in this way, for I have heard that a man should die in peace. . . . (118 A.) He was beginning to grow cold about the groin, when he uncovered his face, for he had covered himself up, and said (they were his last words)— he said: Crito, I owe a cock to Asclepius; will you remember to pay the debt? The debt shall be paid, said Crito; is there anything else? There was no answer to this question; but in a minute or two a movement was heard, and the attendants uncovered him; his eyes were set, and Crito closed his eyes and mouth.

Such was the end, Echecrates, of our friend, whom I may truly call the wisest, the justest, and best of all the men whom I have ever known.

ABBREVIATIONS OF AUTHORS' NAMES

AEL.	Claudius Aelianus
AET.	Aetius Doxographus
AGATH.	Agathemerus
ALEX.	Alexander Aphrodisiaensis
ARIST.	Aristotle
ARISTID.	Aelius Aristides
CEL.	Celsus
CENS.	Censorinus
CIC.	Marcus Tullius Cicero
CLEM.	Alexandrinus Clemens
D.L.	Diogenes Laertius
DIOGEN. OF OENOANDA	Diogenes of Oenoanda
DIONYS.	Dionysius, Bishop of Alexandria
DIONYS. THRAC.	Dionysius the Thracian
EPIC.	Titus Carus Epicurus
EPIPH.	Epiphanius
EUC.	Euclid
EUDOX.	Eudoxus of Cnidus
EUS.	Eusebios
EUSTATH.	Eustathius
GALEN.	Claudius Galenus
GEMIN.	Geminus of Rhodes
HERA.	Heraclitus
HERM.	Philosophus Hermias
HEROD.	Herodotus
HIER.	Hierocles

HIPP.	Hippolytus
ISOCR.	Isocrates
LACT.	Lactantius
LUC.	Lucretius
OLYMP.	Olympiodorus of Alexandria
PHILOP.	Philoponus
PHILOS.	Flavius Philostratus
PLAN.	Planudes
PLUT.	Plutarch
POL.	Polybius
PROC.	Proclus
PSEUDODION.	Pseudodionysius
SEN.	Seneca
SEXT. EMP.	Sextus Empiricus
SIMP.	Simplicius
STOB.	Stobaeus
TERTUL.	Tertullian
THEOPH.	Theophrastus
VIT.	Pollio Marcus Vitruvius
XEN.	Xenophon

LIST OF WORKS CITED

Aelianus, Claudius
Aetius Doxographus
Agathemerus

Alexander Aphrodisianensis

Ammonius Hermeiou
Aristides, Aelius

Aristotle

de Animalium Natura
Aetii de Placitis Reliquiae
Agathemeris . . . Commendiariae Geographiae Expositionum
in Meteorologicorum Aristotelis Commentatio
Quaestiones
Scripta Minora: de Mixtione Aristelis
Topica
Vita Aristotelis
Ars Rhetorica
Orationes
de Anima
de Caelo
de Generatione Animalium
de Generatione et Corruptione
de Partibus Animalium
de Respiratione
de Sensu
de Sophisticis Elenchis
Eudemian Ethics
Historia Animalium
Magna Moralia
Metaphysics
Meteorology
Nicomachean Ethics
Physics
Rhetoric

Bailey, Cyril	*The Greek Atomists and Epicurus, a Study*
Bergk, Theodor	*Anthologia Lyrica sive Lyricorum Graecorum Veterum. . . .*
Breasted, James H.	*The Conquest of Civilization*
Burnet, John	*Early Greek Philosophy*
	Greek Philosophy Part One Thales to Plato
Bury, R. G.	*Sextus Empiricus*
Bywater, Ingram	*Heracliti Ephesii Reliquiae*
Celsus	*de Medicina*
	The True Account
Censorius	*de Die Natali*
Childe, V. G.	*What Happened in History*
Cicero, Marcus Tullius	*Academia*
	de Divinatione
	Disputationes Tusculanae
	Epistolae ad Familiares
	de Fato
	de Finibus Honorum et Malorum
	de Natura Deorum
Clemens, Alexandrinus	*Pedagogus*
	Protrepticus
	Stromateis
David (called the Philosopher)	*Davidis Prolegomena et in Porphyrii Isagogen Commentarium*
Diels, Hermann (ed.)	*Die Fragmente der Vorsokratiker*
	Doxographi Graeci
Diodorus Siculus	*Bibliotheca Historica*
Diogenes Laertius	*de Clarorum Philosophorum Vitis, Dogmatibus et Apophthegmatibus Libri Decem*
	Lives and Opinions of Eminent Philosophers (Editions by R. D. Hicks and by D. L. Yonge)
Diogenes of Oenoanda	*Fragmenta*
Dionysius, Bishop of Alexandria	*On Nature* (cited by Eusebius, *Preparatio Evangelica.*)
Dionysius the Thracian	*Ars Dionysii Grammatici et Armenica in eam Scholia Davidis Philosophi, Anonymi Auctores, Moysis Geroldi, Stephani Sinniensis. . . .*
Dodds, E. R.	*The Greeks and the Irrational*
Eliot, T. S.	*Burnt Norton*

LIST OF WORKS CITED 299

Epicurus, Titus Carus	*Epicurea* (ed. H. Usener)
Epiphanius	*Epiphani Varia Excerpta*
Euclid	*Elements*
Eudoxus of Cnidus	*Ars Astonomicae*
Eusebios	*Praeparatio Evangelicae*
Eustathius	*Commentary on the Iliad and Odyssey of Homer*
Fairbanks, Arthur	*The First Philosophers of Greece*
Ferrater Mora, José M.	*Diccionario de Filosofía*
Galenus, Claudius	*de Elementis ex Hippocratis Sententia*
	de Usu Partium
Geminus of Rhodes	*Introduction (Isagoge) to Astronomy*
Gibbon, Edward	*The History of the Decline and Fall of the Roman Empire*
Gomperz, Theodor	*Greek Thinkers*
Grote, George	*History of Greece*
Harrison, Jane	*Prolegomena to Greek Religion*
Hermias, Philosophus	*Irrisio Gentilium Philosophorum*
	Commentary on Plato's Phaedrus (de Plat. Phaedr.)
Hermeiou, Ammonius	*Vita Aristoteles*
Herodotus	*The Histories*
Hesiod	*Theogony*
	The Works and Days
Hicks, R. D.	*Diogenes Laertius, Lives of Eminent Philosophers*
Hierocles	*Commentary on the Golden Verses of Pythagoras*
Hiller, E. M. J.	*Anthologia Lyrica sive Lyricorum Graecorum Veterum. . . . (Ed.)*
Hippolytus	*Hippolyti Philosophumena* (also called *Refutatio Omnium Haeresium.*)
Iamblichus	*Protrepticus (Protreptikoi Logoi)*
Isocrates	*Orationes et Epistolae*
Jaeger, W.	*Aristotle*
	The Theology of the Early Greek Philosophers
Jowett, Benjamin	*The Dialogues of Plato*
Lactantius	*Institutiones Divinae*
Lucretius	*de Rerum Natura*
Maine, Sir Henry	*Rede Lecture*

LIST OF WORKS CITED

Marchant, E. C. — *Xenophon: Memorabilia and Oeconimicus*

McClure, Matthew Thomas — *The Early Philosophers of Greece*

Munro, H. A. J. — *Lucretius On the Nature of Things*

Mure, Geoffrey — *Aristotle*

Nahm, Milton C. — *Aesthetic Experience and Its Presuppositions*
Aristotle on Poetry and Music
The Artist as Creator

Olympiodorus of Alexandria — *in Platonis Phileb.*

Philoponus — *de Anima*

Philostratus, Flavius — *Vitae Sophistorum*

Planudes — *Scholia ad Hermogenis Rhetoricam*

Plato — *The Dialogues of Plato* (tr. by Benjamin Jowett)
Apology
Charmides
Crito
Gorgias
Ion
Laws
Meno
Parmenides
Phaedo
Phaedrus
Protagoras
Republic
Sophist
Symposium
Theatetus
Timaeus

Plutarch — *Adversus Colotem*
Animine an Corporis Affectiones Sint Peiores
de Communibus Notitiis Adversus Stoicos
de Facie quae in Orbe Lunae Apparet
de Libid. et Aegr.
de Profectibus in Virtute
de Puerorum Educatione Libellus
Quaestionum Convivalium
Quomodo Adulator ab Amico Internoscatur
Solon (Vita Solonis)

Plutarch (cont.)   *Stromateis*
                                   de Tranquillitate Animi
                                   Vitae Parallelas (*Plutarch's Lives*, tr. by Sir Thomas North.)
                                   Vita Pericles

Polybius   *The Histories*
Porphyrius   *de Abstentia*
Preller, L. (with H. Ritter)   *Historia Philosophiae Graecae*
Proclus   *Hesiodi Opera et Dies*
                                   On Euclid
                                   Procli Diadochi in Platonis Cratylum Commentaria

Pseudodionysius   *Ars Rhetorica*
Pseudo-Plutarch   *Stromateis* (fragments, in Eusebius' *Praeparatio Evangelica*)

Ritter, H. (with L. Preller)   *Historia Philosophiae Graecae*
Rohde, E.   *Psyche*
Ross, W. D.   *Aristotle's Metaphysica*
    (*see* Smith, J. A.)
Seneca   *Quaestiones Naturales*
Sextus Empiricus   *Adversus Mathematicos*
                                   Outlines of Pyrrhonism
Sidgwick, H.   "The Sophists," *Journal of Philology*, Vol. IV., No. 8, Vol. V., No. 9.

Simplicius   *Simplici in Aristotelis de Caelo Commentaria*
                                   Simplici in Aristotelis Physicorum Libros Quattor Priores

Singer, E. A., Jr.   *Mind as Behavior*
Smith, Henry B.   *How the Mind Falls into Error*
Smith, J. A. and W. D. Ross   *The Works of Aristotle Translated into English*
   (editors)
Stein, H.   *Empedoclis Agrigentini Fragmenta*
Stephanus Byzantius   *Ethnica*
Stobaeus   *Eclogarum Physicarum et Ethicarum Libri Due Florilegium* (*Sermones*)
                                   Eclogae Physicae
Strabo   *Geographica*
Stratton, George M.   *Theophrastus and the Greek Physiological Psychology Before Aristotle*
Tertullian   *de Anima*
Theodoretus   *Graecorum Affectionum Curatio*

302   LIST OF WORKS CITED

Theophrastus
de Causis Plantarum
de Igne
de Odoribus
de Sensu
de Signe
Physiocorum Opin.

Thucydides
History of the Peloponnesian War

Vitruvius, Pollio Marcus
de Architectura

Wright, Wilmer Cave
Philostratus and Eunapius, *The Lives of the Sophists*

Xenophon
Anabasis
Apology
Banquet (*Symposium*)
Memorabilia of Socrates

Yonge, D. L.
Diogenes Laertius' The Lives and Opinions of Eminent Philosophers

Zeller, Edward
A History of Greek Philosophy (tr. by S. F. Alleyne)